The Invisible Matrix

An exploration of professional relationships in the service of psychotherapy

Edited by
Sasha Brookes and Pauline Hodson

Routledge
Taylor & Francis Group
LONDON AND NEW YORK

First published 2000 by Routledge

First edition 2000

2 Park Square, Milton Park, Abingdon, Oxfordshire OX14 4RN
52 Vanderbilt Avenue, New York, NY 10017

Routledge is an imprint of the Taylor & Francis Group, an informa business

First issued in hardback 2019

ISBN 978-1-900877-27-5 (pbk)
ISBN 978-0-367-32483-4 (hbk)

for Linda Binnington, with love

ACKNOWLEDGEMENTS

We would like to thank Avi Shmueli for recognising the need for this book, for introducing us to Oliver Rathbone and Kirsty Hall of Rebus Press, and for his continued encouragement and enthusiasm on the subject of splitting and sharing. We owe much to the thinking that has flourished over many years in the Society for Psychoanalytical Marital Psychotherapists, and which has contributed to the ideas expressed in the book. We would also like to thank our training organisation, the Tavistock Marital Studies Institute, for teaching us much about boundaries and containment.

We are also, of course, very grateful to all the writers who have contributed their thoughts on various parts of the matrix, and to our colleagues Chris Vincent and Linda Binnington who read and commented on the introductory chapter.

Finally, we would like to thank Noel Hodson for acting as IT consultant to both editors of the book, and for being such a keen supporter of the project.

A NOTE ON TEXTS

Quotations and references to Freud are given according to the *Standard Edition of the Complete Psychological Works of Sigmund Freud.* 24 volumes, translated and edited by James Strachey in collaboration with Anna Freud, assisted by Alix Strachey and Alan Tyson. London: The Hogarth Press and the Institute of Psycho-Analysis; New York: Norton, 1953-1974.

CONTENTS

FOREWORD

Individuals, couples and families who simultaneously consult more than one therapist or helping professional have long presented a fundamental challenge to the traditional concepts of confidentiality and psychoanalytical therapeutic boundaries. These boundaries remain the bedrock of the client/therapist contract and we disturb them at our peril. Whether the patient is an individual, a couple or a family receiving multiple therapies each therapist is overtly or unconsciously aware of the influences of other therapists on their client and, conversely, is aware that his own illumination of the client's psyche is affecting the work of other therapists.

I have encountered the puzzling complexities of this situation throughout my career, both in my private practice, and in larger organisations. At the Woodberry Down Child Guidance Unit, where we attempted for the first time to bring child and family therapy together with psychiatric social work and other supporting disciplines, we felt for a time that when several of us were working with different members of one family it was just too difficult to make contact with each other except in emergencies. This led me then only rarely to address our shared casework with my colleagues. Our clients unwittingly lent support to this decision. I remember on one occasion a patient leaving by the fire-escape to avoid his wife, who was seeing a colleague of mine in the same building.

In the past fifteen years however, the pioneering practice of Woodberry Down has been reflected in the wider therapeutic world. What we contained within an institution now appears in the community at large, so that different private practitioners may find themselves working with individuals of the same family. This raises the question of relationships between professionals just as it did for us at Woodberry Down. How should practitioners best respond to this ubiquitous state of affairs? This book both highlights this situation and draws together a group of psychotherapists who in the following pages have begun a much-needed and stimulating dialogue.

This long overdue, thought provoking and thoughtful book examines what Sasha Brookes and Pauline Hodson have termed 'the invisible matrix' through the practical experiences of its authors. The book provides generous and intelligent insights into the current work practices, theories and strategies of the contributing psychiatrists, analysts, individual and marital psychotherapists who are daily faced with questions about their relationships with their professional colleagues.

I think this book will appeal to and be accessible to both professionals and clients. People in this burgeoning information age often wish to share in the ethical and clinical debate about boundaries in their therapies, and this book will help and inform our increasingly sophisticated clients. For practising psychotherapists this book is both timely and informative. In studying these essays, they will consider their own responses to the invisible matrix, that powerfully accompanies increasing numbers of patients into the consulting rooms of the twenty-first century.

A C Robin Skynner MB, MRC Psych, DPM
December 1999

CHAPTER ONE

THE INVISIBLE MATRIX

Sasha Brookes & Pauline Hodson

Pauline Hodson trained at the Tavistock Marital Studies Institute, and was a founding member of the Society of Psychoanalytical Marital Psychotherapists. She has a private practice in Oxford.

Sasha Brookes has studied literature and psychology, and is a psychoanalytic marital therapist and individual therapist working in private practice. She trained at the Tavistock Marital Studies Institute in couple psychotherapy, then trained in individual psychotherapy at the Arbours Association. She is in private practice in London and a member of the Society of Psychoanalytical Marital Psychotherapists.

Together, Pauline and Sasha have also written 'Learning Through the Looking Glass' (Hodson & Brookes 1989), a short appreciation of their training institute.

This chapter introduces and defines the concept of 'The Invisible Matrix'.

The various chapters which make up the book both reflect and explore the network of professional relationships, visible and invisible, conscious and unconscious, which we have called a matrix. It is the net of psychotherapeutic connections within which the confidential work in the consulting room is held.

We find that there are no generally accepted protocols within the profession for the conduct of concurrent therapies, and as practitioners in this challenging situation we need to rely on ethical principles to guide us to clear thinking. It is evident, however, from the contributions in this book that a therapist can feel very much alone when faced with a complex set of circumstances, particularly when they involve more than one therapy. We hope the book will contribute to the dialogue among analytic psychotherapists about how to conduct our professional relationships for the good of our client/patients when we are working together or alongside one another.

All the authors have generously contributed original papers to the book, and have written from the perspective of the assessor, the supervisor, and from the point of view of therapists working together and alongside each other.

Each author approaches the experience of professional relationship differently, but all work within the discipline of analytic psychotherapy. True to the spirit of the book, however, it is our hope and belief that their thoughts will make connections with and appeal to therapists who work within different disciplines.

* * *

It is five minutes to four o'clock and the new client is due to arrive at four. The therapist checks to make sure all is ready. The diary tells her the name of this new client and who referred him, and she remembers the brief telephone call in which he told her that he had a relationship problem, but his wife wouldn't consider therapy. He told the therapist that he worked at home so could manage an appointment during the day. He sounded brisk and cheerful, but his manner belied the message: 'his wife was about to leave him.'

It is five minutes to four o'clock and the client looks anxiously at his watch. Perhaps he should wait in the car a little longer; he doesn't want to be early: 'don't therapists have a thing about time?' He looks at the house, noticing the geraniums on the step, and the green front door. The house looks welcoming, but he feels a knot in his stomach. She had sounded efficient and gentle on the telephone but had asked him few questions. The tenor of her voice told him little about her age: was she middle-aged like him; married or single; did she have children; would she have any idea of the difficulties he was going through with his wife and children? Was he doing the right thing in approaching a therapist at all?

It is four o'clock and the door bell rings; there is a pause; therapist and client on opposite sides of the green front door gather themselves for their first meeting, maybe the first of very many meetings. They are about to enter what Joyce McDougall has called the theatre of the mind (1986). The stage has been set; the consulting room will remain the same for as long as their relationship continues, and it seems as if there are just two people who will occupy it.

But both client and therapist carry within them invisible matrices. The client's unconscious matrix of relationships, both past and present, will slowly over time be explored and will become visible to both of the people on the therapeutic stage; but what of the therapist's personal and professional matrices? They will remain invisible to the client, but the therapist's professional matrix, which is such a crucial aspect of the therapeutic container, will play as important a part as the client's matrix of relationships, in the drama that is about to take place.

This book is about the therapist's professional matrix, both visible and invisible. It is about how we, as clinicians, manage the web of professional connections that inform, control, bother and console us whilst we struggle with our client's inner world. These include connections with referrers, supervisors, co-therapists in conjoint work with couples, and particularly, colleagues with whom we find ourselves working concurrently. These professional networks of psychotherapists have been helpfully thought and written about elsewhere both from a psychoanalytic perspective, and from a point of view based in systems theory. The papers collected here are all written from a psychoanalytic perspective, and although they deal with various aspects of the professional network, they focus particularly on the issue of concurrent therapies.

As Christel Buss-Twachtmann notes in chapter five of this book, we are more likely now than in the past to undertake to share a patient, for instance with a psychoanalytic colleague offering couple therapy to our individual patient or, as Jason Maratos describes in chapter seven, with an analytic group of which our new patient is a member. Two decades ago concurrent therapies were the exception rather than the rule, and a couple therapist would have thought long and hard before taking two clients into therapy if one or other of them were already in individual therapy. It is now a fact of the economic life of a psychotherapist that she will need to acknowledge and even work alongside other therapists if she is to make a living in a world that is becoming increasingly psychologically sophisticated. We live in a consumer's society and some of our clients make simultaneous demands of more than one part of the therapeutic network; we may share a client both with an analytic colleague and with a reflexologist or aromatherapist, a situation which Penny Jaques reflects upon in chapter four. This challenges our professional identity and ethical standards in a way unheard of twenty years ago.

As our profession grows it is inevitable that more and more of us will, so to speak, bump into each other. Our consulting rooms will have to contain clients whose invisible matrix not only includes personal relationships, but also previous or current therapeutic relationships. Many now consult us who have already had some previous experience of counselling or therapy; and newspapers and periodicals often regale their readers with accounts of therapies that have gone terribly wrong, with therapists who claim to be members of our profession but adhere to no recognisable code of ethics. These stories of misconduct are mitigated by psychotherapists who appear in the media making their, and our, work more accessible to the general public. Susie Orbach reflects on some of these issues in chapter ten.

When there is such an explosion of information and misinformation, such an abundance of therapies and therapists, a psychotherapist who finds herself sharing a patient might well feel she must keep her boundaries by interpreting any potential impact of the other therapy only in the transference to herself. We believe, however, that there are times when not to address the external reality of a concurrent therapy might be to hold too rigidly to boundaries, and so miss a valuable opportunity to challenge the conscious and unconscious assumptions of our clients.

The idea for a book which would debate these issues evolved out of a Study Day that the Society of Psychoanalytical Marital Psychotherapists held in 1997. The day focused on the relationship between individual and couple psychotherapists sharing clients/patients. In thinking about a possible book on the topic we widened this focus to include a larger matrix of professional relationships which surround and, when they are good enough, contain both the patient and the therapist.

This chapter introduces our thoughts about this matrix as it is reflected in the chapters which make up the book. We see it holding patients in concurrent psychotherapies, the guests in a therapeutic community, or patients in the process of assessment and referral. The matrix has visible structures and dynamics as well as invisible ones. For example, an assessing psychotherapist and the colleague to whom she refers the patient communicate in a visible way, have a conscious relationship, and may share more or less information about the patient. Less visible dynamics are inevitably also present in this professional matrix, in addition to the transference dynamics in the mind of the referred patient. Referrals are made in many different ways and spirits and we are often aware that in the assessment process the patient unconsciously communicates something important. What it is may become visible in the referral through the medium of the assessor's counter-transference, as Herbert Hahn shows in chapter three.

The relationship between a therapist and her supervisor also has an explicit basis. They have agreed to work together for mutual benefit, and for the benefit of the patients they will discuss. The therapist pays the supervisor for her time, and receives the benefit of professional support and containment, as well as the benefit of the supervisor's experience and ability to think about the therapeutic work. As we all know, however, and as Evelyn Cleavely so vividly brings to life in chapter eleven, the matrix of the supervisory relationship has powers which are not stipulated in the professional contract, but which can work unpredictably on the patient's behalf; they are some of the powers of the unconscious. A relationship, of which the patient is unaware, can develop between the supervisor and the patient through the medium of the supervisor's counter-transference feelings about the material of the session. The supervisor's counter-transference may make visible an aspect of the material and of the patient which the therapist had not been able to see—for example the presence of the psychotic part of the personality (Bion 1957).

Another familiar experience is that of taking work which feels stuck to supervision. Occasionally the next session has quite a different feeling about it, and the therapy seems to be on the move again. Trying to find a way to describe this mysterious process, which is one of the creative by-ways of the invisible matrix, we say that surely the patient, or the couple, must have been invisibly present at the supervision. Again we are struck by the mysterious and impressive power of minds to communicate at an unconscious level.

We found it helpful in thinking about unconscious communication to remember some of Freud's observations about unconscious mental processes, in 'Formulations on the Two Principles of Mental Functioning' (1911), 'A Note on the Unconscious in Psychoanalysis' (1912) and 'The Unconscious' (1915). He notes in the first of these papers that unconscious mental processes are the primary processes, in the sense that they come first in human development, and are 'the residues of a phase of development in which they were the only kind of mental process.' At this stage of the evolution of his model of the mind, Freud thought of these primary processes as obeying 'the pleasure principle' and therefore as dedicated to getting rid of what he called 'unpleasure', and which we would think of now, following Bion (1957) as 'psychic pain'.

Klein (1946) made clear and vivid the psychic mechanisms of projection and projective identification, by means of which painful feelings are, in phantasy, expelled from the unconscious self into others. In the case of projection, the painful feeling, for example of destructive rage, is then seen in the other, who is felt to have become extremely dangerous. In the case of projective identification, one partner in a relationship identifies with his partner's projected rage which calls up his own anger, and, under the influence of this double dose of fury, he feels and perhaps acts dangerously.

It follows that a patient's unconscious pain is certain to be projected into the invisible matrix of therapeutic relationships. At first, it will itself be invisible there, that is, unconscious. In 'Formulations on the Two Principles of Mental Functioning', Freud writes: 'It is probable that thinking was originally unconscious ... and that it did not acquire further qualities, perceptible to consciousness, until it became bound to verbal residues.' Unconscious pain remains unconscious until, in a phrase of Evelyn Cleavely's, it is 'spoken to'. Once it has been spoken to, and not before, it becomes available to be thought about. Freud tells us that the ability to think, once achieved, 'was endowed with characteristics which made it possible for the mental apparatus to tolerate an increased tension of stimulus while the process of discharge' (that is, projection or action) 'was postponed.'

This postponement, as Freud calls it, is essential to therapeutic work. It allows time to have experience, and the possibility of learning from experience. Bion (1957) developed Freud's notion of a postponement of discharge into his concept of the psychic container/contained relationship, as Stella Pierides clearly outlines in chapter nine. When there is a container/contained relationship in the mind, feelings can be held in the container for long enough to be experienced. When the internal container in the mind cannot hold acute pain, the relational container of the therapeutic relationship or relationships is called upon to do so. The unparalleled importance of this waiting and holding process to emotional life and development had been understood intuitively almost a hundred years earlier by John Keats, who conceived of the 'negative capability' of being able to remain 'in uncertainties, mysteries, doubts, without any irritable reaching after fact and reason' (Gittings 1990: 43).

The mysteries remain, but have become thinkable, and by means of thinking can be linked to the feelings and thoughts of others, until we know we 'suffer in common with all mankind'. Keats wrote: 'An extensive knowledge is needful to thinking people—it takes away the heat and fever; and helps, by widening speculation, to ease the burden of the mystery... The difference of high sensations with and without knowledge appears to me this—in the latter case we are falling continually ten thousand fathoms deep and being blown up again without wings and with all the horror of a bare-shouldered creature—in the former case, our shoulders are fledge, and we go thro' the same air and space without fear' (Gittings 1990: 92).

The therapeutic function which Freud thought of as interpretation, and Bion as alpha function, serves to widen speculation, and ease the burden of the mystery of human experience. Our idea of the invisible matrix of therapeutic relationships is that at its best it serves to hold the psychic pain the patient brings to therapy until it can be seen and interpreted. For the patient, this happens in the bounded space of the consulting room. The therapist, in order to contain the patient, creates a supporting professional matrix which extends beyond the consulting room, to include for instance a supervisor or a colleague to whom she refers her patient with his wife for couple therapy. Because this matrix has an invisible, that is, an unconscious dimension, unconscious dynamics within it affect the therapy, sometimes illuminating and sometimes obscuring the path of the therapeutic work. Splitting and projection may take place within the matrix as well as containment and interpretation, and therapists, like everyone else, can be powerfully affected by projections and may unconsciously identify with them (Menzies 1970, Vincent 1995).

Throughout the book, the contributors, with their differences of emphasis and approach, all think psychoanalytically about the properties of the invisible matrix. Each pays attention first to the framework, defined in terms of time, space, and working contract, which holds the therapeutic work, and makes it possible for the unconscious to appear within it in the form of the transference and counter-transference (Milner 1987). This immediately raises fundamental questions about the nature of the therapeutic frame when the patient is in more than one therapy. Can there only be one therapeutic space in the mind of the patient, in which the two therapies, for instance individual and couple work, must coexist? Or could each therapy be conducted within its own independent boundaries, so that at times there are two therapeutic spaces in a patient's mind? Or should we imagine a more complex situation in which the two therapeutic spaces in the mind are independent at times, and sometimes their boundaries become permeable, so that feelings and problems spill out of one into the other, or are visible in one and invisible in the other?

Psychoanalytic concepts of the unconscious suggest that all these different situations may occur during the lifetime of shared therapeutic work. Theoretically there is only one inner world, which more than one therapist may be exploring with the patient. But within this internal world there may be more radical discontinuities, schisms and uncharted regions than can exist in our outer world, every part of which is now mapped on to the globe. It seems that within the inner world, however, no matter how unexplored, the patient has the capacity unconsciously to join the therapists in the symbolic creation of a *Resolution* or a *Golden Hind*, a therapeutic vessel or vessels, in order to take part in the voyage of discovery during which unconscious processes become perceptible 'by means of consciousness' (Freud 1915).

In a single therapy the vessel or frame may at times feel inadequate to contain the patient's anxiety, and there will be acting out, or feelings may be split off and projected into an extra-transferential object so that they are not available for the therapeutic work. When the patient is in more than one therapy, there is a possibility that, for example, an idealised infant-mother relationship may be going on for a while in the individual therapy, while anger and desire for separateness are being felt only in the couple work.

Questions about the functioning of the therapeutic frame when the patient is in more than one therapy immediately raise other fundamental questions to be considered analytically, of ethics and confidentiality, which are addressed first by Philip Stokoe in chapter one, and then in different ways throughout the book. One obvious question is about the visible relationship which several therapists who are concurrently seeing the same patient might have with one another, and this is discussed by Joyce Lowenstein and Mary Ann Dubner in chapter eight. Elaine Bollinghaus and Helen Tarsh who have worked together for many years as couple psychotherapists share their thinking about the matrix of their con-joint work in chapter six.

The relationships of therapists sharing work will always have visible and invisible dynamics. Freud (1915) tells us: 'It is a very remarkable thing that the Ucs of one human being can react upon that of another, without passing through the Cs. This deserves closer investigation, especially with a view to finding out whether preconscious activity can be excluded as playing a part in it; but, descriptively speaking, the fact is incontestable.' We learn repeatedly from our professional experience that this mysterious fact *is* incontestable, and it is of course the basis of what Searles (1965) called the reflection process, by means of which therapists may find themselves enacting or experiencing aspects of the patient's inner world and its object relationships.

Sometimes, for example, an individual psychotherapist will refer a patient with his partner to couple therapy. In that case, in the mind of the patient as well as in the professional matrix there is a felt connection between the two therapies; the therapists, with the patient's knowledge and permission, have been in communication, although they will not necessarily have discussed the patient, and evidently they feel it is possible and appropriate to work alongside each other. Of course there will be other unconscious dynamics, but at this moment in the professional matrix there is hope of sharing creative work together; a hope based on faith in the good internal objects of the self and the other. Each therapist is able to value himself realistically and is therefore able to value his colleague, and this promotes hope that the therapeutic matrix can contain depressive pain rather than 'emanating persecutory anxiety' (Harris and Meltzer 1986).

On other occasions, however, someone in couple therapy finds herself an individual psychotherapist without reference to the couple therapists. As long as the couple therapists are unaware of the other therapy, they will probably be unable to see the difficulties which are split off and projected into it. When they do get to know of the existence of their colleague and another therapeutic frame in which their patient is working, they will need to think about the couple interaction in the light of this new information. They can then begin to see the reflection of the unconscious dynamics of the couple relationship, as it is reflected in the broader professional matrix which now includes themselves and their colleague.

We assume that if a situation such as this is not addressed by the therapists it is being left to the patient to manage, which she will undoubtedly do in a way which will reflect and perpetuate her unconscious phantasies. There might be for instance an Oedipal phantasy, that the parents must be kept apart, however high a price she may pay in feelings of inadequacy and guilt. When a therapist sharing a patient becomes aware of this sort of acting-in, it is her job to find a way of addressing it, so that the unconscious dynamics become available to be thought about. Is this a situation in which it would be in the best interests of the patient for the therapists to communicate consciously in the external world, and if so, in what way?

A vital concept to keep in mind in such confusing and difficult situations, where there is no obvious 'right answer' or guaranteed good practice, is that of the therapeutic frame holding the container/contained relationship (Bion 1957), because without this relationship no therapeutic work can be done. The therapist, or the co-therapists, must consider first the integrity of the frame, and then how to bring into the frame unconscious conflicts which cannot be seen for what they are, because they are being projected into the matrix of therapeutic relationships.

Confidentiality is a vital property of the therapeutic frame or frames. Feelings cannot be held and thought about in the therapeutic relationship unless the patient is confident that nothing will leak from within it to outside it. In the situation of concurrent therapies we confront the issue of confidentiality consciously, in discussing it with the patient when the second therapy is being established. But this by no means guarantees the safety of the container or containers, and the therapists must continue to be aware of confidentiality, and what it means from session to session, as long as the work lasts.

These preliminary thoughts about the invisible matrix and its properties and dynamics suggest that combined therapies demand negative capability from practitioners working together. They must always be prepared to safeguard confidentiality, boundaries and good professional practice by thinking and thinking again about their conscious and unconscious relationships and what is being reflected in them. They must try to avoid (as Keats put it) 'irritable reaching after' definitive, lasting decisions either about how best to hold the boundaries, or what the relationships mean (Gittings 1990: 43, 92). The invisible matrix is a rich source of transference information. It may also carry feelings of containment and support not only for the patient or patients but also for the therapists working concurrently.

Perhaps the manner of our training as couple psychotherapists fits us particularly well to contemplate these issues. From our therapeutic infancy we were required to manage a set of complex relationships. We trained at the Institute of Marital Studies (as it was then known), now the Tavistock Marital Studies Institute, and as trainees saw couples with co-therapists who were also senior members of staff. We did not need to be told about boundaries: the management of them was taken in with our therapeutic milk; we learned them from experience. Training as we did in a small and intimate institution whose business it was to work with couples, we quickly realised that in order to work with a co-therapist who might also be one's tutor, we had to be a partner in the therapy session; that is: aware of our strengths, but open to learning outside the session; that is: aware of our vulnerabilities. This required a rigorous discipline in boundary keeping, not always managed, but continually struggled with. We became adept at holding a multitude of relationships in our minds at the same time.

It is necessary to reflect on the discipline that our training gave us, because part of the task of this book is to review the axiom that an effective therapy is one on which no outside influence is allowed to impinge; the boundary that encloses the therapist and client should be absolute. As we and many of the contributors have said, confidentiality is the corner stone of any therapy and without it the therapeutic container would not exist; in the therapeutic community however, just as in a marriage, it is only if the boundaries are strong and clear that they can be permeable. If we are clear about our identity as therapists and the area of work that we engage in with our clients, then in a situation of concurrent therapies we can acknowledge the work our colleagues do and allow ourselves to think about it in a way that will be beneficial to our clients.

We have invited the psychotherapists who have contributed to this book to lift their gaze from the clearly defined boundary around client and therapist, and to consider the wider environment of professional relationships within which they work. Each of the authors writes of this bigger picture, which is rarely publicly discussed among therapists, with authority, honesty and clarity. They let us see the complexities of their clinical practices and make it quite clear that in order to be of help to their patients/clients they have to grasp the nettle and acknowledge that they work within a social context. So the authors of this book have come together, each with a strong professional identity, to explore the issues that face all psychotherapists as we approach the millennium.

It is ten to five, and the client after many many sessions, leaves for the last time by the green front door. There are winter pansies in the pot where the geraniums were that summer four-and-a-half years ago. He walks down the steps and turns towards his car. He no longer has an anxious knot in his stomach, but feels a sense of sadness mixed with elation; he will miss the therapist.

It is ten to five and the therapist watches for the last time the back of her client as he closes the green front door. She feels a mixture of feelings, including a sense of loss, but also real pleasure that after many sessions her client has discovered much about himself and his relationships. He can now make decisions and choices based on an intimate knowledge of who he is, and he is enjoying, perhaps for the first time, his family life.

It is five o'clock; the client negotiates his way through the traffic; he is alone but doesn't feel lonely; through his therapy he has discovered a rich internal matrix of relationships which nourish and sustain him; therapy was the right decision after all; he feels a sense of gratitude towards the therapist.

It is five o'clock: the therapist opens the client's file and reads once again the referrer's notes. As she writes the final report she thinks of her supervisor and reflects on the hours of supervision she has had on this client: her supervisor knows him almost as well as she does. Glancing through her notes she remembers with a smile the complexity of negotiating her way through his decision to see a marital therapist with his wife; that was two years ago. The combination of therapies had worked well, but there had been some sticky moments.

By six o'clock the therapeutic stage is empty, the two players have left and the drama that has been such an important part of the client's life, and that has occupied a great deal of time in the therapist's professional life, is over. Different aspects of the client's internal world of unconscious relationships have taken centre stage from time to time, made conscious through the relationship with his therapist, who has remained a willing consort available for the different roles ascribed to her. Her capacity to take part in the drama, whilst observing and interpreting it, has been strengthened by a professional matrix, a supporting cast which now waits back stage for the next play to begin.

CHAPTER TWO

HOLDING THE BOUNDARIES

Philip Stokoe

Philip Stokoe is a psychoanalyst in private practice and at the Brent Adolescent Centre. He is also a Senior Clinical Lecturer in Social Work at the Adult Department of the Tavistock Clinic. At the Tavistock, he has been responsible for designing and running courses for those working in Day and Residential care. He is an Associate Member of the British Psychoanalytical Society, an Affiliate Member of the Society of Psychoanalytical Marital Psychotherapists, and a member of that organisation's Ethics Committee.

Philip Stokoe's chapter speaks strongly to the vital importance of ethical principles when we are considering the complex issues addressed in this book. Through the process of his own creative thinking, based on experience in a wide variety of settings, he establishes a framework for the dialogue of the book within the ethical and conceptual boundaries of psychoanalytic psychotherapy. From this starting point he surveys the conscious and unconscious matrix of professional relationships which surround psychotherapists at work. He shows the reader how clear thinking about professional ethics must be the compass which guides us in the visible and invisible complexities of the therapeutic matrix.

* * *

I am seeking to explore some ethical issues which arise from the situation in which a patient is engaged in two therapeutic processes in parallel. In order to assist in this consideration, I shall be presenting a model of the psychoanalytical type of therapy. I hope that we shall be able to identify some basic principles which seem to me to govern decisions with which we may be faced in the context of one of our patients receiving help from someone else as well. I intend to acknowledge the assumptions and boundaries, define the setting in terms of a container and think about the consequence of task and contract.

Boundaries and containment

I would like to begin by making a few definitions about the work from a particular point of view. In the first place I would like to acknowledge that, like all models of the world, the psychoanalytical approach to understanding human functioning is based upon some assumptions. Physical science is based upon assumptions, principally that events can be connected causally. Our principle assumption is that there is an unconscious, by which I mean that there is a part of our minds that we cannot know about directly but which influences the way we see the world and the beliefs we form about the world. Many of us become caught up in trying to use psychoanalytical insights to prove the existence of the unconscious. It is not surprising that we are then accused of tautology.

It seems to me reasonable to assume that we have an unconscious; I have spent most of my professional life involved in social work or mental health work and the most common event in staff meetings is the effort to understand why a particular client is behaving in a specific way. Whatever the manifest orientation of the individual professionals involved in these meetings, their discussions show that they believe that there is more to the client's behaviour than the client is aware of, in other words, they are assuming that something unconscious is affecting the behaviour, beliefs, perceptions and feelings of the client.

Psychoanalysis, as well as being a form of treatment, is a theory about the functioning of this unconscious. In other words we start from a position of belief; we believe that we are all affected by internal processes which we cannot know directly and then we make a study of that phenomenon. I think that this statement of belief is the beginning of an ethical base because our belief is that discovering these unconscious processes improves the quality of life.

A further ethical position follows from the logical consequence of our definition 'that we cannot know our own unconscious directly', which is that we need help to learn how we are being affected by our internal mental states. The ethical position which follows from this has to do not simply with the provision of help but with the attitude we take to the need for help, that it is a position which applies to us as much as to our patients.

It also follows that we believe that the truest statement we can make about any human behaviour must include some understanding of the unconscious as well as the conscious determinants of that behaviour.

It will be objected that this sounds like a licence to behave irresponsibly, after all I can always blame my unconscious, 'I didn't know I was doing it, my unconscious made me'. But this is to misunderstand the consequence of taking the unconscious seriously; if we recognise that we are affected by such unconscious events, it becomes our duty to do what we can to take account of them. One of the challenges of the psychoanalytic approach is that it does not allow either ourselves or our patients 'off the hook'. Once someone points out to me that I am continually repeating a particular kind of behaviour, spoiling good relationships for example, I can no longer use the excuse, 'I didn't know I was doing it'.

Perhaps it is already clear that we have taken on a moral position and this is the starting point, it seems to me, for an ethical code. I see it like this; we are providing a service in a market and we identify ourselves in a very specific way; we say that we believe that understanding the unconscious meaning of human mental activity (and the consequent human actions) offers the most powerful potential for change. We are part of a profession which has been making a rigorous exploration of the human unconscious and we are offering, to those who feel that they will benefit from it, a technique by which we will try to help them recognise their own unconscious functioning, thereby providing them with an opportunity to use such insights to take control of their own circumstances.

What I want to propose is that the essential nature of the technique is the study of the relationship between patient and therapist. This follows from Freud's famous observation in his paper 'The Unconscious' (1915) in which he says, 'It is a very remarkable thing that the Ucs. of one human being can react upon that of another, without passing through the Cs.' The therapist is aiming to identify how he or she is affected and to try to understand what this means about the way that the patient is being affected unconsciously. In order to do this, the therapist has to be able to recognise his or her own unconscious potentials, so as to exclude them from the data. I do not mean that the therapist is aware of unconscious processes, that would be nonsense (unconscious means that we are not aware of them). What I mean is that the therapist has, as a result of his/her own personal analysis, a good enough understanding of the way that his/her unconscious works as to be on the lookout for tell-tale signs in behaviour, thinking, feeling or perception. It seems to me that this is what we are offering the patient, which means that the patient has a reasonable right to assume that the therapist will be doing this. Now I think that this rather simplistic formula has profound implications for our model of work, it means that therapeutic activity only occurs where there is an encounter in which the therapist is being impacted upon by the patient's unconscious. Segal (1997) speaks of this as the consulting room being a laboratory. I would like to take this a little further by considering how we organise a laboratory in order to maximise the chances of making accurate observations.

If we think of the laboratory as a container in which an experiment is being carried out, we can start to define our terms. In the first place the container should be designed to be strong enough to hold the experiment; it is wise to provide an outer container in case this breaks down, so that all parties can be protected. The container should have as little an impact upon the experiment as possible (bearing in mind that all observations have an impact upon what is observed). The container should be sensitive, that is there should be a maximum chance that encounters are registered because it is these encounters which provide data. One of the major mistakes that institutions make is to reduce the contact between the institution and the patient to nothing; unless there is contact, there is no possibility of work and therefore no possibility of change. Both patient and therapist will be enabled to work at their best if the container is both known and predictable. It is important that both patient and therapist know the principles by which the container is organised, another way to speak of this is that this is the nature of the contract.

If we can be clear about the task and the principles by which the task will be performed, it becomes possible to think about ethics. However there remains the central principle which I defined at the beginning; we believe that a true understanding of anything to do with human behaviour must include the role the unconscious played.

What I would like to do now is to define our apparatus and our method of work; I believe that, once these are clear, some of the issues of ethics will be easier to think about.

Identifying the container, the task and the shared principles of work

My excuse for thinking in this rather pedantic and simple way is that I began to realise the importance of these concepts in the therapeutic community work I was involved in for many years as a social worker. I came to understand that the therapeutic container for the patients was more than the clinical staff. In that environment there was the physical building, the systems of administration, rules, the domestic and ancillary workers and the other professional staff as well as the clinical staff. What made it clear that we were all part of the container was that we were engaged upon the same primary task (treatment for the adolescents) and the patients would express themselves not only towards the clinical staff but to all these others as well; graffiti and other physical damage had meaning, the administrative procedures could often become confused or snarled up, a thoughtful consideration of such difficulties would reveal deeper insights into the troubled patients. Rules were one of the main areas in which work would begin, a challenge to the rules would be a statement about something. The point is that this way of thinking about the therapeutic container makes it clear that a vital part of its function is to register impacts. If our container is predictable and there is good contact between all parts of it, there is the best chance of being able to notice 'messages' from the patient which ought to be thought about. An ethical position follows from this, where there is an engagement of such an intimate sort, we must take a view as to the governing principle of therapeutic engagement and my assumption is that we take the Hippocratic approach of doing no harm. (That is, our aim may be to help but our guide as to how to help has to be that our activities are confined by this ethical rule.)

Turning to the situation of psychoanalytic psychotherapy, I would like to suggest that the container can be defined in the following way. First of all, there is an important distinction to be made between the situation where therapy is provided by an institution (a clinic) and where it is offered privately. There are differences of detail in that the physical setting and the administrative systems are more complex in the former environment (and therefore more difficult to hold onto), but the difference which I feel is the most important one is that the 'outer container' is clear to the patients from the beginning. That is, they know that there is a structure which will be available should the therapy seem to break down. The reason I think this is so important is to do with what I have already said about work, that work is only possible where there is an 'impact' between patient and container. The nature of the enterprise is that the patient makes attacks upon the container and the job of the therapist is to notice and think about these attacks in order to maintain the integrity of the container; when the therapist either does not see the evidence of an impact or else becomes caught up in allowing the container to be distorted, there is a danger of the container rupturing. If this happens it is more than helpful for there to be a sort of back-stop; a structure which can be called up to support the therapy and make it possible to re-establish the container. The reason that I have to be careful with my language is that people often get annoyed with me for using words like 'attack' on the grounds that it seems to be judgmental and it misrepresents the patient's need for help and wish to be helped. I don't mean to do that but I do think that the word 'attack' conveys the lived experience of the therapist when faced with the patient's unconscious attempt to create the world in the image of his/her own internal world. If we provide a container which is our best attempt to give a space designed to perceive the unconscious processes of our patients, then we are attempting to eliminate all other variables than those of the patient's unconscious, and the means by which we can make these observations is that we are made aware of the distortions to the container created by the 'impacts' of the patient's mind upon this laboratory. Since these impacts are invariably of the sort that make out that the environment is of a certain type, *x*, although we have been trying to provide an environment of a different type, *y*, we are liable to experience these distortions as attacking.

Safety

I want to use the language of attack because it helps to make it clear that, even if this is only occasionally how any particular therapist experiences his patient, it shows how important it is to make sure that this sort of encounter occurs in a safe place. It seems to me that it can only be helpful to be clear with patients, from the outset, that we are attempting to provide the best chance for protecting the therapeutic project. We do this in specific ways, we offer certain skills which are the result of training within serious and properly registered bodies; we acknowledge the impact of our own unconscious processes and make every attempt to identify these so as to exclude them (I shall come back to this), finally we maintain a properly professional attitude to our work which means that we seek help from our colleagues to think about what we are doing and we keep abreast of developments in practice. Our ethical stance is to avoid using either our skills or our privileged knowledge of our patients to their detriment.

I want to make the point here about our part of the bargain when it comes to our own unconscious. I believe that we have a duty to our patients to have made an in-depth study of our own unconscious in an analysis or a psychoanalytic therapy. In other words, if we agree that the unconscious cannot be known directly, it follows that each of us needs help to learn about our own unconscious. It would be the height of hypocrisy to believe that only 'patients' need help to know about their unconscious. This means that we are including the results of our own therapy in the collection of skills and knowledge we are offering our patients. But we are also including something else, we are including our awareness that we will sometimes require help to think about our work and the inevitable tangles between our own unconscious processes and those brought by our patients. In other words, consultation with colleagues seems to me an necessary 'servicing' of our own good practice. As soon as we are considering the duty we owe our patients to provide an external check on our own work (because of our own unconscious), we have arrived at a principle and that is that the container of therapy itself needs to be contained, there needs to be a professional matrix to which the therapist turns and which is, therefore, providing a further containment for the therapy. And this brings me back to the point about the difference between providing therapy within an institution and in private practice. The former carries a clear message to patients that we will be discussing our work with colleagues and that they (the patients) have a safety net to fall back on if they feel that something is going wrong with their therapy. This is not so obvious in private practice, however I don't know why it isn't. If we are aware that we might become caught up in something counter-therapeutic with our patients (which causes us to seek advice from colleagues), is it not also possible that this may happen without our being aware of it? In which case would it not be useful for there to be a similar sort of 'safety net' which our patients might call upon to provide a similar service of containing the therapy? I think that this is the function of our professional bodies and that patients ought to be aware, at the point of contract, that such a body exists.

I will summarise the elements of the container:

- The physical consulting room, rituals of access and egress, facilities available to patients and so on;
- Procedures to do with administration, bills, endings, beginnings, and so on;
- A contract in which the therapist offers a professional service in an attempt to address the issues brought by the patient. This constitutes the primary task;
- The exclusion of the therapist's life, especially his unconscious strivings;
- The background presence of a professional body;
- Contact with other professionals.

Now, it seems to me that the ethical issues arise in regard to two main areas: one is to do with confusion about the task, the other is to do with the therapist becoming caught up in a distortion of the container (either as a consequence of the pressures from the patient, or as a consequence of his/her own agenda). I shall deal with them in that order.

Changing the task

I should like to quote a famous example from Pierre Turquet (Turquet 1985: 72) about the teaching hospital: in the crisis of a sudden vascular collapse, does the surgeon go on teaching or does he try to save the life of his patient? In other words, it is important to be clear what the primary task is. It is equally important to be clear about this with the patient at the beginning of the work, even though the task becomes part of the container (it is one of the basic 'rules') and will be liable to 'attack'. Changes in task in mid-stream are very dangerous because they are really an acknowledgement that the original contract is no longer appropriate. The danger is that these changes can happen without that acknowledgement becoming explicit. On the other hand there is the danger that, in spite of evidence that it is no longer viable, we continue to hold onto the task.

The reason why clarity about the task is so important is that it is this alone which provides the therapist with the 'authority' to do his/her job. If it is clear between my patient and me that our task is to explore his/her unconscious, then I am 'authorised' to point out that there is an unconscious meaning to his/her request to have a different time, even though he feels that I am a completely unfeeling brute who refuses to recognise that there is a real world out there. On the other hand, if I am unable to be aware of the wider context in which both of us are working, I am liable to miss the point at which there is a real need to change the task.

The other way that things can go wrong is to change the task without noticing it or without formally acknowledging it with the patient. For example, I found myself agreeing with a couple to see each of them separately and to have joint meetings once a month. I felt that it was a useful approach because the female partner was holding firmly to the line that the other was the patient and needed therapy; I thought that individual work would enable this idea to be explored in a more realistic way. What I had not done was formally to acknowledge that the task was different, that the individual sessions widened the scope of the therapy from the couple relationship to individual functioning. With this hindsight it seems to me reasonable that the woman, who believed the problem was lodged in the man, became very angry with me for making interpretations about her internal world and chose to break off the therapy. This does not mean that I believe that being more explicit about the change in task would have kept the therapy going. In fact, I think that the individual concerned would have refused the new arrangement—what it does mean is that my mistake offered what Segal used to call in her supervision of me, a perch. That is the female partner could claim that it was my fault that the therapy ended rather than have to acknowledge her own responsibility.

Altering the container

This is really a reference to the importance of identifying what, exactly is the container for the particular patient or couple. For example there may be the situation of a patient who is really very disturbed, referred by her GP and to whom she returns frequently in crisis and for drugs. If this GP has been very involved in the referral and also makes it clear that she keeps in touch with the therapist on those occasions when the patient refers to her, then she is obviously part of the container. Difficulties arise if the patient gradually ceases to contact the GP and, perhaps, finds someone else in the GP's place. It would be easy to overlook this in the therapy but the fact is that the patient has tried to alter the container, one of the therapeutic figures in the treatment has been wiped out, and this must be taken up or else the therapy will be undermined.

Some of the ethical issues in the event of parallel therapeutic interventions

What I would like to try to do now is to think about some of the ethical issues which are likely to develop in the context of another therapeutic intervention being provided for one of our patients. I do not want to limit this too much because it seems to me that there are a number of situations which could result in similar questions about good practice. The range seems to me to run from questions about contact with parents when one is working with a child, to questions about contact with the individual therapist of one's couple therapy patient (or vice versa). In between are situations which we are probably very familiar with, for instance the patient who goes to his GP with complaints about the therapy, his state of mind or simply with clearly psychological or emotional problems. How do we proceed? How do we think about the problems? I hope that, in considering some examples, it might be possible to see the way in which the framework I have been describing helps us to think about the issues. I shall be describing situations which have either occurred to me or to therapists or counsellors whom I have supervised or who are colleagues of mine. I have taken some trouble to disguise the material without, I hope, taking away from the point at issue.

Having said that, there are already two ethical issues which we need to acknowledge. Under what circumstances is it reasonable to write about one's patients? A related issue arising from the sources of my material (supervisees and colleagues) is whether it is a breach of confidence to talk to colleagues about one's patients? I think that these are relevant to the wider brief of this chapter because contacting the other therapist might be thought to fall into these categories; the issue might be thought of as confidentiality.

Before I move on to the specifics, I want to pick up two issues which were left hanging at the beginning of the chapter. The first is my statement that it is our duty to take responsibility for our unconscious functioning. Related to this is the serious issue of a therapist using his or her insight into the unconscious mind of the patient to exploit that patient. Perhaps, by putting these two together in this way, it becomes clear why I made the former statement. It is a moral (as well as an ethical) position; I don't think that it is a matter of somehow deducing it from first principles, it is a position of principle based upon a particular attitude to other human beings. However powerful my narcissism remains and however much I would like to resort to an omnipotent state, my analysis has enabled me to discover the truth of Money-Kyrle's assertion that there are three facts of life; that we are going to die, that we were born as a result of the sexual union of our parents and that we are all dependent. It is the last of these which matters here. To put it another way, we are, none of us, able to do everything ourselves, we, all of us, need help. Being able to accept this and not feel oppressed by the idea that being helped is a sign of weakness is, I believe, the secret to true independence. As soon as this 'fact of life' is truly accepted, something really important happens, we find ourselves valuing others, we move into a state of mind in which it is the concern for the object rather than our own survival which dominates. Of course none of us remain in this state of mind continually, we move between states of mind, but the discovery of the concern for the object will help us to return to that state because we always have a shadow of it within us.

Although I have been speaking about my own personal voyage, you will recognise that I am also describing a psychoanalytical model of mind and development. One might say that we are hoping, in our work, to enable patients to discover and value this state of mind. In which case our principles of work must derive from this attitude to the world and our fellow human beings. A different view, for example that my main motivation must be my own pleasure or comfort, is not consistent with the psychoanalytic approach that I know about. It seems to me, therefore, legitimate to say that, as psychoanalytical psychotherapists, our principle must be that, recognising that we are liable to be moved by unconscious agendas, we should be alert to any evidence of their operation and we should take care to limit their impact on our work.

The matter of exploitation of our patients through manipulation of their unconscious functioning is a little more complex than seems at first sight. I don't think anyone would disagree that exploitation for material or sexual gratification is unethical. But it is not that variation of this issue to which I want to draw attention, it is something more subtle and something which will be exploited in us unless we are aware of it in ourselves. What I mean is the situation in which we find ourselves believing that we know what is best for the patient, or feeling that we understand something that the patient does not understand about him/herself. It is under these circumstances that we might find ourselves 'exploiting the patient's unconscious functioning' although we are unlikely to be thinking about it in that way.

Before I started my psychoanalytical training I had trained in an alternative therapy, one which worked with the body and was about releasing energy and trapped emotions. I trained in this technique because I had been through a course of therapy and had felt enormously helped and inspired by it; I had experienced something called a 're-birth' and had found some very early memories, I had sobbed about the way that I had felt as a child and I had discovered something strong and powerful in me which I was told was my inner strength. So I trained and I practised this technique on others. The reason I stopped using the method (although I still use some of the theory in different ways) was because of my growing discomfort. I found myself having to face the uncomfortable fact that my own therapy, though very cathartic, hadn't seemed to shift anything deep inside. Not only that but I didn't think that I was helping my own patients to make any real changes within themselves. However the most difficult thing to face up to was that I had come to recognise that my impact on my patients was manipulative. I began to realise that, in the course of the work, I would form a diagnosis (perfectly reasonable and something I had been trained to do) but I would then use my techniques to 'encourage' the patient to accept my view of their experience. I gave up this way of working because I came to see that I was misusing the patients' strong positive transference to make them take on my view of their world.

Now I don't believe that I did this maliciously, I'm sure that I was probably quite right most of the time about the diagnosis. The point is that the technique I was using didn't allow me to present this to the patient for his assessment and response; the exciting and cathartic nature of the exercise created an atmosphere of high suggestibility and I was using that 'for the best possible motives'. I also don't mean to suggest that all practitioners of these forms of alternative therapies are necessarily operating in the same way that I was. I do mean to suggest that anyone who is working with someone else's unconscious must have had their own unconscious examined in a therapy designed to do that. I also mean to suggest that psychoanalytic therapy is not magically protected from this sort of manipulation and we need to be aware of it.

If there is anyone who has stayed with all of this long enough to reach this sentence, you might wonder why I have gone on at such length about something which does not immediately seem to have to do with parallel therapies. The point is that it is when there is another view of our patient around that we are most vulnerable to a push to feel that it is our view which is correct. We then become caught up in a competition with the other therapist for the loyalty of the patient and for our view to prevail. At this point we are in danger of the kind of manipulation I have been describing.

Confidentiality

Let us begin with an issue about which most complaints seem to focus and which causes us a significant amount of soul-searching, confidentiality. This is often the first area of concern for the therapist who discovers that his patient is involved in another therapy, particularly if this seems to be kept as a secret or if the other therapist's comments are often reported and seem to be either undermining one's own work or else they suggest that the other therapist is being led down a false trail. We feel there may be a case to 'do something' and yet we feel that we have a duty of 'confidentiality' to the patient.

To return to my rather simplistic definition of the work: the provision of a container, the centrality of the primary task and the contract with the patient, our offer of certain professional skills and an ethical context for this in exchange for their conscious wish to engage with the therapeutic process. I have already implied that confidentiality is a relative term; the therapist commits him or herself to protect the patient from any harm as a consequence of the privileged information he or she may have. However the therapist also commits him or herself to providing the best possible practice and this will involve taking advice from other professionals. In other words there will be a certain amount of information passed on about the patients. Of course this will be within the professional boundaries of confidentiality. Nevertheless the fact that we do this creates a confusion which can become exacerbated in the context of parallel therapies. I believe my model helps us with this. The question we can ask ourselves is, 'Is this wish to discuss my patient with the other therapist in the service of my own best practice?' A related question is, 'Would I normally go to this particular therapist to get help about my practice?'

Consider the following examples. There is a marital therapy going on in which the therapists become aware that one of the patients is having individual therapy. The way that this is revealed is that the wife in the couple began to talk about her therapist supporting her view that the problem in the marriage was all down to the husband. Now there were two therapists providing the marital therapy and they both knew the wife's therapist professionally. In the marital therapy one of the themes which was emerging had to do with the way that the wife was actually quite perversely involved in the husband's extra-marital affairs. The couple had come to therapy because the husband seemed unable to stop himself having these short sexual relationships. He claimed that he wanted to stop and that he wanted to have children with his wife. She wanted children but was not prepared to try for them until her husband had stopped his philandering.

The therapists had to work hard to understand what kept this couple together. It began to be clear that the wife, whose childhood in a different country had been very rigidly controlled by a powerfully repressive father, projected her own passionate self into her husband where she could feel that the threat was coming from outside herself, not from within. She could identify with a rigid and controlling father and, at the same time, maintain a sadomasochistic relationship with her husband. It was at the point at which the therapists felt that they were beginning to be able to show this to the couple that the wife appeared to have chosen to engage in individual therapy. However she would bring this into the session in the form of remarks made by her therapist to the effect that she was very clearly a victim of a sadistic husband, i.e. it really was his fault. The marital therapists began to feel stuck because they experienced this other therapist as a block to their own efforts. At this point they began to discuss the idea of talking to the other therapist. They hesitated because of the question of confidentiality.

Now I don't know what you think, but it seems clear to me that any attempt to contact this other therapist would not be in the interests of improving the practice of the marital therapists. For a start they were pretty convinced that they were right about the patient, their agenda was really to alter the work of the other therapist.

So where does this take us? If we establish that there isn't a legitimate reason for talking to another professional about our patient, where do we go? The model which I am presenting offers a clear path; our next question is, 'Has the task changed?' This is the next step because the only way that we can 'do something' (i.e. behave in a different way to normal therapy) is if the context of the therapy has in some way changed. Consider this next example.

A very borderline patient had begun once a week psychoanalytic psychotherapy; she had presented as being unhappy at home and feeling unable to leave this unhappy situation. The therapist had felt that there was evidence of something quite adolescent in the patient (who was still in her early twenties) and felt that the work was something about enabling the patient to take possession of her own body by finding out about her anxieties and phantasies about this. She expected that there would be something quite difficult in the transference but this did not happen, instead the patient treated the therapist as a much valued confidant and support against the array of antipathetic adults and siblings at home. The therapist was concerned that the hostility and dangerousness which had been evident in the initial interview was absent, she wondered where it had gone. At breaks that patient would become very anxious and would express some lurid fantasies about what might happen, however she agreed that she had a supportive GP. (The patient had referred herself for psychotherapy and expressed the wish that the therapist did not contact her doctor.) After a couple of breaks the therapist began to realise that something had happened in them. There was a suggestion that the patient had, indeed been to the GP, who had 'done something', although it wasn't clear what. Meanwhile the patient continued to be easy, compliant, grateful and rather two-dimensional. The therapist began to feel that she ought to speak to the doctor. She had asked the patient about what had happened in the breaks and the patient had merely said that she'd seen her doctor who had sometimes given her anti-depressants and, at other times just talked to her.

At this point the therapist regretted that she had not insisted on contacting the GP at the start of the therapy, because she would have felt that there would have been no breach of confidentiality in contact with the GP under those initial circumstances. On the other hand, there was something wrong. Applying the model to this example, it is clear that the therapist would not normally go to the GP for help in her practice, so that such a contact would not fit with that professional support referred to in the original contract; however there is evidence that something has changed in the original contract. The patient seems to have created a split which allows her to leave a part of herself out of the therapy altogether. This disables the therapist. According to this way of thinking, the next thing to do is to talk to the patient about this, namely that something has changed and the therapy is blocked, that there needs to be a review of the process and that the therapist's professional opinion is that she needs to link with the GP in order to provide a consistent 'container' for the patient's treatment.

The advantage of this approach is that it is consistent, the therapist is not throwing the therapy away but is saying that there is a process which appears to be stopping the therapy working because it has 'breached the container'. The therapist is offering a description of this and that ought to provide her with the understanding to make an interpretation as to why the patient is doing this. In this example that patient has turned 'therapy' into 'supportive counselling'; this is not an uncommon event in once a week therapy.

I think that there is a clear difference between this example and the previous one. I don't think that there is any evidence that the contract has changed, but there is evidence that something is happening. The assumption that the therapist is in some way 'caught up' with the wife's pathology might be thought about in the therapy. The marital therapists were also caught up in something, they felt betrayed, someone whom they thought they could trust appeared to be undermining their work. Of course, once it is put in this way, there is a sense of something familiar, isn't this similar to the picture of the husband, someone who ought to be trustworthy who is behaving in a way which appears to undermine the work (marriage)? The identified patient had moved from the husband to the new therapist but the pattern remained. Once the marital therapists had resisted the pressure to breach the container of the marital therapy, the events which were felt to be an attack on the container, namely the wife's reports of her therapist's comments, could be taken up as material to be thought about.

Confusions about task

In the previous section I have indicated the next question, after the one about confidentiality, is 'Has the task changed?' Sometimes, however, there is no apparent issue about confidentiality leading to this 'next step'. This leaves us with a problem as to whether we notice that the task has changed or not.

There is a common situation which all of us who are working with couples will come across at different times. It is also something which happens in individual work, although it may not be so easy to detect. A couple have come to try to sort out their relationship, they may well have worked very hard on this but the change is that one or other partner seems to decide that it is all over. For them there is no longer the wish to repair but now the therapy becomes the place in which the split should be agreed. This may be so that the one who has decided to end it will not be detected as the decision maker or it may be that he or she feels unable to confront the partner without the presence of the therapist. Either way, the therapist is no longer being asked to help sort out the relationship but is being recruited to enable an ending. In individual therapy this is repeated when the patient is using the therapist as a support against the spouse, the patient is no longer interested in learning about himself, he wants to be able to say to his partner, 'My therapist agrees with me that...' If these changes in task are not detected, there is a real danger that the therapist stops being a therapist and becomes, albeit unwillingly, an accomplice to an act. The ethics of our profession do not cease at the level of conscious involvement, as I have been stressing throughout, we have a duty to attend to our unconscious activity as well. A court of law may judge that I have been drawn unwittingly into a marital dispute as the husband's therapist and that I am not guilty of unprofessional conduct, however I think my own professional body ought to find that the wife's complaint against me, that my comments about her have contributed to her marital breakdown, do constitute a form of professional misconduct in so far as I did not take sufficient precaution to monitor my unconscious collusion with my patient's covert campaign.

Conclusion

I hope that I have been able to give some indication of the sorts of ethical problems associated with parallel therapies and that I have provided a model which allows these issues to be attended to. My aim has been to show that psychoanalytical therapy, like other forms of professional work, can be defined in terms of a primary task and basic principles of work, that these basic principles are already determined by the philosophical status of psychoanalysis and that a shared belief in the unconscious places us in a clear ethical context which ought to enable us to make professional decisions more easily.

Having said that, I must return to something that I find I am often saying to students these days. When I began my professional work I worked in two or three children's homes. In each home the 'house mother' (as they were called then) told me that it would be a sign that I wasn't doing my job properly if I became 'caught up' in the work, if I found myself 'taking my work home with me' for instance. These days I say to my students that I think that it is a sign that you are not in the right work if you do not get caught up, it means that you are not open to unconscious processes. Being caught up is not the sign of bad practice, remaining unaware of it is.

> Psychoanalysis is both a theory of mind and a therapy. The therapeutic situation in the analytic consulting room is our laboratory. Like all sciences, it is the laboratory technique that elicits and organises the data which enables us to form hypotheses, to be checked again with the data. (Segal 1997)

CHAPTER THREE

THE TASK OF ASSESSMENT

Herbert Hahn

Herbert Hahn is a Chartered Psychologist, full member of the British Association of Psychotherapists and founder member of the Severnside Institute for Psychotherapy. South African born, he works analytically with individuals, couples and groups as well as in the fields of Social Dreaming and Group Relations. He chaired the multi-disciplinary Executive Committee of Avon's Child Guidance Clinics, and the Analytic Section of the UKCP at the birth of the BCP with which he is also registered. He has recently contributed to Supervision *(Clarkson 1998) and to* Social Dreaming at Work *(Lawrence 1998).*

Herbert Hahn introduces the reader to the assessment process, and shows us how the therapeutic work begins with the meeting of the client or patient and the assessor. He explores and reviews the task of assessment, and also reflects upon the effect the assessor can have, as an invisible presence in the subsequent therapies, long after his or her visible task has been completed. The assessor's experience of the invisible matrix is often to find himself in a maelstrom of past and present professional interactions with all their conscious and unconscious meanings. He generously shares with us the discoveries he has made about different approaches to the task of assessment, whilst making clear his own definition of the assessor's role. Herbert Hahn shows us how a vital part of his task is to notice, understand, and give meaning to what the client or patient brings, calming the waters in order to launch a new therapy.

* * *

The beginning of psychoanalytic work marks a boundary. Once it has been traversed, all previous significant relationships live in the realm of history available as grist to the transferential mill. Sometimes, the boundary itself may become a permeable region which is occupied by a multi-faceted task; a task in which art and science meet; in which observation, enquiry, and evaluation intertwine with intuition, inspiration and concern: the task of assessment.

Perhaps you'd like to tell me what brings you?
Yes, but where to begin?

These, or similar words often initiate an assessment meeting with an individual or couple: 'a meeting between two almost complete strangers, one confiding and the other thinking, linking and responding' (Hewitt 1998: 116). An assessor will, to varying degrees, in a single session endeavour to accomplish most, if not all, of the following: establish trust; learn about current circumstances (including work, relationships, interests and aptitudes). He or she will endeavour to explore family and personal, external and internal history (including family and kinship background and the development or otherwise of sexual, intellectual, emotional and dream life); to assess for psychiatric illness; to conceptualise a dynamic formulation; to make an internal decision; to express a considered opinion about the advisability of a particular form of analytic therapy and implement the decision made (Mace et al. 1995; Cooper & Alfille 1998). A tall order!

To complete this wide-ranging task in such a short time leaves little space to engage, learn from mistakes, and deal with separation. The assessor listens actively, enquires (and probes) carefully, attunes to transference-countertransference, offers advice and answers questions; makes (sometimes deep) interpretations. All this requires sensitive, thorough, flexible and creative use of psychiatric and analytic skills. It is no wonder that Holmes refers to assessment as 'one of the most taxing and potentially exciting' aspects of his job (Holmes 1995: 27). It is not surprising that phantasies of omniscience, clairvoyance and being a saviour are pervasive (Coltart 1992).

At a more conscious level (Sher 1998), the excitement (and element of seduction) of being the 'first in' and putting the patient 'on track' may be counterbalanced by the frustration and disappointment of not being able to continue. Alternatively, what is discovered may be unbearably painful, and the assessor may have to struggle with uncertainties as to whether treatment is sustainable, worries about to whom and how to refer (together with some relief at the prospect of being freed of a burden). An additional vexed problem for the assessor is that of endeavouring to differentiate between the potential fit of different psychoanalytic modalities for a particular individual or couple. This task is artificially simplified if the assessor is primarily steeped in a particular approach; or if he or she makes little or no differentiation between psychoanalysis and psychoanalytic psychotherapy.

Unfortunately, a search of the literature does not help us with this question, as different assessors offer different and overlapping differentiating criteria for different modalities (e.g. Mace 1995). Once upon a time, psychoanalysis was the 'gold standard', and alloyed approaches were simply second-best. But in those days there were also considered to be clear criteria as to who could benefit from psychoanalysis (Wallerstein 1999). Now, a century on, there are a variety of approaches to psychoanalysis, with varying emphases on the importance of transference and 'actual' relationship dimensions in the work. Furthermore the mutual influence of psychoanalysis and psychoanalytic psychotherapy on each other has led to varying modifications of both. It is therefore nowadays impossible for any assessor to assess 'suitability' in the abstract. At best the assessor can only assess for his or her particular context and professional network. However as assessors have become more and more skilled at their task, they may find ways of connecting with their assessees in a way which may be more a function of their own expertise than a general indication of suitability for psychotherapy, whatever the modality.

The process of assessment may reflect that aspect of the analytic process which, from the moment it begins, is always promoting the patient's or client's self-discovery, so that there will come a time when the external therapist can be relinquished. But the processes differ too, in that when conducting an analysis the analyst is committed to receiving all that the analysand brings, and faithfully continuing towards an uncertain and unknown outcome for as long as it takes. In contrast, initial assessments must take about ninety minutes, predict the future, draw conclusions, make decisions and implement them. This is the shadow of the heroic period of psychoanalysis. Assessors who aim to 'wrap up' the assessee in a diagnosis, or even a dynamic formulation, pre-empt an ongoing process of discovery which requires patience as well as interest.

Could it be that the pressure to 'assess' quickly relates to the anxieties generated by our therapeutic task? These are not ameliorated by the increasing range of analytic therapies available, and the continuing modifications in and developments of technique, which continually stretch and permeate our boundaries. Many assessors are also under pressure to provide 'evidence' of the usefulness of their work, and such pressures may force us to develop a form of assessment which looks contained and precise, but may also deprive us of the wonder of observing, exploring, and working with unconscious processes in individuals, couples, groups and organisations. It seems to me that the current ethos in assessment is somewhat driven by the hope that assessors can protect us in advance from the risks and fears inherent in the therapeutic task. It is also difficult to identify the good enough assessor, as any form of intense experience of assessment can cast the shadow of the assessor forward over the therapy. Excellent assessments can be hard, or even impossible 'acts' to follow, and poor assessments may put the applicant off the idea of therapy completely.

For the person coming for an assessment, the experience of being carefully and thoroughly heard, and 'seen' by a stranger who is presumed to be safe and professional, is often experienced as movingly memorable. This may be all the more so, and fuel highly charged unconscious significance, if deep interpretations have also been proffered. Thus, despite the brevity of the encounter, it may nevertheless induce a powerful and enduring sense of attachment. Concomitantly the speed of the prescribed separation and the rejection often implicit in being passed on, may be painful, especially if the assessor fails to warn of this at the outset. Difficulties in good-enough transfer may also be a result of the active nature of assessments being too much of a contrast with the stillness of the therapist. For example, Hewitt (1998) describes a crucial moment in an assessment when the assessee rose to end the meeting prematurely. The assessor's intervention turned this round, and the outcome was that the assessee sought long-term therapy. Of course, there is no guarantee that the subsequent therapist will be as skilled as the assessor, and it is interesting and relevant to note that in giving his account of this assessment, Hewitt refers to the task as an assessment, but to himself as 'the therapist.'

The style and approach adopted by assessors also links with their internal relationship with their role models, by a process which reaches back to our trail-blazing analytic pioneers. Holmes (in Holmes & Lindley 1998) records that his mentors were Henri Rey and Heinz Wolf, who themselves learned from Klein and Winnicott. In assessment meetings Rey specialised in 'deep' interpretations, and his patients cried 'throughout'. Similarly, Wolf's patients would be bathed in 'cathartic tears' and 'promised the earth', which registrars then had to deliver. One is reminded of the Count in Mozart's *Marriage of Figaro,* who seeks to exercise his traditional right to deflower the peasant bride before she marries one of his servants. Holmes, while himself more muted, nevertheless emotionally likens his approach to assessments to that of anticipating a 'theatrical performance'. He 'confesses' that the interview has not really worked for him unless the patient has 'cried or at least come close to tears' (Holmes & Lindley 1998: 27-8).

This approach to assessment and referral finds a representation in myth: Semele asked Zeus to show himself to her in his majesty. This he did, but Semele was unable to endure the sight of the lightning which flashed about her lover, and was struck dead. Zeus took the unborn child, which was still only in its sixth month, from her womb and sewed it up inside his thigh. In due course it was born alive and perfectly formed. This was Dionysius, the twice-born god. Is there an archetypal assessor, a god-like (male) figure who exploits the patient's need as an opportunity to flash his interpretative bolts, deflowering the psychic hymen of the patient? (Kuprat 1999). The therapy which is conceived out of the coming together during the assessment is then as it were prematurely handed over to another therapist, who as an extension of the god, receives and contains what has been started and brings it to life.

Denford (1995), one-time director of the Cassel (a psychoanalytic inpatient unit) pays tribute to his charismatic mentor, Tom Main. But while Main largely saw his assessments as distinct from the rest of the therapeutic process, Denford emphasises that he considers himself as representing a therapeutic team, which includes staff, other patients, and also the referrer. He therefore seeks to establish 'attitudes and assumptions in the culture which will give juniors, nurses and patients, the confidence to say what they think and the expectation that it will be heard' (Denford 1995: 47). In his initial consultation, Denford considers it an intrusion of privacy to 'interpret primary processes' to a person he is only meeting once. He feels these interpretations to be the exclusive province of ongoing work.

Hinshelwood (1995), however, successor to Denford as director of the same hospital, argues his case for including 'a trial of interpretations' in initial assessments (Hinshelwood 1995: 164). He also develops an argument for the value of a dynamic formulation, as contrasted with a formal diagnosis. While this argument is useful as far as it goes, it assumes that it is always possible and constructive to pursue this aim of dynamic formulation. Pressure on the assessor to produce *the* one-off psycho-dynamic X-ray, may leave little room for puzzlement, confusion or simply not knowing that much about another person as the result of a shared single meeting. Furthermore, the degree and appearance of clarity and of authority which the assessor holds, may discourage the subsequent therapist(s) from actively taking into account their own subsequent discoveries.

Jane Knowles (1995) has further developed Denford's way of sharing the work of assessment. At her unit, where a range of analytic options are available, the whole therapy team becomes part of the process at different stages. The senior nurse is consulted in relation to the preliminary information which has been garnered, then the analytic psychiatrist has an individual session with the prospective patient. The case material of this session is subsequently presented to the team for dialogue, as an aid in mediating the assessor's therapeutic zeal or pessimism. When the team recommendation is for in-patient analytic therapy, the existing patient group also participate and have a vote in making the final decision. Such empowerment of a therapeutic group will evidently also require a readiness to work with the destructive aspects of large group dynamics (Nitsun 1996).

Many assessors consider it essential to establish a firm 'contract' relating to time, task and boundaries at the outset. Such information is clearly useful to the recipients, especially if further referral is to be the outcome of assessment. Furthermore, patient agreement to such a contract can be drawn on to deal with later resistance (Stokoe, this volume). We may then ask why we as assessors tend to pre-empt the making of a contract, by referring to those who come to see us as 'patients' even before they have entered our consulting rooms. It is as if we have unconsciously already made an assessment. Might this reflect a way in which as assessors we split off and project our own ill parts, as a way of defending ourselves against the anxieties generated by the assessment task? Such anxieties would nudge us in the direction of following a standardised set of procedures and leave us less open to 'a unique intersubjective encounter' (Tonnesman 1998: 12).

Within the psychoanalytic culture, there are inter-professional bridges and areas of cohesion and co-operation, and also inter-professional rivalries and tensions that may detract from mutual respect between assessors and potential therapists for the validity and usefulness of each other's approaches. Linda Binnington (1999) believes that it is sometimes an appropriate outcome of marital psychotherapy, whether brief or longer term, for one or both partners to seek individual therapy. This could be viewed as part of the process of individuation so central to much marital therapy. The fact of having a period of couple therapy first can strengthen the couple by enabling them to understand and be better prepared for some of the impact of individual therapy on the couple relationship. Binnington expresses concern that many individual therapists who assess and refer a member of a couple for one-to-one therapy appear to ignore the meaning and implications for the couple of the prospect of this new relationship. Further, once therapy is in process, the way in which the treatment can drain or undermine the couple relationship, for example by splitting between therapist and partner, may also not be considered. This type of splitting can be greatly lessened if both partners are somehow involved in sharing the decision for one of them to go into therapy.

The process and outcome of an initial assessment may be significantly influenced by a variety of environmental factors. For example, practitioners working in an institution often feel contained and supported by its collegial and other personal and structural resources which cater for their dependency needs. But they may also feel constrained and sometimes even oppressed by other aspects of the organisation. In private practice, freedom and solitude is counterbalanced by absence of immediately available professional and organisational support and possible loneliness. An absence of external checks and balances for both assessor and assessee may need to be made good by seeking out external resources. Those coming for an assessment may be affected by aspects of the assessment environment, including the manner in which their initial referral or enquiry was dealt with and length of time they have been required to wait. A good experience of assessment may not only be therapeutic in itself, but also serve as an encouragement to engage in therapy; too positive a transference-countertransference link may adversely affect a subsequent therapeutic alliance.

One common feature of assessments in organisational contexts is that they invite a shared or split transference: to the institution and the assessor. Symbolically, there is then an assessing couple comprising the assessor 'father' and the assessing organisational 'mother' (or vice-versa) in dynamic relation to each other. The length of time involved in waiting for an assessment and then therapy has a bearing on the way each patient experiences these dynamics, as does the extent and quality of communication between the professionals involved. In private practice, a therapist (or patient) may wish and need, early on, if not at the beginning, to draw in another professional for a second opinion, or specialised further assessment (e.g. where there are intimations of serious organic or psychotic processes at work). Such a referral may also become relevant at some later stage in the process—again evoking the experience of a working couple. Complicated cases may also, at some stage, involve other forms of assessment by GPs, social services and so on. Over the course of a long or crisis-laden therapy there may be an interweaving of formal and informal assessors, to whom patient and/or therapist relate with varying degrees of intensity and with underlying dyadic, triadic, family and group dynamics.

Mary Morgan (1998) of the Tavistock Marital Studies Institute reflects on her personal experience of being an assessor:

> ...despite always saying at the beginning that I won't be the ongoing therapist, a good proportion of couples still hope by the end of the consultation that it will be possible to work with me. However, I also think that a good consultation, i.e. where there had been a good emotional contact, usually makes for a good transfer. (Morgan 1998)

Her colleague, Chris Vincent, adds:

> I believe very strongly that it is the first assessment rule that the assessor makes clear the context (including length of meeting and nature of referral process) before clients start to talk about their difficulties. If you do not do this or are forced out of it by some unconscious enactment, then you are in for big problems in ending the assessment process. (Morgan 1998)

Hinshelwood (1995) provides an instance: during an assessment meeting he realised that the patient was expecting to continue working with him. When he told her he would not be available, her initial reaction was 'catastrophic' and she terminated the interview prematurely. An exploration of the dynamics of his 'forgetting' to warn the patient in advance, leads him to relate this to her pathology. He adds that successful referral for therapy was nevertheless effected.

A more lasting effect of transfer is reflected in the following: a supervisee reported that a good year into thrice-weekly analysis, his patient referred in passing to his therapist's double-barrelled name. The patient added that she knew her therapist did not use this name on his bills so as not to show off and intimidate his patients, and that this was also the reason that he worked from a small terraced house rather than his much more palatial home. In fact, it was the original assessor who had a hyphenated name and had conducted the assessment in his substantial premises. This patient yearned to have aristocratic connections and often became disillusioned and angry when her glamorised expectations of her therapist and of others were not met. A further elaboration of Morgan's and Vincent's concerns about the long shadow potentially cast by the assessor on future therapy is provided by the following two vignettes:

A therapist reported to his supervisor that his analytic patient of several years standing had made an unexpected 'confession' the previous week. He still yearned for the assessor whom he had seen just once and with whom he would have preferred to work. A week or so later, the supervisor happened to meet the assessor in question at a professional meeting and found herself being asked how the therapy of this same patient was going. The supervisor registered the keenness of the enquiry and intuitively felt that the assessor had also not relinquished the patient. The supervisor's unease had been stirred much earlier because she knew that the original assessment had lasted for two hours, and the assessor had emphasised to the patient that the therapist would be 'a trainee'.

Dorothy Judd (1998) recounts the way in which a male assessor featured in her couple work with a female co-therapist. The couple, Mr and Mrs B., described how positively they felt towards the assessor. He infused them with vitality and sexuality. On the night after the assessment, they made love more passionately than ever before. However, the next day Mrs B., anxious that she was pregnant, took the 'morning-after' pill and was sure that an abortion ensued. Months of gynaecological problems followed.

In their therapy they frequently referred to the assessor, idealising him and regretting the absence of a male therapist in their present therapy. The therapists felt that potency had been split off into the assessor, Mr F, while their work was often attacked and 'aborted' by means such as forgetting the entire content of previous sessions. The couple's experience of the assessment posed a challenge for the therapists. Could they use and interpret it, or would they as therapists become identified with the aborted pregnancy?

Writing about interprofessional dynamics, Rosalind Stumpfl (1998) reminds us that: 'as assessors we all come to an assessment interview carrying our own personal history of thoughts and beliefs; philosophical, socio-economic, political, ethical' (Stumpfl 1998: 111). Assessors take conscious account of these factors and monitor counter-transference for unconscious indicators. But it may be far from easy to consider ways in which certain biases may operate. I refer here to certain assessor attitudes and feelings which are taken for granted. Anthropologists who work cross-culturally describe these as 'doxic' (second nature), and therefore not likely to be accessed by counter-transference intimations (Krause 1998). For example, group analysts, psychoanalysts, couple therapists and family therapists, even if all endeavouring to tune in to unconscious processes, tend to be operating on different (though overlapping) wave-lengths.

Although the majority of analytically-minded assessors emphasise the importance of keeping initial assessment time to a minimum, Garelick (1994) takes an opposite view. Drawing on work with 1,000 patients, he concludes that the assessment process and the aptness of subsequent referral for psychotherapy benefit from a full and proper process of assessment over several sessions. Patients, including those who are unsuitable for analytic therapy, are also more contained by such an approach. Indeed they can make a better positive connection with a therapist after a full assessment than after a brief one. An implication of Garelick's work is that in restricting their meetings to a single session, assessors are unconsciously projecting and acting out their own fears about doing more harm than good. However at the other end of the spectrum, I have very occasionally found that a single meeting may be all that is needed. In the example of Hewitt's assessment quoted earlier, a fleeing assessee was transformed into an eager patient by some initial therapeutic work. In the following instance, what might have been an assessment apparently turned out to be all the therapy that was required:

A mutual acquaintance asked if a Mr Evans might consult for a professional chat about his career. I suggested that Mr Evans might be encouraged to write to me directly. This he did, and his letter referred to a general feeling of underachievement and an inability to live life fully. When we met he spoke in a positive way about the recent ending of an absorbing and successful project at work. His head of department was encouraging him to seek promotion, but he lacked the confidence for this. He went on to speak in a flat voice of his closeness to his wife and children and their attachment to him. I commented on the contrast between his words and his tone. He responded: 'I'm surprised at hearing you say it, but it's true!' I asked whether this way of expressing things had any links with his past. He then recalled, with surprise, the way his mother used to 'put the damper' on his achievements as a child. He then mentioned that he had recently heard a radio programme that referred to 'anxiety dreams'. He said he did not attach much importance to his dreams but asked if I might be able to explore them with him. Time was running out so I suggested the possibility of a further meeting.

We arranged this for a fortnight later. He arrived apologising for only bringing a notebook containing twelve dreams, which he quickly proceeded to read through and to associate to at length. Although I felt somewhat overwhelmed, I managed to register and comment that there were several references to childhood memories. He said he had noticed this too and added that since our first meeting the thought had struck him that childhood experiences were still affecting him strongly. I wondered aloud whether his feeling that twelve dreams today were not enough also had a link with high expectations, perhaps from his parents, during his childhood. He laughed and said 'Yes ...I feel a sense of relief!' It was time to stop. I asked what he would like to do. He replied that a lot had come up that he wanted to think about and that he would like to come again in three weeks' time.

At the third meeting, he said he was a lot clearer about the nature and origins of the dissatisfaction he had come with at our first meeting. He also narrated a single dream, which with the help of his associations we were able to relate to painful unresolved feelings and memories of sibling rivalry. As we ended the session he expressed appreciation for the work we had done together and stated that he now felt able to proceed on his own. Two months later he requested a 'follow-up' session. On arrival he told me with satisfaction that for the first time in his life he had had a person-to-person talk with his father. But subsequently he'd had one of his lows. He then proceeded at some speed to narrate several dreams he had had over the previous weeks, and went on to reflect and associate to some of the dream content. He also said that he felt uncomfortable with those parts of his dreams which had to do with animals and seemed 'primitive'. He said that in thinking about his dreams at home, he had also remembered some of the things I had said previously. He felt he was discovering a middle ground between conflicting points of view within himself. He also felt optimistic about developing his interests outside his work without having to give up his job. He said he now felt he could cope on his own, but would like to be able to come and consult me from time to time if things became difficult again.

He did so three months later. First he reported 'progress': people were commenting on the fact they were finding him much more positive and helpful. He would probably also be offered the sabbatical year he wanted. Then he began energetically to produce a stream of dreams. By the fourth one, I interrupted him linking its anxiety content with a possible fear on his part that, despite good evidence of progress, he was at times finding himself out of his depth in his inner world. Perhaps he might even be finding it difficult to cope. He gave a deep sigh and said he felt he needed help. We then arranged regular sessions. He said that he was looking forward to beginning his sessions, and ended on a reflective note: 'I do not think that I would have been able to consider the idea of regular sessions until now; first I needed to have a few pointers to what was going on inside myself, and then it took time to discover that I could not sort it all out on my own.'

On reflection, it seems that I was here holding two roles and tasks in mind simultaneously, being the assessor and also the potential therapist. A matrix was established in my mind during the long assessment process, within which the internal assessor and therapist roles engaged in a pre-conscious dialogue with one another. In the example given, it could be said that these roles were also shared with Mr Evans, who then tested out the scope and limits of his own internalised precursors of therapist and assessor. The matrix in my mind included the function of monitoring, or in a sense supervising, the process we were both engaged in, and this role was also shared with Mr Evans. The reader may not be surprised to learn that Mr Evans' subsequent career flourished in the field of *adult* education.

Assessors carefully evaluate many patient-specific factors including the potential to establish a therapeutic alliance, but rarely consider therapist-specific factors in making a referral (Mace et al. 1995). A striking exception was Nina Coltart (1992) who 'knew' many analytic workers and prided herself on an intuitive approach to good and fast matching. Most assessors are not in such a felicitous position, and refer on the basis of organisational and network affiliations. They thereby ignore Adam Limentani's (1972) conclusion that many unsatisfactory outcomes in analysis are the result of a combination of factors in both analyst and patient. Tantam (1995) furthermore points to research conclusions that a moderate similarity between therapist's and patient's values is associated with the greatest improvement. There appears to be a gap in the literature with regard to criteria for matching. However some general guidelines are offered by Karl Konig (1997). He suggests that therapists with strong depressive character traits may be particularly vulnerable to working less well when their self-image is being devalued, and may not be suited to patients likely to develop a strong negative transference. However they may be particularly suited to long-term work. Obsessive-compulsive therapists may put emphasis on structure and even rituals and be less useful where a flexible approach is indicated. They may also be unconsciously inclined to try and control their patient's lives and find it difficult to settle for less than a 'cure'. Therapists with phobic tendencies tend to work best with self-confident patients who need to be accompanied rather than led. Hysterically oriented therapists may be less suited to taking sole responsibility for long-term treatment and may work best in a hospital or clinic setting where the work is shared. Overall, this relatively unexplored area is crying for further attention.

Sher (1998) reflects upon referral from the assessor's point of view. Assessors are sometimes ambivalent about referring on, and thus losing someone with whom they have had a gripping and exciting encounter. There may also have been elements of seduction which arouse guilt. They enjoy the privilege of having had the first opportunity to see people on their way. It can be a problem to think about how to refer a patient whom an assessor thinks will be difficult to work with. Should the assessor lay out the facts as he or she sees them, or try to 'sell' the patient by being economical with the truth? This experience of being on the receiving end of a referral is illustrated by the following vignettes:

Hodson (1998) was referred a young man by a colleague who assessed him as having 'a little Oedipal problem'. He turned out to be in a borderline state. Her feelings were mixed and conflicted but she certainly felt that she had a lot to handle. Unfortunately her colleague's boundaries did not allow for any further thought about the patient by both therapists.

In my supervisory practice, a therapist reported that a senior colleague who was an experienced assessor had sent her 'a man with a little marital problem. Just the sort you're good at.' This patient turned out to be ruthlessly playing off his wife, lover and mother against each other, as well as being dangerously suicidal and directly threatening to the therapist. While this may raise some questions about the assessor's skills or unconscious motivations, another line of enquiry would lead us to consider whether the patient unconsciously applied great skill in 'passing' his assessment, before he revealed himself more fully.

Some analytic therapists consider the whole of analytic work as a process of continuous assessment and re-assessment. For example, a patient in therapy suddenly experienced what he called a memory 'fade out'. The circumstances were as follows:

On a Sunday morning when he woke quite early he quietly went to relieve himself. On his return, he drew the curtains a little and was amazed to find a totally strange woman sleeping on his partner's side of the bed. He knew he had had a lot to drink the previous evening, but while the woman continued to sleep, it gradually came back to him that he had 'picked up' this woman for a one-night stand, knowing his partner was away visiting her family. The analytic work focused initially on his unconscious motives, but when he had another 'fade out' both of us were alerted to the need for a neurological assessment.

The following account written up after a supervision session reflects something of the complexity of choosing between therapeutic modalities (Mellett 1998):

I brought to supervision a middle-aged woman who is in the process of ending her therapy. The therapeutic work over some years has revolved around the tragic death of her eldest child. The ending of therapy feels like a concrete gesture towards moving further from the trauma, which she finds hard to symbolise. Throughout the therapy I have experienced myself as working with a couple in the room, either my client and her partner, or my client and her lost child. At the time of the tragedy, her partner could not cope at all, and she had to manage alone. Her anger about this overwhelms her whenever she is alone with him. Now the youngest child is leaving home, emphasising the enormity of the space between the couple. She is terrified of sharing her feelings with her partner for fear of being overwhelmed by her memories and by her rage at his emotional absence. In the meantime, he, too, had sought individual therapy.

I brought to supervision the question of how appropriate couple therapy might be at this stage. As I reflected with my supervisor on referring this couple on, I recalled a therapist colleague who had originally seen my client before myself, and had then offered couple therapy. My client had chosen not to work with her. I wondered whether my colleague had thought first of couple issues and couple therapy because of her experience in that work. On the other hand my client may have been defending herself against couple work in choosing to work with me.

My supervisor suggested in the light of all this, it might be appropriate for me to see the couple, not for couple therapy as such, but to initiate within the couple a process that might connect my client more with life. I suggested 'help her grasp the nettle of their life together' and my supervisor reflected that nettles have to be tightly grasped to avoid stinging. I found myself imagining how this grasp might anchor her more in life, as opposed to the therapy, which was associated with the trauma and death. She had been locked into the specialness of her relationship with her lost child; trying to find what she did wrong; undo the tragedy. In sessions subsequent to this supervision, it seemed that she had an increasing need to close the gap between herself and her partner. This now possible shift in her is reflected in my own exploration about my way of working and the role of my colleague.

What if, we might speculate, the original couple therapist had at the outset offered just a session or two of consultative exploration and then herself made a referral for individual therapy? Could the couple have come back to her later for further help?

A marital therapist colleague working in co-therapy found that reviewing or re-assessing a couple with the individual therapist can address important Oedipal issues that have been avoided in the separate therapies. She offers the following example: their clients were living separately and fighting over their child. One of the partners was subtly denigrating both their couple work and the parallel individual therapy. The therapists, after careful consideration, sought the client's permission to consult with the individual therapist. The client agreed on condition 'that you tell me what you say to each other'. The therapists refused this condition, but nevertheless obtained the client's angry permission. While the content of the ensuing discussion between the therapists seemed of little import in itself, the client made great strides afterwards, becoming much calmer. The couple also ceased fighting over their child.

Drawing on detailed clinical material the therapists concluded that their stance in insisting on being trusted to meet in private on behalf of the client confronted and contained the client's Oedipal wishes to control and split 'the parents.' This contrasted with the client's experience of her own estranged parents, who only met in order to fight over her.

In contrast, Philip Stokoe (this volume), a psychoanalyst who also works with couples, writes that his supervision enabled him to resist the temptation of liaising with a parallel worker, despite the client's wish for this to happen. This decision paved the way for the patient to make strides in the development of his separate identity. It will be evident from these examples that the therapeutic outcome of such decisions based on re-assessment is determined, not by what is done or avoided, but by the way in which action is taken or resisted and the meaning which this then carries for the client. In both cases it was the opportunity to 'think again' which proved useful.

Both assessor and assessee often have to cope with the experience of intimacy followed by the swift and total loss of each other. The loss is often felt as premature. I recall long ago reading a short story, I think by Guy de Maupassant. It concerned a couple entombed in a tunnel after a train crash. Convinced they were going to die, they made love tenderly. When they were in fact rescued, they suffered guilt and shame. In assessment, the intimacy which develops may take on the intensity of a pair who know that they only have this single chance with each other. In spite of being a fine experience, it may also leave an undercurrent of frustration and even guilt—perhaps echoes of a one-night stand. Mrs X, for instance, spent a night with a visiting old flame. She found the sexual matching perfect, but she also felt used and abandoned—dumped. She needed something more reliable. Idealising a lost assessor may be a manic defence against the pain of abandonment. In desperately attempting to preserve something good, negative feelings may be split off and projected onto available others. On the other hand, if the assessment is experienced as having gone wrong, the assessee is deprived of the opportunity to confront the assessor with a view to putting things right. A search for a family metaphor for a good-enough assessment takes us into the realm of triadic relationships. If the assessor represents say the father and the therapist the mother, therapy may feel like being in a one-parent family. The image of the assessor as an uncle or aunt—someone who is close to and concerned about the family, but not too close—may make for a more benign transfer.

I saw a woman in her early thirties for an initial consultation and referred her on to a colleague. Soon after meeting and embarking on regular therapy with this colleague, she wrote asking if she could see me very occasionally 'to talk about important questions.' When I replied requesting her permission to share her letter with her therapist, she agreed. Her therapist then told me that the work had got off to what seemed a good slow start. She said she thought the patient wanted to know that she could maintain a link with me at a time when her recent losses (including betrayal by her lover and an abortion) were still so painful. With the therapist's agreement, I wrote briefly saying that I and her therapist were agreeable to her coming to see me occasionally if and when she still felt she wanted and needed to. I think that may have been all she needed, because I did not hear from her again. The initial impact of my referring her on may have felt both like another betrayal and like an abortion—in identification with her never-to-be-born baby.

Is it ethical to endeavour to carry out a comprehensive thoroughgoing assessment involving responsive engagement, intimate enquiry and interpretation in the space of a single 90 minute session? It all depends. The process of researching the material for this chapter has led me to the view that when an initial assessment is likely to lead to treatment by another, it often behoves the assessor to hold back from intimate engagement. However, there will paradoxically be times when an engaging initial therapeutic consultation may be sufficient in itself, or facilitate positive transfer. In a deeper sense assessment, like interpretation, can and should never be finished—it is always in the process of becoming. Good enough interpretations in effecting change, become part of history; and a good enough initial formulation, in promoting re-search, encourages re-formulation of what was and what has changed or is changing. Perhaps we need to reconsider the role of those who do brilliant assessments but are hard acts to follow. Might they serve better if they involved themselves less, and left more for the work of therapy?

At an unconscious level, assessors are vulnerable to idealising their own form of assessment and preferred treatment, and selectively perceiving and projecting bad practice elsewhere. Such splitting, when it occurs, puts a persecutory emphasis on what are nevertheless important and valuable guidelines relating to time, contracts, confidentiality and so on. The propensity to idealisation of assessors, which may include omnipotent and omniscient phantasies, comes from difficulty in containing the uncertainties inherent in the task itself. It may also be the outcome of defensive projection by the analytic system as a whole into its specialised assessment sub-culture. Within this sub-culture, such projections may make it difficult to hold in mind the interrelated values of analytically inspired individual, couple, family, group, inter-group and organisational assessments

All analytic work involves an ongoing process of exploration, assessment and discovery. Assessments may be useful before the beginning of therapy, or at a variety of subsequent choice points. They may usefully be carried out by one or more individuals in a variety of permutations and time scales. As we are tending towards longer life spans, it becomes increasingly important for assessment to cease to be the prerogative of powerful 'seniors', who may have their less conscious reasons for creating a mystique around and retaining control of the assessor's role. Methods of assessment and their active re-evaluation must be covered in our training courses.

If the process of assessment aims to exclude all those who are deemed unsuitable or unsafe, we risk losing our vocation. Our future may be healthier if initial assessments set the style and tone for an ongoing readiness to approach what is new with wonder as well as anxiety, fear, care and concern. The sub-culture of assessment may need continually to reassess itself, and to be open to new insights in which sharing and separateness take on new meanings. For example, an ethos which promotes valuable specialised training in assessment, may in its shadow foster a powerful self-perpetuating elite. At an opposite pole, Foulkes (1971) suggested that assessment may be practically unnecessary for group-analysis, which 'is a valuable experience for everybody' except 'those who are too sick or 'too normal' ... [and] those will usually find a good reason to keep away anyhow.' As we endeavour to stand on the shoulders of our predecessors, in a spirit of growth as well as emulation, we need to bear in mind the importance of encouraging development in our successors. Our pursuit of excellence and our protective concerns must not deprive those who seek to learn from and with us of support in doing their own assessments, and learning from their own experience.

CHAPTER FOUR

RELATIONSHIPS CUBED: SHARING PATIENTS FROM AN INDIVIDUAL PSYCHOTHERAPIST'S POINT OF VIEW

Penny Jaques

Penny Jaques is a member of the British Association of Psychotherapists in private practice in Oxford. She works with individual adult patients and occasionally with couples and she is involved in supervision and case discussion with trainees and colleagues. Penny came to psychotherapy training from a career in child care and psychiatric social work and was for many years a member of the multi-disciplinary team in the St Albans Child and Family Clinic, where the sharing of patients was intrinsic to the clinical practice. She is the author of Understanding Children's Problems: Helping Families to Help Themselves *(Unwin 1987).*

Penny Jaques is an individual therapist of many years' standing, who combines rigorous analytic thinking with openness of mind. She writes this chapter from a viewpoint informed by her therapeutic practice, and also by her experience in the roles of supervisor, assessor, and training therapist. She pays attention to the complexities of working alongside—and sometimes sharing patients with—both analytic and non-analytic therapists, and emphasises the importance of being able to open a dialogue with one's colleagues, whilst acknowledging the difficulties in doing so. She gives detailed consideration to reflections of unconscious issues which can appear in the relationships between therapists, and lets us see the need to take account of the external world, whilst keeping faith with our belief in unconscious mental processes, our internal worlds.

* * *

This chapter is written from the point of view of a psychotherapist working alone in private practice, with patients seen between one and three times a week, long and short term, who present with a wide range of problems. While some patients are psychologically sophisticated and welcome the opportunity to embark on the analytic journey (the open-ended intensive work in depth which is the essence of psychoanalytic psychotherapy) others have little or no idea about what may be involved in the therapeutic relationship.

Many people consult a therapist in a crisis, often before, during or after the breakdown of a relationship and then the space needed to think with the patient may be filled up, not only with unprocessed and often unconscious feelings and phantasies belonging to aspects of the patient's past relationships, but with very disturbing and distressing events and emotions in relation to the significant people in the patient's current life. A very varied caseload presents a therapist with many challenges, not least, the need to be flexible enough to modify technique without sacrificing the basic tenets of psychodynamic practice.

Therapists in the public or voluntary sector who work within financial and staffing constraints may envy the private practitioner who has greater freedom to make choices about whom to work with and for how long. But this freedom brings its own problems, for unlike the therapist who works within an institution or clinical team, the psychotherapist working alone has to provide the total therapeutic environment; the external set-up and the psychological space which will allow for the exploration of the patient's inner world. The therapist may need to seek out or even create support structures, whether in the form of professional consultation, peer group discussions or active participation within a professional organisation. All these activities will involve a certain degree of sharing both of oneself and of one's work with patients.

We share our patients whether we like it or not. We share them all the time with the significant people in their lives outside the consulting room. We may also find ourselves sharing them in ways which will inevitably have a powerful impact, consciously and unconsciously, on the course of the therapy. This may be because the patient chooses to seek some form of alternative therapy, or perhaps someone in a close relationship with the patient enters their own therapy. Perhaps the patient is being taught or supervised by colleagues and friends of the therapist; almost inevitable in small networks. Then there are occasions when a therapist may support, or even suggest, that the patient start a parallel therapy such as marital therapy. These situations provide fertile ground for the development of serious splitting and therefore require the therapist to be vigilant in monitoring not only the patient's feelings and phantasies, but also what is provoked in the therapist which may or may not belong also to the patient.

In intensive analytic work the therapist will listen carefully to what the patient says with an assumption, based on an understanding of object relations theory, that what the patient says may express an unconscious aspect of the patient's self. When the patient speaks about people outside the consulting room, whether from the past or the present, the therapist will be sensing and responding to the underlying, often unconscious, connection to the patient's feelings about the therapist. The therapeutic relationship becomes the forum for the exploration of the client's internal world and through the developing transference the therapist will feel the impact of the patient's unresolved emotional pain, conflict and longing. This work with unconscious processes within the crucible of the transference/counter-transference situation is the *sine qua non* of psychoanalytic therapy.

Whether or not, and if so how much and in what way, a therapist should be drawn into discussion about the patient's relationships to people outside the consulting-room is a subject of on-going debate. Fine (1989) argues that there are always at least two significant transferences, one to the therapist and one to someone outside, and working only through the former cannot be done properly without working on the other. His formula is: 'This is your life in miniature. What you do with me you also do with other people'. This helps the patient to focus on all the transferences in his/her life and not to isolate the therapy from the rest of life.

As Josephine Klein (1995) has argued, some patients are not ready for interpretations of any sort. With other patients, particularly those seen less intensively or short term, Malan's (1995) model, extended by Molnos (1995), of the 'Triangle of Person' and 'Triangle of Defence' is helpful in showing the links which need to be made between the conscious and unconscious feelings associated with the patient's significant relationships: in the distant past, in current or recent life, and in the developing transference. Within this framework the therapist will speak about the patient's relationships with people outside the consulting-room, although Malan has demonstrated that ultimately it is the interpretation of the transference to the therapist which is the most powerful agent of change in the patient.

Given the debate and controversy over the place of extra-transference interpretations (Blum 1983, Stewart 1992) it is hardly surprising that it feels much more difficult to consider situations of the actual sharing of patients, making the dramatic shift from a focus primarily within the therapist/patient relationship to one which encompasses the patient's relationship to another therapist. This topic of sharing patients is one that would seem, at least on first view, to be a challenge to the very core of best practice in individual psychoanalytic psychotherapy. But there are situations which occur in our work when either we find ourselves having to share our patients, or even, on rare occasions, we may initiate the sharing.

Each of us has made our own journey to becoming a psychotherapist. We bring to our work our life experience, our previous professional training and experience and our self awareness derived from our own therapies. I have always been intrigued by the interlocking systems of society, family, couple and individual—conscious and unconscious—and how first as a social worker, then as a family therapist and now an individual psychotherapist, I have had to make different choices about where, when and how to make an intervention. We do not stop knowing what we know about couples and families when we work in an intense one to one relationship with a patient in psychoanalytic psychotherapy. In the same way marital psychotherapists will not stop thinking about each partner's individual psychopathology although the interventions will be in the 'in-betweenness' of the marital relationship and the reflection of that in the counter-transference.

Through discussion with colleagues and supervisees and particularly in relation to my own practice, I know that issues around sharing cause concern and confusion. Where the therapy network is small and therapists have opinions about other therapists' work, the problems inherent in sharing are extraordinarily complex and provide fertile ground for splitting with attendant idealisation and denigration. In our training we learn the fundamental importance of boundaries, containment and confidentiality so perhaps it is not surprising that we feel uncomfortable when we decide to get involved in decisions which appear to disobey these rules. Therapists who are keen to discuss the problems of sharing when they are in informal groups or supervision, are reluctant to do so in formal discussions and written papers.

Perhaps it is the guilt arising from the feeling that one is doing something improper which accounts for the fact that some therapists who do get involved in sharing their patients seem to have difficulty extending their analytic understanding to matters that lie outside the one-to-one analytic relationship of therapist and patient; the territory is forbidden so perhaps it is also best avoided.

An example of this which many therapists meet from time to time is when a patient asks for help in finding a therapist for the patient's partner. (I am taking for granted that the therapist has done a lot of analytic work with the patient about the meaning of this request). It helps if there is a clinical referral service in the area but there are few of these and they tend to be concentrated in the larger metropolitan areas. Where this is not an option, the therapist may chose to give the patient a name for the partner rather than risk the partner finding someone unsuitable. The therapist may then feel relieved that the matter is now being attended to and the therapy that has been interrupted by this episode, can now proceed. But what needs to be borne in mind from that moment on, is that the patient's material will be imbued with phantasies about the other, unknown therapist and the imagined relationship between the therapist couple and the (other) therapist-patient pair. The original therapist and patient are now part of a matrix with interpersonal and intrapsychic dimensions.

The metaphor which came to me when thinking about this complex set of relationships was of a 'Rubik's Cube' puzzle where interlocking squares with different coloured faces can be turned to face inside or out while remaining in obvious or hidden relationship to each other. The turning of one part of the puzzle affects the whole picture and brings previously hidden aspects to the fore. When the face of one brick is turned away it has still to be born in mind because of its relation to the whole.

It has proved exceedingly difficult to find out what leading psychoanalytic writers have to say about this whole complex area of sharing patients. Individual psychotherapy is essentially a therapy within a boundaried one-to-one relationship and therefore to think beyond that boundary provokes feelings of unease and fears of chaos. Bollas and Sundelson (1995) alerted therapists to the need for extreme vigilance in maintaining confidentiality particularly against the intrusion of third parties. Searching through the references at the back of favourite books has proved fruitless; under the subject headings of 'boundaries', 'containment' and 'confidentiality' the message within the text is to demonstrate a failure by the therapist to gather everything into the transference and maintain a proper analytic attitude. Perhaps it is not surprising that it is within the literature of marital and family psychotherapists that fuller discussion about sharing has taken place (Scharff & Scharff 1991, Ruszczynski 1993a).

Symington (1986) writes about a patient who was so upset by the way her therapy was going that she had gone back to the counsellor who had referred her to ask her advice about it. In the next session she told Symington what she had done. He writes:

> Then she was silent. After a while I asked her what the lady had said. She said her reply had been, 'It sounds as if he cannot hear the screams of a distressed baby'. I was about to say something when I was gripped at the very centre of myself by a dawning realisation of the truth of what she had just said... I was deeply moved and it took me a few minutes to gather my composure, and then I said to her, 'I think what you have just said is quite correct', and she burst into tears. (Symington 1986: 292-3)

Symington did not become defensive in the face of the attack implicit in the patient's decision to go back to the counsellor. He chose instead to allow himself to be open to hear the true message and in doing so he was willing to 'share' his patient with the counsellor so that her interpretation could help him and his patient.

What follows are some examples from my clinical practice which have confronted me with the need to think very carefully about different sorts of sharing.

Sharing with General Practitioners

Every psychotherapy patient has a general practitioner who may or may not be a significant person in the patient's life and therefore in the therapy. Patients who are being medically treated, whether for physical or psychiatric illnesses, particularly those suffering from psychosomatic conditions, present special challenges for psychotherapists working alone in private practice who need to be free to work with the psychological aspects of these problems, but also to be sure that someone is looking after the patient's physical health. If the more disturbed patients are to benefit from private psychotherapy, it is essential that the therapist is familiar with the various mental health services in the community and knows which psychiatrists are supportive of analytic therapy and may be available for consultation if needed.

Where there is professional rivalry or a lack of mutual understanding or respect, the patient will not feel safely held and the therapy may come unstuck. This is much more complicated for a therapist working alone than for those who work in clinical teams where the overall containment is provided by the agency within which the different professionals have structures and procedures for setting up treatment and providing consultation. In private practice it is crucial that the different professionals agree their separate roles and responsibilities and that the patient is clear from the beginning about who may or may not communicate with whom and about what. I learnt the hard way very early in my role as a therapist working alone.

Mr Shah came to see me on the advice of the personnel director at the company of which he was a director. He had mentioned to her his difficulty in asserting himself both at board meetings and in relation to his eldest teenaged son. Following two consultations we agreed to meet regularly on a once-a-week basis and with Mr Shah's agreement I notified his GP.

Two months later Mr Shah took one of his sons to see the GP who then told Mr Shah that he did not know me and suggested he go to a medical colleague of the GP's. He offered to telephone his colleague there and then. Mr Shah had politely declined the offer but was completely thrown by this suggestion, not least because he came from a culture in which male authority was paramount. For my part I felt humiliated and upset at this attempt to 'steal' my patient and at that very early stage in my career was too lacking in confidence and, as I realised later, too angry to speak to the GP. Mr Shah had found it very unsettling but made the decision to stay with me and I went along with his declared wish to put the matter behind him.

Only much later was I able to acknowledge that my lack of courage in tackling the GP had recreated the drama of Mr Shah's childhood; he was forced to protect his mother/me from his father/GP's violent rages. He was identified with, and protective of, the victim/mother/me and unable to own and make use of his assertive and angry feelings fearing he would become like his dangerous and destructive father. It was a long time before Mr Shah was able to accept that he would have preferred a male therapist.

Rather then getting involved in taking action in the external world the therapist's task is to hold the boundary within which the patient and the therapist can continue to explore the hidden, unconscious dimensions of the patient's conflicts. But sometimes the patient's internal conflicts get projected into the other involved professionals who may then act them out in such a way that the therapy is undermined.

Jenny was a brilliant student in her first year at university. She had been anorexic for several years and had one hospital admission at sixteen, organised by her mother, a doctor, who had been divorced from Jenny's father, a businessman, for ten years. Jenny welcomed the opportunity that therapy offered to explore the unconscious meaning of her anorexia, and settled in twice-weekly sessions paid for by her father and supported by the college medical staff who would continue to monitor her physical health and understood that I would not contact them without Jenny's permission. Her mother had said Jenny was old enough to make her own decision about starting therapy, but also made it clear that she thought psychotherapy was probably a waste of time.

To cut a long story short; Jenny's therapy proceeded well and her obsessional symptoms eased. I was therefore very surprised when the nurse telephoned sounding anxious to tell me that Jenny had not been attending her regular weighing sessions and her mother had turned up unexpectedly and was quite critical of the nurse for not having up-to-date information. The nurse said she thought Jenny's mother might be right, that what Jenny needed was to be admitted to a hospital near her home. I felt quite alarmed at the apparent turn of events and though I listened attentively, I was careful to say nothing about my work with Jenny and clarified that I would need to tell Jenny that we had spoken.

At her next session, Jenny seemed unusually withdrawn and sulky. In her opinion, both her mother and the nurse were being over-anxious and controlling . With a definite note of triumph in her voice she said that she had been seeing the college doctor in his town practice and had asked him not to tell the nurse. She liked talking to him because he treated her like an adult. In the face of such obvious splitting, I made a link to her problems growing up with warring parents and interpreted her fear of losing the good me if she brought her angry feelings into the open between us. She denied any negative feelings towards me, saying that it was the nurse who she resented because she was bossy.

Before her next session I had the doctor on the telephone saying rather angrily that Jenny had told him I had been 'very cross' with her for talking to him. He wanted to discuss what to do for the best and said that he and the nurse did not agree about Jenny. He thought it would be a very retrograde step for her to leave college and in his view she did not require hospitalisation. I replied in a general way about the level of anxiety some patients cause and how the professionals can feel wrong-footed and misrepresented. Though he had originally agreed that I could not discuss Jenny's therapy with him I could sense his frustration with me.

This case illustrates some of the particular problems facing a therapist working alone and sharing a patient with other professionals. Had I been consulting to the college medical team, I could have focused on the way Jenny had projected aspects of the splits in her internal world into the different team members who were then acting them out. Changes in the way the team functioned would then have had an impact on Jenny. If I had been a family therapist I could have suggested a meeting of all the professionals with Jenny and both her parents, to help Jenny to be more open about her divided loyalties and unexpressed distress about her parent's divorce. But as Jenny's individual therapist, I had to find a way to maintain trust with the other workers without losing the therapeutic boundary within which Jenny and I could continue to explore the meaning of her symptoms and her behaviour. The splits which were acted out at the interpersonal level were indicators of the deeper intrapsychic disturbance which then became the focus of my work with Jenny.

Some patients will use the relationship with the doctor to attack or undermine the therapy.

When the going got tough in Mr Gordon's therapy he fled to his doctor and demanded Prozac. Where previously he had turned to alcohol, he now used the medication. It was important that I stayed well away from any decision about the Prozac—I had no contact with the doctor—but continued to explore the symbolic meaning of his need for something real inside him. I interpreted his profound fear that I, like his mother, was incapable of understanding him and was withholding the unconditional love which he believed would 'cure' him.

Casement (1985) gives a full and graphic account of work with Miss K who, whilst in therapy with him, consulted a number of doctors and even went as far as having her jaw wired to stop her eating. Casement describes in fascinating detail his struggle to maintain an analytic attitude and understand the meaning of her behaviour. Had he got involved in stopping her from doing things that he believed were unhelpful to her, he would have been responding to Miss K's unconscious provocation to behave like the intrusive mother of her early life. His position, which subsequently proved to have been very wise, was not easy to maintain, particularly when he was seriously worried about what was happening to her.

Sharing patients with 'alternative' therapists

I work in a district where 'alternative' therapies thrive. It is hardly surprising that patients who are troubled enough to enter psychotherapy may at some point in the therapy also seek other forms of help. We should not fall into the trap of assuming that such an action is always an 'acting out'; an attack on the therapy, therefore bad. Of course, the patient's action is a very powerful communication, but what it means in terms of a particular patient at a specific time can only be understood within the context of that individual's therapy, and the quality and intensity of the transference.

James, an attractive and intelligent man in his middle thirties had been in twice-weekly therapy for about a year following his wife's sudden exit from the marriage. He had quickly developed a dependent, rather idealised transference and saw himself as the innocent, misunderstood partner in the marriage. He cried a great deal and initially elicited a sympathetic feeling in me which gradually changed to irritation. I understood this as a counter-transference response and attempted to interpret his anger and frustration with me which he denied. I knew enough about his early life experience to hypothesise that he had never managed to cope with the intense rage he must have felt towards his mother who had doted on his sister, born when he was three years old. Near the end of a Friday session he mentioned, very much in passing, that he had been having a number of aromatherapy sessions in a house round the corner from mine. Given that I do not disapprove of many alternative body therapies and knowing that an aromatherapist is unlikely to be wanting to understand the client's unconscious, my intense feeling of anger at this information could only be understood as projective identification. I was in no doubt at all that the correct thing to do was to interpret his frustration and angry resentment with me who, like the mother of his early years, withheld her soothing, loving caress.

In setting up the two therapies James had recreated in the external world the split in his internal world which, from early in his life, had been his means of keeping his mother idealised and 'good'. James had made me feel left out and frustrated just as he had felt, but having stirred these feelings up in me it became possible to begin to help him to think about and reintegrate these powerful and forbidden emotions.

Isabel had been in three-times weekly therapy for several years. She had grown up in a large, poor and chaotic family where all the children had been physically abused by her mentally ill mother and Isabel had been sexually abused by her father and some of his work-mates. As far back as she could remember, she had been watchful and independent and developed a way of coping and caring which had served her well as a defence against the terror of feeling that her mother might kill her. Inevitably her 'true self' was deeply buried and though highly intelligent, with a coping external self, she seemed to be in an emotional 'deep-freeze'. Though I often felt exasperated by her schizoid withdrawal she also elicited from me a longing to 'mother' her, to hold and feed her. Whether on the couch or in the chair she remained rigid and motionless. She ran for miles every day to keep her body ready for flight from imagined threat and only ate food when the clock showed her it was a meal time for she had no sense of what it felt to be hungry. She was profoundly out of touch with her body.

One day Isabel reported that someone at the running club had organised an aromatherapist to come on a Saturday afternoon to give anyone who wanted it a trial session. She found the idea both disturbing and strangely alluring, an ambivalence which was captured symbolically in a series of dreams of meals that appeared and disappeared, leaving her frustrated and miserable. She hung around the club when the aromatherapist came and peeped into the room hoping no one would see her. She copied the name and address from the card on the club notice board and carried it in her purse for several weeks. Her head told her she would be quite safe with the aromatherapist and she could even imagine she might find it pleasurable. but we had to do a lot of work before she felt able to allow her terrified and vulnerable body to be at the mercy of a potentially dangerous 'mother'. In the end she was able to have the massage and had found herself crying. The aromatherapist had not been at all fazed by this; in fact, she had told Isabel that very often people who are not used to being touched find themselves weeping.

From the day Isabel first spoke about the aromatherapist I had been careful to avoid giving any indication about what she should or should not do, but I had explored the meaning to her of both the fear and the longing associated with being touched. Early in the therapy when she was on the couch she had developed a near-psychotic transference with terrifying episodes of believing I was going to kill her. She knew at an intellectual level that I would hold the analytic boundary which included no physical contact, but it was several years before she could begin to introject aspects of a benign therapist/mother. Only then did it become possible for her to imagine how it might feel to allow herself to be physically touched. The aromatherapist just happened to come along at the moment in Isabel's therapy when she was ready to risk an experience of real physical contact.

There was another benefit from this sharing. Having grown up in a household where there was no affection or communication between her parents so that being closer to one parent meant rejection by the other, Isabel had no experience of, nor could she even imagine, being in a three-person relationship. Her struggle in getting to the aromatherapist was partly based on her unconscious dread that I would seek revenge for her disloyalty. I recognised but resisted my wish to reassure Isabel, and by maintaining my neutral position she could discover for herself that current life experience can be different from what happened in the past. Unbeknownst to the aromatherapist, she and I were having shared care of Isabel as she dared to risk letting herself be held, psychologically and physically.

Therapist, patient and supervisor

Many therapists belong to small professional networks in which boundaries can easily get broken or seriously muddled. Trainees and trainers live and work in the external world where organisational politics and theoretical arguments take place. If the therapist is to maintain the open mind necessary to understand how the trainee patient uses these external events to carry unconscious wishes and conflicts, then it is essential that the therapist keeps his or her own feelings and opinions outside the therapy relationship.

Trainee therapists will be aware that their therapists and supervisors may know each other; a triangular situation full of potential for Oedipal rivalry and splitting. This particular sort of sharing depends on supervisors and therapists holding firm boundaries within which their different focus of work with the trainees takes place.

The Rubik's Cube metaphor is particularly appropriate to the following clinical vignette because of the difficulty I had in finding a focus for thinking about what was happening. It illustrates the confusion that can arise between the external and internal boundaries; things known and unknown, consciously and unconsciously. Turning one part of the puzzle to the foreground changes the whole pattern; what was previously understood easily becomes a muddle.

Initially it seemed a straightforward matter; a young man, Mr K. came for an assessment and help in finding a therapist. He told me he had been given my name by his wife's therapist, Sarah Jones. This was a surprise and a complication because Sarah was a patient of mine and she had said nothing to me about giving my name to her patient's husband. (Sarah had successfully completed her training as a psychotherapist and we were only meeting once a week as we moved towards the ending of our therapy relationship, although we would continue as colleagues in our small professional network.)

I was able to refer Mr K. to a therapist who, as far as I could surmise, would not be on any of the same professional networks as Sarah. He was rather taken aback when I discussed fees, as his wife had been paying a very low fee which I assumed meant that she had been Sarah's training patient, not something I could tell him.

At her next session Sarah told me that she had given him my name because she wanted him to have a good experience of therapy with someone who shared her own approach to the work. When I wondered why she had not mentioned anything to me prior to giving him my name she talked of being confused about 'professional protocols'; the unwritten 'rules' which no one explained to her and which she experienced as restrictions on her freedom. She then revealed that she had initially tried to refer Mr K. to her clinical supervisor but he had not had a vacancy.

Finding a focus to think about this was not easy. I acknowledged Sarah's genuine wish to do the best to help her patient and I tried to look with her at the meaning of what had happened in terms of her relationship both to me and to her supervisor. I was already aware of feeling quite critical towards the supervisor—someone I knew and respected—because it had become clear that neither he nor Sarah had thought about the boundary of confidentiality if Mr K. started treatment with the supervisor, who already had intimate knowledge of Mr K through the supervision of Sarah's work with Mrs K. When I referred to this aspect of the situation Sarah understood my concern but, not surprisingly, felt criticised by me.

(Sarah's internal world contained aspects of her relationships with the three significant people of her early life; a self-absorbed and frequently absent mother who swung between intense demonstrations of love and long periods of emotional distance; a hated great-aunt who looked after Sarah and her siblings and with whom Sarah could do no right, and an emotionally immature father who was often violent towards Sarah. I had known what it felt like to be on the receiving end of projections from these internal object relationships.)

As the session progressed I realised that I had allowed my focus to shift from what was happening between Sarah and me out to the external world of Sarah and her supervisor and the question of what was, or was not, ethical practice. I think that my strong critical feeling towards the supervisor was a convenient, albeit unconscious, device of mine to deflect a possible attack from Sarah. Much easier to ally myself with the part of Sarah who could justifiably complain about her parents' (supervisor's) thoughtless and insensitive care of their child (trainee) rather than risk an attack from Sarah for being in her eyes, an unhelpful and critical therapist (parent/great aunt).

On the positive side I wondered about Sarah's wish to have joined me in becoming the 'parents' to the shared 'children' of Mr and Mrs K. For then she would have had the proof that she had so long sought, that I was happy for her to grow up and become an equal, something she felt her own rivalrous mother could not tolerate. If I had taken Mr K. into therapy while Sarah continued her work with Mrs K, Sarah could also have avoided facing her feelings about the impending loss of her special relationship to me. There were many layers of meaning and feeling arising from this incident which Sarah and I continued to explore together.

Sharing with marital therapists

Taking one partner of a marriage (I am including in the term 'marriage' all committed relationships, whether legally married or not) into individual therapy will, sooner or later, have an impact on that marriage for better or worse. Adult partners choose each other not only for what they know at a conscious level but also because of an unconscious recognition of disowned and denied aspects of the self which are projected into the other. This system of mutual projective identifications creates an unconscious contract which has come to be termed the 'marital fit' (Ruszczynski 1993b) and it is this 'fit' which is likely to be unsettled and threatened when one partner enters an individual psychotherapy relationship.

The mode of work with an individual adult patient is to set up an exclusive one to one relationship between therapist and patient and to work with the strong transference and counter-transference which this promotes. Changes in the patient's internal world may well lead to significant improvement in the quality of the marriage, and as Morley (1994) has argued, it is sometimes necessary to adopt a marital focus within one to one therapy. But de-stabilising the marital fit can also be destructive to the real-life partnership, particularly if the partner who is not part of the therapeutic endeavour reacts by becoming more rigidly defended in the face of pressure to change.

The relationship between the therapist and patient may threaten the marriage by seeming to be in competition with it and becoming preferred to it, alternatively the therapeutic relationship may be rejected because it is felt to be too threatening to the couple relationship. Sometimes the partner may decide to seek their own therapy which may be the best option, although there is a risk that each one-to-one relationship of partner and therapist can lead to a rigid and stuck system in which the patient couple is psychologically held apart as a defence against a coming together that is dreaded, and so the therapies become interminable and ultimately unproductive.

How can an individual therapist working alone know when it might be in the patient's best interests to start couple therapy? Just having the first thought about such an idea should alert the therapist to the need for some serious self questioning. Perhaps the therapy is feeling stuck and the therapist wants to be rescued, to hand over the problem rather than wrestle with the underlying reasons for the stuckness. Where the marital therapists are a couple—particularly a man/woman couple—the therapist may have the feeling that a 'parental couple' will be able to manage the therapy in the way a 'single parent'-therapist cannot.

Perhaps the therapist has quite properly been exploring and interpreting a patient's contribution to difficulties in the marriage only to come to the point of believing that the partner is as troubled or impossible as the patient reports. Or a patient may be appropriately concerned about their partner who is suffering emotionally but unwilling to be seen alone. In either case, referral to marital therapists may be the best way forward.

There are very real difficulties for individual therapists working alone as compared with marital psychotherapists who have much greater flexibility working conjointly and separately when this seems necessary, and can retain the open communication between them which allows the counter-transferences to be aired and shared and taken back into the therapeutic work. Individual therapists have to contain and process projections which arrive from various parts of the wider system whilst keeping their focus on the relationship in the consulting room.

Mr Smith started therapy with me at the request of his wife's therapist. As my work with Mr Smith progressed he talked a lot about what went on in the marriage and reported long discussions with his wife in which she told him what her therapist had said about him. I started to feel burdened by a growing sense that Mrs Smith and her therapist had decided Mr Smith was the really disturbed partner and that I was expected to 'do something' about him. I started to feel ganged up on and my counter-transference reaction was a strong sense of wanting to protect him—and myself—from their critical attacks.

It took me some time to understand what was going on between Mr Smith and me partly because I had my own feelings about Mrs Smith's therapist, someone I knew had a rather negative view of men. Thinking it through and reflecting on my counter-transference lead to the realisation that I had colluded with Mr Smith in feeling misunderstood and victimised by the wife/therapist couple. In this way, I had avoided facing Mr Smith's negative feelings towards me, and I had recreated in the therapy aspects of Mr Smith's relationship to his over-protective mother. Once the focus was back onto our relationship, I heard much less about Mr Smith's wife and her therapy

Family therapists have long realised that the child presented as 'having' or 'being' the problem is likely to be the standard bearer for family disturbance, often within the parental couple. Similarly a psychotherapist working with individual adults may come to feel that the patient is carrying the problems for the partner and is taking too much responsibility for the emotional health or ill-health of the relationship. Alternatively, the patient may be using the absent partner to carry many of the disowned—denied and projected—aspects of the patient. Of course the therapist can never really know the absent partner who is brought into the therapy through the distorting mirrors of the patient's transference both to the partner and to the therapist. Nevertheless, over time and from the understandings gained from the analytic exploration of the patient's level of object relationships within the transference/counter-transference situation, it is possible to gain some understanding of the problems between the patient and the partner. The therapist can also get a feel of what it might be like to be married to the patient.

Complex but potentially productive sharing arises when a patient in individual therapy enters marital therapy to run in parallel. The disadvantages resulting from the loss of the exclusive one-to-one relationship can be outweighed by the therapeutic benefit to the patients. But it is a way of working fraught with complications for everyone involved and its success depends to a large extent on a close, mutually respectful professional understanding between the different therapists.

Quite soon after settling into twice-weekly therapy, Mrs Lewis began to express negative feelings towards me; she experienced me as rejecting, disapproving and rivalrous. My counter-transference remained positive and warm except for occasional and fleeting moments of irritation. She was married to a man whom she trusted and with whom she had many shared interests, but for whom she could feel no physical desire. He would often tell her of his love for her, but her constant complaint to me was that if he really loved her she would feel it, and as she did not feel it, then he obviously did not really mean it. As I attempted to gather all this into the transference and make links between Mrs Lewis's feelings towards her husband and towards me, I could get a sense of Mr Lewis's predicament. When Mrs Lewis began to think there might be value in being seen as a couple, I did not interpret this as an attack on me or her individual therapy, rather as her acknowledgment that she and he needed a space to gain understanding about the difficulties between them; how they could not hear or make sense of each other's needs and longings. Mrs Lewis feared that unless her husband took some active part in the therapeutic journey, he would get left behind and the relationship would be seriously under threat. Mrs Lewis' individual sessions were cut back to once a week for the duration of the marital work; this was partly for financial reasons, but it also demonstrated, in a very clear way, Mrs Lewis's commitment to the marriage which had been under increasing strain. In the shared sessions, she was surprised at her husband's willingness to begin to look at his part in their distress, she had thought him repressed and withdrawn—rather like her own father—and she also gained real insight into the part she played in setting him up to fail to reach her. Throughout this time of shared therapy my position in relation to Mrs Lewis would subtly shift, either from session to session or even within the session, from being 'beside' her as she reflected on the marriage and the marital therapy to being in an intense one-to-one relationship in which some of the marital problems could be experienced and worked on in the transference.

By the time the couple therapy came to a planned end Mr and Mrs Lewis had gained some understandings about their relationship and

Mrs Lewis was able to acknowledge the degree to which she had used her husband to carry aspects of her own unresolved conflicts. She had been surprised to learn that he, too, felt disappointment and regret, and she had reached the point of accepting that she did not have a monopoly on feeling misunderstood and lonely. This joint work of disentangling the projections, recognising what was shared and belonged to each of them separately, challenged Mrs Lewis' long held belief that if only the 'other' would be different, she would be happy. Then she was able to accept her need to increase her individual sessions to three a week.

For marital psychotherapists the 'patient' is the marriage and the focus is on what the two partners create between them. It is the marriage that is the arena in which the internal world of each partner is explored. Warren Colman writes:

> ...whereas the individual psychotherapist's focus is on the internal world per se and he addresses himself to the interaction between himself and the patient in order to reveal this, the marital therapist's focus is on the interaction between the couple as an end in itself. (Colman 1993)

Nevertheless, there is a large area of overlap and the individual therapy will be profoundly affected both by the process and the content of the other therapy. Feelings and phantasies can travel round the larger system and land up in the psychological lap of the individual therapist who can find it difficult sorting out what belongs with whom. Sharing patients depends on the therapists having a very high level of mutual trust and respect founded on shared theoretical principles. They need also to be aware of their own vulnerability to criticism or tendency to feel rivalrous.

Mr and Mrs Grove started marital therapy after several years of Mrs Grove's twice-weekly individual work. She would tell me how much she admired and liked the woman therapist, whose interpretations, though often similar to mine, had also produced some new and interesting ways of understanding Mrs Grove's contribution to the marital difficulties. I began to wonder to myself how I had failed to reach those understandings. Was the other therapist right and was I being very stupid? Maybe the other therapist was forming a low opinion of my work or perhaps my patient was being misunderstood. Then, during one particular session, Mrs Grove reported that the therapist had said to her: 'what on earth have you learnt in your individual therapy?' In recounting this Mrs Grove spoke in a very arch and denigrating tone. My immediate feeling was of being hit by the other therapist and momentarily I felt weakened and useless . My internal supervisor was alerted by the strength of this feeling and I was then able to think about what had just happened and know with absolute certainty that my colleague, the marital therapist, would never have spoken with this tone of voice; it was imperative that I heard and interpreted the attack on me as coming directly from Mrs Grove.

...and what about the children?

Many people who come to therapy have serious difficulties in relating to their children. Insight gained from explorations of the patient's own early life relationships and their working through in the transference, can bring about quite dramatic improvements in family life. But sometimes children continue to suffer and their behaviour becomes so disturbed that the therapist is no longer able to focus exclusively on the patient's inner world.

Mrs Morgan came to therapy initially at the behest of her husband who had already had two years of therapy. She appeared to have accepted his view that she was responsible for their unhappy marriage and the problem behaviours of their three children. As the therapy proceeded it became clear that the Morgans' embattled relationship was an example of 'malign mirroring'; a complex web of projective identifications resulting in a confusion of self and other leading to endless battles and mutual blame.

The children were caught up in the uncontained chaos of their parents' abusive relationship and, not surprisingly, were showing increasing levels of disturbed behaviour, both at home and at school. Mrs Morgan was genuinely very worried about the children and whilst I tried to focus on the way she used them to carry her own unresolved unconscious conflicts, I was beginning to think that a marital or family focus might be more appropriate.

Following a particularly upsetting episode in which the eldest boy made an alarming suicidal gesture, Mrs Morgan told me that her husband and his therapist had been discussing the possibility of referring this son to a child therapist. My heart sank because I could imagine a sort of 'domino effect' in which, as each member of the family went into individual therapy, so the next one down the line would bear the responsibility of carrying and acting out the family disturbance.

The boy's behaviour was too serious to be ignored and it seemed clear that the other therapist felt the same. I was mindful of the risk that the fights between the patient couple could get re-enacted by the therapists, so while agreeing that individual therapy was certainly one option, I introduced the idea of family therapy for the whole family, or marital psychotherapy for the couple with the possibility that their individual therapies could continue in parallel for as long as necessary.

Mrs Morgan talked to her husband, he talked to his therapist and the message came back that both Mr and Mrs Morgan wanted to have a consultation with a marital therapist but would like their two therapists to talk to each other about how to put the idea into action. This request had a significance beyond the practical, in that it carried both patients' wish to have therapist/parents who could get together to contain and protect them. The conversation with the other therapist was brief and did not include any detailed discussion about the couple.

The Morgans started joint sessions with the marital therapist and continued their individual sessions. The final outcome was that the couple decided to separate whilst continuing shared care of the children who, freed from the unremitting tensions of their parents' angry frustration and unhappiness, settled down at school and at both parental homes. The parents' individual therapies continued for several years.

Conclusion

As a therapy relationship works towards an ending, there is often a recapitulation; a recalling of the feelings and events that occurred at the start of the therapeutic journey now seen with the benefit of insights gained through the shared exploration within the transference/counter-transference situation. In the same way, as I come to the end of this chapter I want to return to the point I made at the start about the particular challenges for individual therapists in private practice who must provide the total 'set-up'; the bounded space—both actual and psychological -in which the therapy takes place.

We are faced with an on-going paradox which is that in order to 'be' we have to 'do' and one of the things we 'do' is cope with the pressures and demands from the external world whilst maintaining our focus on the internal world and being prepared to think about the links between those two realms of experience.

As I have tried to demonstrate in the clinical examples above, there are times when we are forced to share, and there are situations where we may even initiate the sharing of a patient. We must guard against doing anything which seems manipulative, controlling or omnipotent, but as we monitor the progress of a therapy we may need to change our goals. Sometimes to do nothing may masquerade as analytic purity but actually deprives our patients of the maximum opportunity for emotional development and the possibility of more satisfying relationships and happier lives.

CHAPTER FIVE

SPLITTING AND SHARING IN CONCURRENT THERAPIES

Christel Buss-Twachtmann

Christel Buss-Twachtmann is a graduate of the Tavistock Marital Studies Institute diploma training in marital psychotherapy, and a full member of the Society of Psychoanalytical Marital Psychotherapists (SPMP). She works with couples in private practice in London, individually and with a co-therapist. She is a member of the executive of SPMP and the chair of the Continuing Professional Development sub-Committee. Christel has a degree in Psychology, and trained and worked as an individual counsellor with a Westminster Pastoral Foundation affiliated counselling service for many years.

This chapter is written from the perspective of a couple therapist who, working on her own, recognises the need to pay attention to the difficulties and challenges presented when her clients are also in individual psychotherapy. Christel Buss-Twachtmann shares her thinking process with us while she carefully considers her relationship with her couple's individual therapists. She explores and describes how this visible professional matrix is managed in every day clinical practice, and the unconscious meanings and dynamics it can also come to reflect. In doing so, she highlights the central issues of containment, boundaries, and the complex transferences in combined therapies, and gives us an insight into the internal dialogue which is needed to promote sharing and mitigate splitting in concurrent therapies.

* * *

Introduction

I first became interested in the effects concurrent therapies have on each other many years ago. I was seeing two couples; in each couple, one partner was also in individual psychotherapy. While the other therapy had not come into the work with me in any very obvious way, I was forced by events to recognise that it had affected the couple therapy greatly, but in each case, very differently. This led me to think about the factors which had given rise to such different experiences.

How far were the differences a reflection of the internal processes of the couple, and how much were they linked to the different ways the two therapists involved managed all the aspects of the therapies? I began to look more closely at the issue of concurrent therapies; at differences in the development of the transferences and at the crucial question of containment.

In my experience of practising in London, it is becoming rare to see couples who have not had any prior experience of psychotherapy or counselling. More than 75 per cent of couples in my current practice have had either past or present experience of some form of therapy. In almost half of my cases one or both partners are in couple therapy at the same time as in individual psychotherapy. Given that two thirds of my cases are influenced by another psychotherapy experience, I feel I have to take note of this fact and find a way of thinking about the effects it has on the therapeutic work with me. I discovered, however, that very little has been written on this subject. Perhaps the reason is that working alongside another therapist is a recent phenomenon and not enough experience has been gathered, or that we as therapists find ourselves confronted by too many dilemmas to begin to think and write about this topic.

A friend and colleague said recently: 'I wish I never had a couple where a partner is in individual psychotherapy. It makes life so difficult.'

In this chapter, I am going to explore the various complex dynamics I have encountered and struggled with when seeing a couple while one or both partners are engaged in another psychotherapy. I will outline some of the ways the couple therapy can be profoundly influenced, and how partners are affected when one or both are exposed to two forms of psychotherapy and two or three or even four therapists. My work is also affected by the knowledge that there is another therapist working with my clients; and I imagine that my presence too must affect the work of the other therapist.

So where is the thinking about the overlapping systems to be done, and how do two or three therapists process and contain the various effects and conflicts inherent in concurrent therapies? Can we continue to think in the same way about containment when we work in this complex framework? I shall use case material to describe how splitting and sharing of emotions and experiences, and of their expression in the transferences to the therapists, always occurs between the various therapies. I shall explore how and where the marriage, the meaningful link, is made between the work in two separate arenas, when each arena displays a different aspect of the same client(s). This marriage will enable split elements to be brought together for the benefit of the couple relationship. When concurrent therapies promote splitting rather than sharing, it is because a container of all the therapeutic endeavours cannot be created; an overarching 'third position' from which thinking can lead to understanding, cannot be taken (Britton 1989).

In the beginning

Let us begin at the beginning and explore how and why partners undertake two forms of psychotherapy at the same time. In my experience of concurrent therapies, the couple psychotherapy usually begins when one or both partners are already in individual psychotherapy. It is rare in my experience that a partner decides to seek individual psychotherapy during couple work; when this does happen, it is often at my suggestion because I begin to feel that this partner would benefit from a more private exploration of issues less linked to the couple. Frequently, in these cases the other partner is already in individual psychotherapy, and it seems probable that the need for couple therapy is in some way linked to the work being done in individual therapy. The links I have come across are varied but can generally be found in two areas. The first is related to the feelings stirred up by one partner entering into another intimate relationship which excludes his/her partner. This can be experienced as an 'affair', and can lead to feelings of abandonment and an awakening of strong Oedipal anxieties which have remained unacknowledged and undermined the marriage contract to the point where continuation of the relationship is threatened.

The second area is related to the effects that the individual therapy has had on one or both partners and therefore the couple relationship. In these cases the individual psychotherapy of one or both partners has upset the status quo between them. Their conscious and unconscious contracts have been disturbed, old ways of functioning are challenged, new demands are made on the partners, and the partnership is struggling to adjust. Their shared defences are challenged, the system of mutual projections breaks down and previously hidden problems come to the fore.

The suggestion for couple work might come from the individual therapist when his/her work is overshadowed by couple issues, and another container for these has to be found. I believe that these referrals come about because certain aspects of the individual are too lodged in the couple relationship to be available in the transference to the individual therapist. The hope is that if the partners are able to use the couple therapy, the unconscious projective system between them can become more conscious, and more separateness can be achieved, which will allow the individual therapy to progress.

Sometimes the referral from an individual therapist is a crisis referral. I am asked to see a couple very quickly because there is a crisis in the family: for instance, violence between the partners or danger to children. It is vital that the two therapies together provide the necessary containment, though how this can be achieved varies from case to case. Even though a link between the two therapies is easier to make when the suggestion for couple psychotherapy comes from the individual therapist, the fact that the referral came at a crisis highlights the couple's inability to contain feelings, and their tendency to act out. There is a greater likelihood that splitting will occur between the two therapies, and a good outcome depends on the ability of the various therapists to create a strong enough container.

Setting up a container for shared work

Setting up a container for therapy starts with the assessment. One of the fundamental questions I ask myself when a couple come to me is whether they can use the kind of help I offer. In order to explore this, I need to know what has brought them, and if there is sufficient agreement between partners about the goal of couple psychotherapy. When one or both of the partners are in individual psychotherapy as well, I need to be as sure as I can be that seeking couple psychotherapy is not an acting out of a difficulty in the other therapy. One way of addressing this is to have permission to contact the individual therapist.

The response to this request can yield valuable information, and the request itself is an attempt on my part to keep the other therapy in mind. If the individual therapist has not been informed about or is opposed to the couple psychotherapy, there will be a greater possibility of each therapy being used as a defence against the other.

My usual practice is to write a formal letter to the individual therapist informing him/her of the request for couple work, and inviting comment if this seems appropriate. The aim of this letter is to acknowledge that the two therapies are linked. In a most basic way at least the parents/therapists know of each other, even if they never directly work together. I feel that this initial contact is very important, and my hope is that it will establish in the mind of the couple a connection between the two therapies which can lead to thinking about them in relation to one another. Asking the couple's permission to make formal contact with the other therapist opens the door for the exploration of their conflicting feelings about the concurrent therapies. I have often found that not making this initial contact proved to be detrimental, especially when it was not made because one partner or his/her therapist refused permission.

My experience of working alongside another therapist is obviously closely linked to the unconscious processes of the couple and to how they manage the concurrent therapies. I form different views of my colleague with different couples, although I usually have no real information or knowledge of the other therapist. When I do not know or at least know of the other therapist, I find myself relying on reports and my counter-transference in the session to form an image of my colleague. Evidently this experience will be influenced and distorted by conscious and unconscious processes in the matrix of relationships, but if we believe in the unconscious we must believe that my phantasies will affect the way I think about my clients and their other therapist(s).

I therefore try to make the other therapist as real as I can by writing an initial letter and by acquiring some basic information. It will be helpful to know if the other therapist also works analytically. If not, I will assume that the transference is not being worked with, which has implications for my approach. My pre-transference view or fantasy of the other therapist is that he or she works in similar ways to myself, is respectful of my work, and has the capacity to process reports about the couple therapy in terms of the unconscious functioning of his/her patient. I find myself assuming that his/her view of our shared patient is not too different from mine. This fantasy will of course be challenged, and will probably change from time to time, in the course of the therapeutic work. Both therapists in this situation must work with assumptions and uncertainty, and will rarely have the opportunity to find out about the reality of the other therapist's views of and work with the shared patient. Their ability to work effectively will be undermined if the separateness of the two therapies is being used defensively, either by the couple or by the therapists.

The development of the transference in shared cases

A committed couple relationship is a forum of deep unconscious meaning for both partners; the feelings evoked there are often primitive and tremendously powerful. It is therefore not surprising that for some couples this is the arena where aspects of their internal world remain firmly lodged despite long, and in many ways effective individual therapy.

The effect of individual therapy on the couple's shared inner world can be explored in the couple therapy, and this can help them to find out if new insights can be internalised which would allow their marital container (Colman 1993) to be more flexible, or whether they have to consider separation. Couples are at different points along this spectrum when they come into couple therapy, some being determined to hold the relationship together and others being closer to break-up.

Some couples come into couple therapy because, despite long and effective individual therapy, sometimes for both partners, the couple relationship is not improving. Often each individual has changed greatly, has achieved more integration, better relationships with parents and children and a more satisfactory work life, yet both feel the relationship between them is not satisfactory. Something is stuck and they cannot bring about movement on their own or in their individual therapy. One woman said: *'My life has changed so much because of my therapy but I still feel trapped in the same relationship with my husband. Why do my insights not change my marriage?'*

In these cases a mutually reinforcing recreation of childhood patterns may prevail between the partners, and aspects of each partner may remain projected into the spouse, and will not be available for work in the transference in the individual therapy.

One of the most important topics to think about in the situation of concurrent therapies is what is happening in the transferences. The transference relationship in the individual therapy, and the feelings the other partner has about it, will affect the transferences to the couple psychotherapist. When the individual therapy has been experienced as largely positive, there can be expectations that the couple therapy will be as positive and that the therapist will behave in similar ways. The couple therapist can be seen as an extension of the individual therapist, and it will be difficult to allow each forum its distinct features. When the differences become apparent, great anxiety can occur and disappointment and anger come into the work. The phantasy that both therapists are the same may be necessary as a protection against the struggle with difference, and against the anxiety that the good link with the individual therapist will be disturbed.

When the experience of the individual therapy is less positive there may be the hope that the couple therapy will be different and more helpful. This can turn into despair about the appropriateness of any therapy when progress is not made as fast as hoped for, and engagement in both therapies becomes threatened. A comparison between therapists and therapies cannot be avoided and some splitting is inevitable. Engaging in a second therapy brings some idealisation and denigration of both therapies at different times.

It has been my experience that in all cases of concurrent therapy feelings of competitiveness, confusion about differences and conflicts of loyalty are present. Whether these feelings can be worked with and contained depends on the degree of splitting resorted to in the shared internal world of the couple, as well as on the way the two therapists manage the resulting conflicts and inevitable acting out. For some couples, the past or present individual therapy can come to dominate the couple sessions, and a working alliance with the couple therapist is difficult to establish. All too often, however, I have found that the conflicts between the different therapies remain hidden and can silently undermine the work in each therapeutic forum. The unconscious avoidance of Oedipal issues is very powerful, and all participants 'forget' there is another therapy.

Sometimes in the transference the two therapists are seen as in competition with one another. I hear reports of the other therapist's criticism of my work, and of our conflicting interpretations; my perception of my colleague as a partner comes under threat, and I wonder fruitlessly about the reality of his views.

I may find myself in the counter-transference becoming uncertain about my approach, concerned about how my work will be reported to my colleague, and constrained in my interpretations. Alternatively, my counter-transference may be to see my colleague as a partner not a rival, and in a very difficult case to assume he is struggling as much as myself. I may find myself fused in phantasy with the other therapist, as a defence against despair, envy and competitiveness.

My experience has been that it is vital for me to keep the other therapy in mind if I am to allow the couple to become aware of and work with all the effects of shared and split transferences created in two or three concurrent therapies. Keeping the other therapy in mind is also vital if I am to monitor and process my counter-transference feelings about my colleagues. This is easier when I have some real knowledge of the other therapists and the way they work.

Mr and Mrs Thomas

I shall now describe the work with a couple which shows the different transference issues that arose with their couple and individual therapists.

Mr Thomas had been in therapy for a short time many years ago, and had not found it helpful. Mrs Thomas had been in intensive psychotherapy for many years; she valued her therapist and felt her life had changed for the better in most ways, yet her marriage had not improved. The referral for couple work was instigated by Mrs Thomas with the support of her therapist. She experienced herself as being exploited and abused by her husband and felt that his denial of these events and his aggressive withdrawal made it impossible for her to stay in the relationship. Her husband did not share her view and felt the marriage was largely fine. Later, in the couple therapy, he confessed that he felt that her individual therapy had made her aim for perfection.

It became clear in the course of the therapeutic work that Mr and Mrs Thomas were stuck in a mutually neglecting and abusive marriage; a re-enactment of a victim-tyrant relationship which linked closely to their childhood experiences. I was very aware of the shared aspects of this dynamic because in the sessions it was often Mrs Thomas who was the demanding and aggressive partner, with Mr Thomas remaining more quiet and compliant. In the transference I felt pressured by Mrs Thomas's powerful insistence that I bear witness and acknowledge the tyrannical aspects of Mr Thomas. Her collusion with her partner, which was enacted in the couple sessions, had been harder for her to see in the transference in her individual therapy. I was able to experience and interpret how the abuser-abused dynamic was re-enacted between the couple, and between the couple and their therapist.

The couple therapy was necessary to bring the mutual projective system to light. A central aspect of this work seemed to be that I act as 'witness' to abuse when it happened in the here and now of the session. Having a third person present, Mrs Thomas tried to achieve the acknowledgement of abusive behaviour so missing in her childhood.

Only when a reality was confirmed, or a secret out in the open, could she begin to believe her own perceptions in a different way and make a start on letting go of old patterns. This was a major step in the couple relationship. Both partners were able for the first time to reach a shared platform for discussions about various events.

In time, I came to understand that the individual therapy could not progress further because Mrs Thomas's experience of being exploited in intimate relationships had become so deeply lodged in her marriage. Her own tyrannical and abusive aspects were so firmly projected into her husband, where they found a ready hook, that they had not appeared in the transference to her own individual therapist. I wondered if Mrs Thomas needed to preserve her therapist as the good parental object in order to do the work on her troubled past. Perhaps this seemed all the more necessary to Mrs Thomas as the bad and persecutory aspects of her inner world were emerging more fully, increasing the need to project them into Mr Thomas.

It seems that sometimes couple therapy is essential despite successful individual therapy, because certain constellations from the past need to be recreated in a forum where an observer/witness is present. For some individuals a weak sense of reality originates from abuse and neglect remaining unacknowledged in the original family. The couple therapy provides in a concrete form the experience of a 'third position' (Britton 1989), from which vital understanding of inner and outer reality can be gained.

Understanding the transferences

The case of Mr and Mrs Thomas illustrates particular dilemmas which arise when only one partner is in individual therapy. The feelings and phantasies about the partner's therapy can lead to resentments and resistance in the marriage and in the couple therapy. If the couple therapist is not sensitive to this, and these feelings cannot be expressed and interpreted, the couple therapy can become ineffective.

Mr Thomas's feelings about his wife's long therapy and close relationship with her therapist had never been expressed, and became apparent only in the couple therapy. Mr Thomas was often silent and unresponsive and repeatedly late for the sessions. I was aware that his reluctance to engage in the couple therapy might be related to his feelings about Mrs Thomas's individual therapy. Eventually, his fears about the couple therapy and his anger with Mrs Thomas, her therapist and me became clear. He felt his wife had abandoned him when she started her therapy and he was angry that it had changed her and made her demanding and critical of him. He was liable to see her therapist as an enemy. It became clear that I was seen as an extension of her therapist and as working on her therapist's behalf. Obviously, for Mr Thomas to trust me took considerable work and time.

The partner who has no therapy experience can feel disadvantaged in couple therapy, and that their partner holds all the knowledge about therapy. Mr Thomas feared being 'ganged up on' by myself and his wife, being made into the problem and responsible for all the difficulties. The partner in individual therapy can exacerbate this fear, by maintaining that the major problem in the relationship is that the spouse has not been in therapy, and by behaving like another therapist in the room with me and at home. This was not the case with Mr and Mrs Thomas, and is to the credit of the work she had done in her individual therapy. She was able, without feeling too excluded, to give space to her husband and allow me to help him express his feelings. It is not uncommon for partners who are used to their individual therapist's exclusive attention to resent having to share the attention of the couple therapist and to be unable to ally themselves with her.

A partner in individual therapy can also use their insights defensively against the partner and the couple therapist, so as to keep their vulnerabilities out of the challenging couple arena. It can appear as if the value of the individual therapy will come into question if remaining pathology is acknowledged in the couple therapy. Mrs Thomas found it very hard to acknowledge her part in the couple difficulties and to talk freely about her childhood struggles. Often childhood issues are less alive in the couple therapy, and are reported without emotional content because they have been worked on repeatedly in the individual therapy. My interpretations can feel like an intrusion into that arena. This limits my ability to understand the partner in individual therapy, as well as limiting the scope and effect of my interpretations.

Mrs Thomas's positive experience of her individual therapy and the fact that her therapist had recommended me gave her hope and allowed her to engage in couple therapy with a high degree of trust. In the beginning she was able to work with my interpretations about her part in the couple problem and make links to her past. She frequently acknowledged the importance of the work in her own therapy, describing it as complementing the couple therapy rather than as a competitive arena. She saw the two therapists as allies, with the hope of a parental couple working together for her benefit; and at the same time this enabled her to defend herself against a struggle with our differences.

When the differences between myself and her therapist appeared more strongly, however, Mrs Thomas became angry and upset. She often challenged my interpretations, especially when they questioned her beliefs about herself and about her husband. I was often seen as wrong, if not unprofessional. This struggle was fought out over issues of my procedure on fees and, on one occasion, about changing the session time, as well as over my interpretations about her collusion with her partner. Mrs Thomas became insistent that I adjust my policy in line with her therapist, perhaps in an attempt to make us the same as a way of managing the differences and the conflict of loyalties. She began to feel exploited and abused by me when I held on to my policy, and misunderstood and angry about my interpretations of the couple interaction, which differed from those of her individual therapist. I felt I had to be very firm in order not to become part of the victim-tyrant dynamic which was recreated in the room. Surviving, understanding and interpreting these interactions became a vital part of the couple therapy.

It became clear later in the work that Mrs Thomas had experienced herself very differently in the couple therapy. She was disturbed and humiliated by her own abusive behaviour and rage in the couple sessions, and was able to say in the last phase of the therapy that her individual therapist had never seen her like that. Only at this point could I be sure that my assumption about the aspects of Mrs Thomas which I thought had been split between the two therapies was correct.

Like Mrs Thomas, the partner in individual therapy is invariably very sensitive to interpretations which are different from those of their individual therapist, and may feel that I do not support the individual work. The conflict about real or perceived differences is disturbing and leads to confusion and to various defences against it. If this is not interpreted it may undermine each forum to the point at which one or the other therapy is ended prematurely. This struggle is an integral part of the work in concurrent therapies and not all couples are able to engage in it. I believe that a capacity to develop trust in each therapist and a capacity to manage conflict are essential.

For the Thomases, the two therapies worked well together. Mr Thomas's feelings about Mrs Thomas's therapy and fears about the couple therapy could be contained and worked with. Mrs Thomas felt contained enough to struggle in the transference with competitiveness and conflicts of loyalty in both arenas, and her challenges to me seemed to be essential to bring about understanding. Mrs Thomas was able to bring the insights from each therapy into the other, and to continue to work on them in both. She continued to use her individual therapist to help her manage the challenges from the couple therapy and to help her understand the links to her past. Both partners now used the safety of the couple sessions to share painful aspects of themselves and came to a new understanding of themselves and each other.

With Mr and Mrs Thomas, the relationship between myself and the other therapist worked well. I experienced him as supportive and generally valued the work he did with Mrs Thomas. Despite this, in the counter-transference I still wished at times that Mrs Thomas's feelings about the couple work were not being discussed and analysed elsewhere. When Mrs Thomas challenged or attacked me I found myself questioning the effectiveness of her long therapy, and sometimes felt tempted to contact her therapist to alert him to the 'other side' of his patient. I assumed that the individual therapy was freer of conflict, and was concerned about the splitting of the transference and the negative effect this could have on both therapies. I struggled with feelings of exclusion in the counter-transference; and I managed not to make contact and to continue to trust that the two therapists were partners rather then competitors. We had 'shared' a number of cases and I had known of the other therapist for a long time, and this helped greatly in processing my feelings.

All the above shows that the transference relationship to me develops in relation to both partners' existing transferences to the individual therapist. My capacity to understand and interpret the internal world of each partner is greatly affected by what is going on in the other therapy, as is the impact of my interpretations upon the couple. It shows us graphically that in concurrent therapies it is never a case of 'splitting *or* sharing' but that the total transference situation is always both split and shared between the two therapies.

Splitting in the transferences

The task of the couple psychotherapy is to provide a safe forum for exploring the marriage as a psychological container (Colman 1993). This container is under stress when partners enter couple therapy and they are likely to have resorted to a more paranoid-schizoid way of functioning and are less able to be in the depressive position. This means that splitting and projection are more prevalent ways of defending against psychic pain at this time. Engaging in two therapies can provide the opportunity for partners to use each forum to explore and understand their internal worlds as well as being understood and supported. At the same time two therapies may provide a further opportunity for splitting as a defence against psychic pain.

The question that has to be considered in each case of concurrent therapies is whether the splitting can be known about, understood and worked with so that it highlights the internal object relations in a useful way. If the splits remain hidden the ego of the individual will remain split and development towards integration, the recognition of oneself as a whole person, is hindered. How can splitting be contained and understood so that it becomes useful to the therapeutic endeavour in each forum?

The degree of splitting and defensive use of concurrent therapies will depend on each partner's capacity for internal containment, their ability to struggle with differences, and on the strength and flexibility of the marital container. The strength of the relationship existing with each therapist, especially that with the individual therapist as this is often the longest established, is also vital. These are the major factors which I believe determine the extent of containment that can be achieved in each forum and across the therapies. Another important factor is the way the various therapists contain and work with the inherent dilemmas of concurrent therapies.

I have seen a number of couples where the individual psychotherapy was ended soon after the couple therapy began. In most such cases the individual psychotherapy had begun only recently, and its purpose was seen as limited or as crisis management. At times, the individual therapist has become a denigrated object and I am idealised. (Of course, sometimes the reverse is true and in either case, this needs to be interpreted.) The individual therapist may either have been idealised as having done such a good job that the psychotherapy had come to a natural conclusion, or have been denigrated and seen as useless. When there is a lot of either denigration or idealisation I know that the couple have difficulty in integrating opposing emotions, and when occasionally I have had contact with my colleague after the individual therapy had ended, it has been no surprise to learn that he/she did not share the couple's view of the reasons for ending.

Often the opportunity to interpret and contain the conflicts is not given because the individual therapy ends without any discussion in the couple therapy and sometimes without being mentioned until months later. Such an ending of the individual work feels like a fearful retreat from the conflicts of loyalty between the two therapies. Each partner fears exposing differences, and what might be revealed if the various relationships are thought about. It feels too hard to be in two intimate therapeutic relationships at once, especially when the purpose of each is seen as different and the two therapists remain unconnected. If such a conflict cannot be thought about, it has to be acted out.

Sometimes the individual therapy is ended after a short time because it was intended to resolve one partner's dissatisfaction with the marriage. When it becomes apparent that the problem remains in the couple relationship, and that couple therapy would be a more appropriate forum, the individual therapy no longer seems necessary. Sometimes, however, it feels as if the individual therapy has become too much of a threat to the marriage to be sustained. There may be a shared phantasy that the couple can only be preserved by one or other sacrificing their individuality, and the ending of the individual therapy symbolises this. The degree of struggle between autonomy or individuality and relatedness is thus highlighted, and will be a major part of the work in the couple therapy. Sometimes the couple work reveals that the ending of the individual therapy reflected an inability to become dependent in a committed relationship.

In some cases, where the individual therapy is well established, it is likely to continue throughout concurrent couple work. I assume that a strong and trusting enough relationship exists with the individual therapist, within which dependency is possible. As with Mr and Mrs Thomas, work in concurrent therapies may benefit the individuals and the couple. But occasionally it is used defensively, and I begin to suspect this and to wonder about splitting between the two therapies when the individual therapy is never mentioned in the couple forum, and I find myself failing to keep it in mind. The conflicted feelings about the two therapies remain hidden. In these cases, I find that invariably the couple live somewhat compartmentalised lives and have strict boundaries around intimate contact. The effect of being in two forms of therapy can only be managed by the two arenas remaining totally unconnected in their minds, and no meaningful links can be made. This will quickly lead us to the Oedipal conflict, and each partner's capacity to reach a 'third position', to struggle with difference, and with the knowledge that an intimate relationship is made up of two separate individuals. Sometimes in these cases my attempts to keep the other therapy in mind, and look for evidence of splitting in the room, seem to fail because of these powerful Oedipal anxieties which prevent any sharing between the two therapies. Here the couple and the therapist risk colluding in staying away from painful issues, the exploration of which is an essential part of psychotherapy—issues of reality, truth and difference. Not mentioning the other therapy can be understood in this context as a measure of the defensiveness prevailing in the couple therapy (and perhaps in the other therapy too). The whole meaning and purpose of therapy is being undermined.

Eva and Brian

This case provides an example of how three therapies can work against each other when too many aspects of each partner are split between the therapies and when the conflicts and splits cannot be contained. In this case, the couple therapy ended prematurely and the couple separated.

Brian and Eva struggled with a fear of, and longing for, intimacy, with Brian holding the fear of intrusion for the couple, and Eva holding the wish for intimacy and the fear of abandonment. This had been contained for a while when Eva's compliance had allowed Brian to feel in sufficient control of the distance between them. When Eva's need for commitment increased (she wanted to get married) Brian began to feel threatened and withdrew from her. This activated Eva's fear of abandonment and made her more emotionally demanding, leaving Brian feeling overwhelmed, intruded on and out of control. He often threatened to throw Eva out and sometimes became violent in his need to distance himself.

Some of these conflicts were recreated in the relationship between the three therapies, and Eva and Brian only achieved a very limited understanding of these processes in the couple therapy, because both found full engagement too difficult, and they took refuge in defensive conflicts between the therapies.

Eva had been in individual therapy for six months and had a very antagonistic relationship with her therapist. He was opposed to the couple therapy and was reported as saying that it was another sign of Eva's attack on her therapy with him. A conflict between the two forms of therapy was set up and overshadowed the couple therapy from the beginning. When Eva was helped and understood by me she very quickly felt she was betraying her therapist and feared punishment. These conflicts resonated too closely with Eva's traumatic childhood experiences of antagonistic parents and punishing step-parents, with no place of safety.

When the interpretations of the two therapists were very different, the conflict became almost unmanageable and Eva felt her mental stability was at risk. Each therapist interpreted from a very different experience of Eva, and as so many aspects of Eva were split between the two transferences, the interpretations were often in direct conflict. I would interpret Eva's compliance and desperation to hold on to the relationship at the cost of assertiveness. Her therapist was reported as saying she was too aggressive and not working hard enough to maintain the relationship, refusing Brian's love as she refused the food her therapist offered. Eva was torn between two very different views (and aspects) of herself.

It became clear in retrospect that Eva's rage and anger had been expressed in her individual therapy, which was often under threat of ending. Her neediness, compliance and fear of abandonment was expressed in her relationship to Brian. Both of these aspects of her found expression in the couple work in her appreciation of me and her attacks on me, but were hard to work with sufficiently because she was so torn between her two therapists. This reflected aspects of her troubled childhood, which had been painfully recreated in the transference. As in her past and in her relationship to Brian, she was not able to escape from unsatisfactory relationships nor was she able to improve them.

Brian had been in individual therapy for many years, and even though his therapist had suggested the couple work Brian never allowed any links to be made to his individual therapy, and even felt his childhood experiences only belonged in that forum. He became very remote in the couple forum and found the differences between the two arenas difficult to manage. I only learned in a letter from Brian after the couple therapy had ended the extent to which he had used the two arenas defensively against each other, and deprived each forum of vital elements. His therapist was unaware for instance of Brian's aggression and violence, which was only expressed in the relationship to Eva and only known about in the couple work.

Brian explained that he had felt too exposed and out of control in the threesome to reveal his feelings and work on the relationship. He had always felt in control with his therapist and, as in his relationship to Eva, he could not function when he was not in control. The couple therapy was so disturbing that he had to withdraw, as he withdrew from Eva and had done from many other relationships before. His individual therapy was used exclusively to help him manage the feelings brought up in the couple therapy. Unfortunately, the benefit of this work never came back into the couple therapy, and the total transference situation of each of the partners was split between the three concurrent therapies.

Forbidden zone: contact between therapists and Oedipal issues

In the process of thinking about concurrent therapies, I have come to believe that in some sense it feels that we are entering a forbidden zone. In keeping the other therapy in mind we are reminding ourselves and the couple that there is another on-going intimate relationship from which we are excluded. Facing the feelings exclusion arouses is never easy. In concurrent therapies we are in the middle of the Oedipal dilemma and its difficulties for patient and therapist alike. As couple therapists, especially in a threesome, we are working with an ever-changing triangle (Britton 1995). The partners are either being a couple while being observed, and know they are excluding the observer; or one or other of them is in the position of being excluded and observing a couple made up of one partner and the therapist. These triangles, which are present in the room, are open to exploration and at least in potential can be thought about and worked with.

In the situation of concurrent therapies we are adding another triangle. This triangle is not available in the room, not as open to exploration and harder to think about. It could be that sometimes the Oedipal situation within couple therapy, and also within another or two other therapies, creates too much internal conflict; especially when there is no contact at all between therapists, and no forum where the overlapping systems can be thought about. All participants are open to the development of phantasies that are hard to investigate and therefore to contain and work with.

When the therapists have no contact at all it is as if the patient is confronted by a separated parental couple who never talk together. Where is the welfare of the child held, when there will be obvious differences between the parents? In a functioning family these feelings can be managed by the parents coming together as a strong couple that has a life of its own as well as a shared concern for the child. What would be the equivalent for therapists when there are concurrent therapies?

I have come to realise that just as in family life there are no easy answers: no protocols in place which one can follow to stay safe and keep one's therapeutic integrity. Each case is different and each case needs careful thought. For some patients, boundaries between individual family members are too permeable and little individual identity or space is accepted; fusion and keeping it in the family are their shared phantasies. In a case like this, the therapist might find herself caught in the counter-transference, and too readily considering intruding into the other therapy and not holding to strict boundaries, in a collusion with the couple's belief that any separateness is an exclusion that cannot be survived.

Other couples keep their lives very separate and the shared phantasy might be about keeping everything within the individual, with overly rigid boundaries. When this happens, the therapist might find herself forgetting that there is another therapy, and dismissing too quickly any thought of enquiring about it. Not suggesting some contact between therapists would collude with the couple's belief that boundaries are concrete walls and must never be broken.

The issue of making or not making contact with one's colleague is a different one in each case. In most cases I have no more contact than my initial letter, or some information given when the referral comes from the other therapist. Occasionally, however, it is helpful when the therapists do make contact during the work; and occasionally, I become aware of the detrimental effect the lack of contact has had, after the couple therapy has ended. We could well imagine lack of contact between therapists could result in the impoverishment of both therapeutic endeavours, vital elements being split instead of shared between them, as happened with Eva and Brian.

These vital elements, which consist on the one hand of transference feelings in inner reality, can also consist of information about important experiences which reflect this inner reality in the outer world—in either therapy, or in either partner's past. I have occasionally discovered long into the couple therapy that matters like childhood abuse, mental illness, or affairs were known and worked on in the individual therapy, but withheld from the couple forum. The opposite is also true, and violence between partners and against children may not be disclosed in the individual therapy. Both therapists may have been working on the mistaken assumption that these vital elements of the partner or of the couple are at least known, if not worked on, in the other therapy. The therapeutic container is under threat when secrets are kept, and when the transference is split rather than shared.

In our therapeutic work we see the defence of splitting as one of the opportunities of understanding our clients when it occurs within our arena of work and we can interpret it. The same must apply to splitting between two therapies, if the splits can be known about and understood. But within what container can this understanding be gained? As therapists we believe that we have to be able to reach a 'third position' within the consulting room to reflect on the total situation of the transference and counter-transference as it is displayed in front of us. Patrick Casement called this capacity 'the internal supervisor' (Casement 1985).

How can we gain this 'third position' when the split and shared aspects of the transference are not fully open to investigation by either therapist? Can we conceive of creating this third position on occasion by means of the two, three, or four therapists seeking consultation with a supervisor who could be seen as consulting to the total situation?

When I am the only therapist for a couple, it is clear that the couple therapy alone has to provide the containment for therapeutic work. When there is a parallel therapy, the frame is more complex. I believe that in this more complex situation, we need to think about the issues of boundaries and containment on the basis of the contract that each therapist has made with their patient or patients. In an institutional setting all the therapists involved have the remit to think together about the 'system': the partners or the family have implicitly given this permission when they sought help from the institution. The contract is with the institution: a framework which offers to contain more than one therapy. When we do not have institutional containment the therapists in private practice need to be aware of the possibility that the therapies could be used as a defence against each other. In private practice we do not have a contract for on-going contact with one another, and there are few if any protocols in place to support us in our struggle to avoid splitting. When a couple come to me at the suggestion of the individual therapist, or if I refer one partner to a colleague, it might be helpful to think of this as forming an 'institution' for shared work. In all cases, however they may be managed, confidentiality in each forum is essential to the creation of a therapeutic container.

Conclusion

I should like to return in conclusion to the case of Mr and Mrs Thomas. How did both partners manage the conflicts of two therapies, and what provided the necessary containment for the two therapies to work so well together?

For Mrs Thomas, the parental couple had not protected her from abuse, but colluded in denying it. Mr and Mrs Thomas managed the rearing of their children by remaining very separate, each having strictly boundaried individual contact with the children, which reflected their fears of a combined parental couple. We could therefore imagine that in the transference Mrs Thomas would be very concerned that the two therapists could collude against her. Perhaps the only way for her to manage concurrent therapies was to make sure the two therapists had no contact, leaving her to make the links between the two arenas. In this way, her fear of a combined parental couple was contained enough not to split the therapists, but to allow each of us to hold the other therapy in mind.

We could well assume that Mrs Thomas needed to bring the parental couple together in a careful and controlled way as part of her unconscious task in her therapy. My experience certainly was that she valued her individual therapist throughout the couple therapy, and came back to valuing what her couple therapist had to offer in the end. But for this development to happen, it was essential that the experience of the individual therapy be thought about in the couple work, and vice versa. In general, in managing the complex task of working alongside colleagues, our aim must be to minimise splitting where we can, and by keeping the other therapy in mind to promote sharing, so that each therapy can support and enrich the other.

This chapter was born as an idea for the theme of a Society of Psychoanalytical Marital Psychotherapists Study Day, with the title Splitting and Sharing. *Some readers may remember that Diana Daniell and I gave a talk on this subject at that conference and many of the themes in this chapter come out of the work she and I did at that time. I therefore want to express my thanks to her for generously allowing me to build on our joint work and for her support in this project.*

CHAPTER SIX

CAT'S CRADLE: CONJOINT OR SINGLE SESSIONS IN COUPLE THERAPY

Elaine Bollinghaus & Helen Tarsh

Elaine Bollinghaus has a degree in medieval history, and subsequently studied psychology. For many years she worked as a Relate counsellor, before becoming a graduate of the Tavistock Marital Studies Institute's Diploma training in psychoanalytic marital psychotherapy. She currently works with couples in private practice, both on her own and conjointly with Helen Tarsh. She is a founder member of the Society of Psychoanalytical Marital Psychotherapists. She is co-author with Helen Tarsh of 'The Prism: Object Relations Theory at Work' (SPMP Bulletin 1996) and of 'Shared Unconscious Phantasy: Reality or Illusion' (Journal of Sexual and Marital Therapy, May 1999).

Helen Tarsh trained at the Tavistock Marital Studies Institute (TMSI) after a previous career in Law, and is a founder member of the Society of Psychoanalytical Marital Psychotherapists. She now works in private practice both on her own and conjointly with Elaine Bollinghaus. She has taught psychoanalytic theory for some years as a Visiting Lecturer with the TMSI to groups of mixed professionals undertaking the Psychoanalytic Study of the Couple Relationship.

Helen Tarsh and Elaine Bollinghaus have been in practice together as co-therapists for nine years, and write confidently from that position. This description of their clinical work in marital psychotherapy gives us a valuable insight into conjoint work with couples. Using the metaphor of 'the cat's cradle', the chapter explores the effects of changes within the foursome framework which these co-therapists regularly use. They describe the historical context in which the framework originated, and pay particular attention to the reasons for, and results of moving from this familiar way of working. The chapter clearly describes a professional relationship, a matrix within the consulting room, which can be flexible and robust, and which has the capacity to reflect and contain the couples' transferences.

* * *

The theme of this book, *The Invisible Matrix*, is an exploration of how concurrent therapies, or other relevant activities such as supervision, may affect a couple's on-going psychotherapy if not consciously addressed or held in mind. A penetrating focus upon that multifaceted arena exposes the dangers emanating from defensive splitting and projection between all these various functions that can unconsciously and adversely impact upon the couple work. The debate in this sense is about what best facilitates a creative, rather than a destructive, coupling of one therapeutic or relevant endeavour with another—to the general enhancement of both and with the hope of finding a shared and enlarged container that can accommodate all the emotional turbulence that may be aroused.

To this debate we would like to contribute our experience as couple/marital (we shall use the terms interchangeably) psychoanalytic psychotherapists. We see our task as one whereby we seek to promote integration within each of the partners, to facilitate the growth of a creative internal marriage, and to enlarge the 'marital' container. Because many couples in trouble have not had the opportunity to internalise a creative coupling, their own adult coupling becomes deeply problematic. We therefore struggle with them to move from their joint intrapsychic position dominated by rigid defences such as splitting and fusion—fission or fusion—to one where a creative 'intercourse' characterised by separateness and sharing can be thought about, tolerated and thus release the partners to engage more freely with each other.

We work in foursome therapy because we believe that the idea of an internal marriage is symbolised by the co-therapy partnership. It is the ability of the co-therapy partnership to concretise, model and symbolise a 'marriage' that gives conjoint foursome therapy its cutting edge. At a conscious level a co-therapy partnership models a relationship. Some heterosexual clients know and express this when they voice their disappointment on first being told that the co-therapy relationship we offer them is that of two women. Clients' interest in and feelings about 'our marriage' are a reflection of their fascination with the idea of marriage itself, for as Britton wrote: 'the idea of a couple coming together to produce a child is central in our psychic life, whether we aspire to it, object to it, realise we are produced by it, deny it, relish it, or hate it' (Britton 1995).

As Colman made clear in his thinking about marriage as a psychological container (Colman 1993), marital therapy primarily works not with the couple's conscious but with the couple's unconscious shared internal image of a relationship, which is essentially the image of the couple in intercourse. The changes therefore that occur in a couple in marital psychotherapy refer not so much to changes in the individuals but to a change in the quality of their relationship. Through allowing the therapists to participate in their interaction the nature of a couple's relationship is altered and a different image of relationship becomes available for introjection. If the shared unconscious image of a relationship in which a male and female mate is conceived of as a fruitful intercourse then some creative outcome will result.

However, working in this way as a foursome, seeing and keeping both partners together with two co-therapists, as opposed to seeing them individually, was not historically, and still may not be considered by some to be either the treatment of choice for all couples or even always expediently manageable. It is our intention to explore this particular issue more fully. Our usual framework as co-therapists is largely to preserve the foursome framework working with both partners in the room together. It is when this particular boundary is altered for whatever reason that the marital therapy may become vulnerable to splits in the patients' inner world in the same way that a seemingly insoluble conflict between couple and individual therapies may also echo splits in the psyche of the shared patient.

We shall divide this chapter into three sections. Firstly we shall set the context of the theoretical assumptions behind our work as couple psychoanalytic psychotherapists. We shall give a brief psychoanalytic understanding of how we perceive a couple's attraction to one another and what it is that underpins their choice of one another and we shall give an overview of the particular psychoanalytic approach on which couple psychotherapists draw. We shall link this understanding of couples with a consideration as to their suitability for conjoint and/or singles therapy.

We shall then revisit the debate about seeing couples with the partners singly or together. The context for our exploration derives from our experience of working as lone therapists in threesomes as well as within a long standing conjoint co-therapy partnership, with couples some of whom we have never thought of separating and some of whom we have made, with the couple, the conscious decision to separate and work with each partner singly, and some of whom indeed we wished we had worked with separately.

Finally we shall explore the experience of therapists and couple when the conjoint framework risks breaking down. This may be because the couple have been separated, expediently or intentionally, either from each other or from one of the therapists.

In total this complex web of parallel split-off issues and multiplicity of interactions with all the participants moving actually or psychically in phantasy, between twosomes, threesomes, and foursomes—every which way—but all nonetheless optimally held together and contained by the therapists—is what we refer to as the cat's cradle. How this containment is provided by the co-therapy relationship and how change is enabled to occur, is the question we would like to pursue.

Theoretical assumptions: the intrapsychic dilemma for marriage

It is not surprising, wrote Pauline Hodson and Sasha Brookes in their introduction, that the idea for creating a space, a dialogue to think about concurrent therapies originated with marital therapists, who are trained to think about the nature of partnership. For of all partnerships, marriage (or a long-term committed relationship), is the one which, par excellence, can provide for each partner's most fundamental needs. It has its roots in our archaic longings for intense primitive closeness, as well, however, as in our archetypal conflicts. Above all else every marriage carries within it the tension of balancing the needs of the individual and the needs of the couple To put the dilemma another way: at the core of every emotional conflict lies the longing for a close intimate relationship with a significant other, a longing to be part of a couple, and the longing to be self-sufficient, to develop one's own wholeness and capacity for individuation. Indeed, crucially, the very task of being in a relationship with another is not only to meet conscious and unconscious dependency and intimacy needs, but paradoxically it is also absolutely vital for the very purposes of being able to define one's self and determine one's identity against that of significant other(s).

> There is no such thing as a single human being, pure and simple, unmixed with other human beings... That self... is a composite structure... formed out of countless never ending influences and exchanges between ourselves and others... we are members one of another. (Riviere 1991)

In this inherent oppositional aspect of the psychic developmental dilemma lie the seeds of later difficulties for many couples with entrenched problems.

That being said, however, both kinds of longings—for a primitive sense of fusion and oneness or for a profound desire for autonomy and self definition—contain their own associated anxiety. The longing for fusion or closeness arouses the fear of being swallowed up, of being taken over, of losing one's self. The longing for autonomy and selfhood can be accompanied by the dread of the loss of the other, of abandonment, of destroying the other. In the face of such tensions between desire and fear, we all have to find ways of managing loving and hating the same other, the same person who appears to arouse such inner turmoil. With luck a state of mind can be developed where 'marriage does not have to be a place where I can entirely be myself, but it can be the place where I discover some of the possibilities for becoming myself' (Colman 1993). This paradox situated at the heart of all marriage is beautifully expressed in the phrase of the Australian poet quoted by John Bayley in his account of his marriage to Iris Murdoch where he describes marriage as a place where the partners in it 'move closer and closer apart' (Bayley 1998).

For couples who find their way into marital psychotherapy however, this possibility, this state of mind, does not exist, or if once existing has been lost sight of. More often than not the couples whom we see, instead of being able to feel themselves to be separate and yet together, are likely to feel split or fused. Like Schopenhauer's porcupines, they can never find a comfortable distance between them. Feeling alone and cold they huddle together for warmth, but the minute they do this, they find themselves pricked by each other's long spines, and they spring apart. Once apart they feel alone and cold again, desperate for warmth. Indeed, this image expresses well the couple dilemma that where there is fusion paradoxically there is also fission; and where there is fission there is also fusion. When the fused porcupines were too close they needed to split, and when they were too far apart they needed to fuse. It is only those couples where the partners can feel separate enough from each other, therefore with sufficient self identity, who can come together to share, able to find a mutually comfortable distance from which to move in and out of their compact. By fusion and splitting we are referring to an intrapsychic process, a state of mind, rather than a physical reality. Two case vignettes will illustrate the point:

Professor and Mrs A lead on the surface two very separate lives. It was difficult even to negotiate with this couple over a consultation process as they hardly spoke to one another about anything other than the bare minimum of practicalities. From the outset we found ourselves caught in the cross fire of their inability to come together. Only answering machines mediated between them and us. However when this couple eventually came into therapy we realised that, despite their overtly separate existences, their emotional thinking was utterly fused. For example, Mrs A had bought an expensive set of fishing rods for her stressed-out husband without consulting him, only to be shocked to discover that he hated the whole idea of fishing. In Mrs A's mind there was no separation between her perception of her husband's needs and his. When it was suggested to her that she had bought the fishing rods for her idea of her husband and not for him, she reacted with puzzled astonishment. Likewise, Professor A simply could not understand the way in which he left his wife feeling totally isolated, assuming that she always knew what was in his mind and he need take no initiatives nor communicate with her. The feeling associated with this particular couple's form of fusion was one of no marriage, but a relationship in which each partner's fragile identity was persistently written out by the other.

By contrast, the feeling of the relationship conveyed by Mr and Mrs B was one of a battle for survival. On the surface, they did everything together, unable to make a step without the other's agreement for fear of arousing the other's wrath. Nothing was too trivial to let pass or to fight over. They gave each other no respite. But the paradox was also in the fight. They fought to force the other into fusion and they fought to preserve their own identity, to avoid being taken over and written out like the As.

Both these couples experienced no emotional or sexual intimacy. The As split with deadly quiet efficiency. The Bs split with murderous anger and quarrelling. However, in phantasy both couples lived in a state of fusion. They lived in each other's minds, inside each other's skins, they put part or even all of themselves, psychically, into the other. They saw the other as an embodiment unconsciously of their own fears and phantasies, not as a separate other with reality questioning and testing available to them.

Psychoanalytic theory underlying partner choice and interaction

Underpinning our understanding of marital interaction is Object Relations theory. The premiss is that a stable or long-standing (sexual) couple relationship provides an arena in which the internal world, the unconscious phantasies, of each of the partners is externalised in the relationship between them. In this sense the couple relationship can be thought of as a mutual transference relationship in which the unconscious choice of partner will be determined by each partner's receptivity and cathexis to the split-off disowned and projected aspects of the other. The marriage can therefore be seen as a shared system with each partner acting to some degree as a container for the other's unconscious hopes of repeating that which was good, repairing that which was bad or missing, and re-visiting that which once felt unbearable, in earlier primary relationships. The mutual acceptance of the other's projections constitutes the unconscious attachment which the couple will have for each other and consists of shared phantasies and shared defences (Bannister & Pincus 1965). By making their partner choice couples are therefore embarking upon a relationship which can veer from being a very powerful arena for change on the one hand, to being conversely a compact for the purposes of defence and resistance to altering the status quo, for fear of something worse, held within their unconscious minds.

The nexus of this psychic system between the couple is that of projective identification, a mechanism first described by Klein (1946). She hypothesised projective identification as an essentially life-saving phantasy to protect the infant from persecutory experiences and fears for its own survival, in what she called the paranoid-schizoid position of psychic existence. Among such prototypic phantasies thought about by Klein and others were deep-seated fears for the safety of the self, with terror of annihilation uppermost, dread of the loss or destruction of the object, early Oedipal glimmers arousing fears of exclusion and spoiling envy (Klein 1975b). The concept has been developed extensively and controversially since. At its broadest, projective identification is an unconscious primitive (defence) mechanism, whereby, in unconscious phantasy, parts of the self and internal objects are split off and projected into an external object, which is then identified with that which has been projected. Thus, for example, an infant who has experienced a rejecting mother and has split off that internalised aspect of him or herself may grow into an adult who will seek out a partner with whom to projectively identify this aspect of himself and will then experience that partner as the rejecting one

Bion developed the notion further by suggesting that the person doing the projecting acts in such a manner as to evoke in the recipient of the projection feelings appropriate to those being projected (Bion 1962). The recipient of the projection therefore unconsciously identifies with that which has been projected and is thereby recruited into action by the projector. He is, in part, influenced in his thinking, feeling and behaviour unconsciously by the projector (Ruszczynski 1992). Thus, in the previous example, the partner perceived to be rejecting becomes ever more actively rejecting.

Bion also expanded our understanding of projective identification by suggesting that it could be thought about as normal or abnormal, the difference being in the degree of violence in its execution by the projector. Normal projective identification has as its aim a communication to the object, a desire that the object contain certain states of his or her mind. In the infant-mother relationship this communication by the infant of its emotions may then be contained by the container-mother and processed in a way that will convey meaning to her child's otherwise inchoate state. With good enough mothering (Winnicott 1960a) or active containment (Bion 1962) the infant can move more easily into that which Klein (1952) called depressive position functioning. The infant then fears less for itself than for its object. The associated prototypic anxieties will then be more to do with fears of loss, exclusion, concern for harming the object or denial of the object's importance, as well as ultimately a desire for genuine reparation.

Abnormal projective identification, by contrast, has as its aim, not that of communication, but that of the desire to evacuate violently a too painful state of mind which leads to entering forcibly an (internal or external) object in unconscious phantasy, often with the aim of intimidating control of that object. Meltzer has suggested that this extreme form of the mechanism, be referred to as intrusive identification, and that the inside of the object penetrated by the subject through this intrusive identification be referred to not as a container but as a claustrum. (Meltzer 1982).

It would seem that Bion's definition of normal projective identification could help us to understand those couples whose 'marital fit'—their unconscious compact, or mutual transference relationship—is of a creative and developmental nature. Whereas Bion's thoughts on massive or abnormal projective identification, enhanced by Meltzer's ideas of the claustrum, help us to understand what is happening in a defensive, stultifying or cruel relationship in which the aim of each partner's projections is likely not to be for the purposes of unconscious communication and understanding, but rather violently to get rid of, or dump unwanted parts of the self into the other. Such couples who use massive evacuative projective identifications are described by Mary Morgan to be in a 'gridlock' (Morgan 1995). Of course in practice couples are not so neatly divided and many couples will find that their interactions may oscillate between using projective identification as a means of communication and as a means of evacuation.

Part of the intensity felt by 'gridlocked' couples can be understood by thinking about Esther Bick's (1968) and Meltzer's (1966) elucidation of another primitive defence that they perceived, for which they coined the phrase 'adhesive identification' (Bick 1968). This term describes a form of narcissistic identification characterised by imitation. Whilst observing infants closely Bick noticed that in the absence of the mother, some would fix their gaze rigidly on any object, or move frantically, as if they were having to hold themselves together, as if to create their own psychic second skin, for without the mother's containing presence it was as if they had no skin to hold them together. In later life, this behaviour seems to be manifested by those who, in the face of intolerable separation anxiety, cling to their object as if glued adhesively. The object for them does not function as a separate other but rather as a second skin without which they would cease to exist. Such is the nature of this form of adhesive identification that in the case, for example, of couples who so function but try to separate physically or even psychically, it feels to them as if their skin has been ripped apart, part of the self has been torn away and a gaping wound has been left raw and bleeding.

Recently Fisher has extrapolated from the thinking of Bion, Bick and Meltzer to help us understand better what is happening to such 'gridlocked' couples who are linked together in a sadomasochistic 'folie à deux' (Fisher 1999). These are couples whom he describes as being neither able to live together nor yet separate, but for whom the relationship is torment. He considers that an insidious pattern of mutual projective identification is structured around an ability to be all too porous to massive projective or intrusive identification, powerfully but unconsciously required for the purposes of staying super-glued or adhesively identified with the life supporting object. Whilst this is effected as a defence against separation it likewise creates its own crisis. A partner who feels him or herself to have no psychic skin, no sense of inner containment in which their own psyche may dwell, also has no protection, no way of shutting orifices and boundaries against intrusive attempts to penetrate, against massive projective identification into their skinless psyche. Partners who adhere to their objects not only to stay attached in a limpet-like manner, but also to find and create their own sense of identity, inexorably run the concomitant risk in the relationship of never feeling themselves, but only a 'someone' defined by the other—an other whom they then have desperately to try to shut out, or by whom they feel they will be totally overwhelmed. As one partner said, 'It is important not to let the other person know how much a part of them you are otherwise they'll destroy you'.

Couples like the As and the Bs present a formidable challenge to marital psychotherapists, for these are the couples that can neither live together nor live apart. For them it is hell with the partner and hell without them. Their mutually destructive interaction may well induce phantasies in the therapists that if only these two people were seen separately then levels of destruction would subside, rather than being apparently exacerbated in the therapy. Therapists imagine that such a couple could come back to conjoint work now able, with greater ego strength, to use less primitive defences instead of the hailstorm of persecution, blame, vicious attacks, omnipotent control, denial and projection that they inflict upon each other to protect themselves against their deeply unconscious fears for their own psychic survival. The atmosphere in the room with such a couple can be unbearable with not a millimetre of space for thinking and with any sensitive revelation of one partner, being used by the other as a free gift with which to attack the donor.

Such was the case with Mr and Mrs C who could not use the conjoint sessions. This was a couple whose initial love for one another had been too early disillusioned through pressures of step-parenting and work. In their disappointment they turned their backs on one another in a mutually escalating tit-for-tat. In the sessions, each found ways through silence, withdrawal or attack to undermine the other, fearing to harm as well as be harmed. Blame was all. The therapeutic space for thought and reflection became what another couple once described of their marriage—'a knacker's yard'. Single sessions were offered and although accepted each of them continually bemoaned the lack of their joint sessions and eventually single sessions broke down and joint sessions were reinstated. Therapists may propose but clients dispose. At some level, the separateness for the Cs tore away at each partner's containing skin or membrane located in the other. Their projections were mutually retaliatory in response to the other's intrusive identification but each was ruthless in refusing to take the other's projections on board. It was the only way they knew to find out their own identity. To find out who he was he needed to know the boundaries as to who she was, and vice versa. This mutual resistance to accept any projection was paradoxically in the healthier service of creating a self, albeit that it was experienced as totally annihilating of the other. The hatred of being in any way defined by the other manifested as a massive resistance, in a way that any interaction was taken in, experienced as defining and then instantly ejected. To this end the couple needed to have therapy together; there was an unconscious wisdom in this choice although the outcome also demonstrated at another level that they could not live together and they could not survive apart.

All these couples are classically in the paranoid-schizoid position, classically 'gridlocked', classically unable to separate yet unable to be together; their relationship is 'torment'. The degree of unconscious fusion between the partners, with their 'fit' of super-glued adhesive identification and massive projective identification, would if they were divided, only allow the splits to be displaced and an alternative container found outside of the therapy. It is true that in single sessions scope is provided for a positive or even powerfully negative transference to develop with the therapist(s), but the partner remains in the background as an additional subversive container for some or alternative projections. Indeed, with couples like this the treatment of choice could well be conjoint couple work (if it can be contained and survived) before individual therapy.

Development of marital therapy: conjoint sessions and/or single sessions

When couples like the As, Bs, and Cs were first seen in a therapy that began to be recognisable as psychoanalytic marital therapy by the Family Discussion Bureau (the forerunner of the Tavistock Marital Studies Institute) in the 1950s, each partner would have been seen on their own. This thinking was based on the paradigm of individual psychoanalysis (Haldane & Vincent 1998).

By the 1970s however marital therapy had built up a body of clinical experience and its own theoretical underpinnings were well established. Following Dicks, Alison Lyons (Lyons quoted in Ruszczynsky

1993a) and Robin Skynner (1976), in separate publications, thought about the criteria for making an informed choice between one to one therapy—singles—for each partner, or conjoint therapy whether carried out by one therapist in threesomes or two therapists in foursomes. There seemed little (if any) disagreement between practitioners then or since that conjoint therapy was indicated for the couples who were functioning in the paranoid-schizoid position. Recently, Ruszczynski has affirmed the view that:

> If the couple use excessive splitting and projection, as well as blame, denial and other more primitive defences then they need to be seen together, so that the two sides of the splits can be located in the same room. (Ruszczynski 1993b)

However Skynner and Lyons also believed that individual sessions were most strongly indicated when couples were thought to be on the cusp of the depressive position at a point 'when partners have begun to see and to feel worried and sad about what each is doing to the other... the couple need individual help to bear this painful guilt...' Skynner argued that such couples needed a 'secure, reliable dyadic relationship'. They are at a point where they are in the early stages of the depressive position,

> ...where the synthesis is still insecure and the capacity to keep the image of the loved ones present and intact is precarious and easily threatened by arousal of frustration and rage through absence and rejection. Such individuals... like infants between about six months and two years of age, are deeply dependent on positive relationships with each other and with the therapist, *and are made severely anxious by any threat of loss, separation or rejection.* (Skynner 1976: 228, our emphasis)

Skynner seems adamant in his view that people with a history of early loss, deprivation and separation should particularly suggest a need for individual sessions. Lyons (op. cit.) believed that when couples were more easily able to bear their awareness of guilt and separateness, then either conjoint or individual therapy seemed to be equally appropriate.

Whilst we concur with the arguments for keeping couples who are in the paranoid-schizoid position in therapy together however difficult it is, our experience does suggest that only the most psychically mature couples who are well entrenched in the depressive position can tolerate the anxieties induced by single sessions for each partner. It has been our experience that cases where we have worked in single sessions—and either kept up regular but intermittent joint sessions or returned after a spell of single sessions to joint sessions—have not proven successful in that format.

These were couples who in Skynner's terms, had reached a state of improvement, who were on the cusp of depressive position functioning, splitting and denial were diminished, responsibility was being owned and awareness of their destructive actions and phantasies towards the other were to the fore. Nonetheless, undertaking separate sessions provoked regressions in the marriage. The couples found it difficult to bear the jealousy and envy aroused by their partner's therapy relationships that excluded them. The basically fragile linking that had been developed was not secure enough to withstand separation taking such a concrete form and attacks on all links (Bion 1959) were renewed between the couple and in the transference.

We will now present clinical examples and discussion to illustrate the cat's cradle of some of the differing constellations of single and conjoint sessions. References to therapists include lone or co-therapists, the point at issue here being whether or not the couple is kept together in principle, or divided into singles for a period of time. To make a truly comprehensive survey of all the issues involved would take us beyond the remit of this chapter. Whilst every case demands that its own particular needs are met, and there are as many needs as there are cases, we are inevitably writing schematically for the sake of making generalisations and raising questions in all that follows. Furthermore, it would also be impossible to say what would have been the outcome had we done the opposite to that which we did, and divided couples into singles or vice versa. We are writing inevitably from our own experience, and do not intend to promote a dogma.

Mr and Mrs B were just such a couple whose marriage regressed when we decided to work in single sessions. They had come together after an on-off relationship in which Mr B had initially pursued a reluctant Mrs B. Realising he would never marry her, she left the area, only to be pursued by Mr B and proposed to just at a time when she had at last found another relationship. Twenty-five years on, they both felt that only their children had kept them together. Mrs B was bitter and frustrated by Mr B's lack of overt affection and caring. Mr B felt harassed, badgered and emasculated by her constant criticism. Admittedly provoked by fortuitous reasons connected with Mr B's work disabling him from attending any longer in the daytime, but nonetheless fitting in with our sense that this couple both desperately needed and were ready now for individual dyadic work, we changed into single sessions with monthly joint sessions. Mrs B was particularly grateful to start with and Mr B soon began to use his time more fruitfully for himself. However it was not long before Mrs B became internally preoccupied with what went on in her husband's sessions. She could not value changes that he seemed to be making. She felt that she had lost touch with him and they were more isolated as a couple than ever before as he could not or would not really or fully tell her what had been talked of in his sessions. She resumed her earlier hostility to her husband. In the transference, she became anxious about what was or was not confidential between the therapists and would or would not get back to the partners. She became anxious for her own safety and began to become impenetrable and attacking with her therapist. Mr B for his part began to withdraw from his prior use of the sessions and, indeed, gradually withdrew from the sessions altogether, arriving so late that they became almost useless and eventually pulling out totally. Possibly had the new format lasted we might have been able to explore the way in which Mr B became more and more his unapproachable father and Mrs B more and more one of her cruel siblings. However, in our view this negative constellation between them and in the transference to us needed to continue to be worked through together in stable conjoint sessions. The disruption itself supplied an extra transference focus that could no longer be contained.

Such regressive tendencies might argue that these couples were in fact not sufficiently secure in the depressive position and should not have been separated. That is indeed our point. Skynner's reasoning for putting couple like the Bs and the Ds (below), who are apparently on the cusp of the depressive position into single sessions is to provide a positive dyadic experience at this vulnerable developmental time. In theory, going along with Skynner's view, the couples could work through, within their individual sessions, their internalised, and now externalised recapitulated experience of loss played out in the transference to the lost co-therapist and partner. However, to our minds this is far less favourable than working through losses in the transference together. Crucially, we feel that it is vital for partners to experience together the psychic survival of each other, as this will relate to their own unconscious phantasies about the state of their internal objects, and the destructive or envious attacks, persecutory guilts, fears and compulsions connected to the safety of the other. Above all, conjoint work would be necessary in our view for those couples where there is experience of early loss.

Our view, contrary to that of Skynner, is that it is just at this early stage of depressive position functioning, when synthesis is insecure that the couple definitely should not be divided and seen separately. Skynner himself says: '...such couples are made severely anxious by any threat of loss, separation or rejection...'; he draws different conclusions from ours, however, from this evidence.

For the reasons already given, we would now be chary of dividing couples into single sessions. There is, however, an often almost irresistibly powerful impulsion to separate them where for seemingly plausible, expedient reasons, it appears that one or both partners have individual needs that demand it. Nevertheless, it is generally, in our view, a mistake to do so. The mere fact that there are, on the face of it, good reasons to divide the couple does not mean that this couple is sufficiently outside the paranoid-schizoid mode of functioning. Possibly far from it—and the very problem itself may be seen as a diagnostic indicator to suggest the lack of containment within the partnership that calls for understanding and interpretation rather than a potential collusion. When for example both partners are already in their own individual therapy, or are leading very separate lives, or where secrets, affairs or other known traumas have been boxed up and kept out of the marriage, any demand for separate sessions is potentially a massive counter-transference impulsion which needs interpretation. If this pressure is understood with the couple, it often loses its force as a potential enactment and can then become a shared crisis. Its long shade, which had darkened the couple's relationship, whether unconsciously or consciously, can, once exposed with all its ramifications, gradually diminish, leading ultimately to a heightened cathexis between the partners.

The kinds of reasons forwarded by couples for consideration of singles are multifarious and may be apparently practical, as for example partners, like the Bonds, who can no longer attend at the same time so that the therapy would have to end unless their different needs can be accommodated; or partners who appear to have different agendas, as for example where one partner already, consciously or unconsciously, wishes to leave the marriage, or another is coincidentally engulfed with grief over the loss of a beloved (extra-marital) relationship, or partners who have a particular encapsulated trauma pre-dating the relationship which appears to be quite outside the marriage. The pressure of any one partner only to seek single sessions, for whatever reason, needs a great deal of exploration and intense counter-transference reflection. The danger of an unforeseen enactment—of an unconscious historical or phantasised repetition—is very great and provides that necessary warning against the potential risk of altering an established conjoint container.

Mr and Mrs D were seen for many years together. Separations at holiday breaks had been an especially difficult time for this exceptionally fused couple and the wife would always become ill, scarcely able to breathe. During the therapy, however, the marriage improved, the couple were rewardingly more aware of their effect on each other. There was more space. Then the marriage deteriorated in ways that seemed not adequately understood. Eventually, the wife brought out into the open her desire for a formal separation from her husband and single sessions with us. This fitted the strong counter-transference feeling of one co-therapist from the start of therapy, who had always believed that Mrs D came to therapy in order to leave the marriage. The other co-therapist however was more doubtful perhaps in identification with Mr D. In these differences of feeling were reflected the ambivalence of the couple as to preserving the marriage or to separating. The wife wanted no more to do with her husband whom she was now experiencing as actively dangerous because he had 'accidentally' backed his motorcycle into her, maintaining that he had not seen her standing there. The pressure to move into single sessions was enormous and the therapists agreed with her that their shared agenda had now changed. Single sessions continued and eventually their separation was legally formalised. Thereafter, the wife had a breakdown and attempted suicide. She was by then the same age as her mother when she had successfully killed herself against what she had perceived as the growing impossibility of her husband.

It is significant to note in relation to this couple however that where an agenda difference is connected with the certain end and/or legal separation of the couple, continuation of conjoint therapy could be considered a collusion, in those circumstances where the couple cannot separate psychically. It is also important to keep in mind that if at the consultation stage there is a suspected or confessed affair or other trauma in the background it may well be that individual single consultations with the therapist(s) prior to regular therapy might be important to allow partners freedom of expression in circumstances which would otherwise be totally inhibiting, to the ultimate detriment of any future conjoint work. Such individual consultations might also allow one or both partners to claim any unconsciously longed-for phantasised intensity of fusion with an object—in this case the therapeutic object—that the secret or trauma represents, or fails to represent.

The goal of all couple psychoanalytic psychotherapists, be they proponents of joint or single work, is to increase the potential or actual psychic space between the couple, or in other words, to enlarge the couple container. This goal is achieved by a reduction in splitting, withdrawal of projections and, therefore, greater ego strength. Theoretical support for the idea of single sessions for each spouse, as a means of enlarging the psychic container, could come by analogy, from a source in individual therapy. In a paper entitled 'Patients who are not ready for interpretations', Josephine Klein identifies a group of people whom she describes as utterly lacking in a sense of themselves, egoless, skinless people as it were, with insufficient psychic structure (Klein, J. 1990). People who lack ego strength in this way cannot experience themselves because as yet there is no experiencing person there to effect the processing of experience, thus inhibiting their capacity to think about and evaluate themselves. Their thinking is concrete, they lack any capacity for symbolic thought and function. For such persons, she writes, it is essential to build a good-enough ambience of trust and safety, in which ego processes can develop naturally. She holds that classic transference interpretations, for example, may have to come much later, after potential space—the precursor of analytic space—has been created between therapist and patient. Such thinking in the context of couple work would support the idea that where individual partners could be thought to be insufficiently robust, lacking a sense of self adequate to the rough and tumble of couple work, there might need to be at first a secure, reliable dyadic relationship in which to strengthen their own hold on themselves.

The case of Mr and Mrs E offers a vivid example of the kinds of patients of whom Josephine Klein writes. This couple had had a great deal of couple therapy in which they had repeatedly been put into single sessions as therapist after therapist found it impossible to work with them together. Mrs E concretely expressed her psychic symptoms physically. She could not resist scratching and tearing at her skin, especially at times of great stress in her marriage. She would arrive at sessions with large raw red patches on her face and arms. She seemed literally skinless. Every comment pierced her. Her husband had long learned to say nothing and did so in the sessions. He lived away from home all week and stayed out all weekend. By contrast, her words poured out seamlessly through her skinless body as it were, and thus metaphorically speaking, she emptied herself out into the room. Concretely she filled the room, there was no potential space for anyone else to come in and no room for any thought including her own.

Josephine Klein's thinking is involved with the question of how people experience themselves as individuals, 'how are they formed and how best to treat them when they are overformed, underformed or deformed' (Wright 1991). Winnicott also asked this question and in all his writings tried to understand how an individual grows through infantile dependence towards a personal way of being. He highlights the developmental necessity for the infant's primitive ego to emerge through the expression of his or her 'true self' manifest in the 'spontaneous gesture' to which the mother responds, as opposed to the infant having to respond to the mother in what would then be a distortion of the infant's own sense of psychic continuity, its 'going on being'. (Winnicott 1960b). An infant who suffers from undue external and internal impingement can only develop a defensive 'false self' with which to face the world and its inevitable (presentiment of) anticipated onslaughts on his deeply hidden self. Winnicott came to think of psychopathology as originating from breaks in that continuity of being, caused by gaps in holding, intrusions, impingements and deprivations of which the infant could not make sense and for which he could not find a place within himself.

With a 'good enough' developmental start an infant may gain a sense of its own omnipotence, its own sense of selfhood, its own belief in the goodness of a responsive world that it may internalise. Thus in adult therapy single well contained dyadic sessions in order to develop this sense of selfhood would be valuable, or, in another paradigm, provide a secure base (Bowlby 1979). That of course does beg the question of circumstances where a persecuting object lies between a couple. Perhaps maximum therapeutic effect in couple work would be achieved by offering the most disturbed couples both conjoint and single sessions on a weekly basis. This work was done in America and reported in an interesting and comprehensive discussion of the literature and a detailed case study, by McCormack in his paper 'The Borderline Schizoid Marriage' (McCormack 1989). However his treatment was offered as an adjunct to in-patient treatment of one of the partners and would be an expensive option unavailable within the UK's National Health Service or indeed probably even privately, unless offered serendipitously.

In several years of work experience with couples (seen in a NHS outpatient unit) who attended separately in parallel single sessions, it was clear that for the most part, the individuals benefited from this single session mode of treatment and reported some improvements in their relationship (Chiesa & Brown 1990). The maximum success of parallel single work is highly dependent on the therapist's capacity to hold the marriage through making sense together of their separate counter-transferences to their own client; whilst each partner works on their individual problems linked always to a marital focus. This work can be replicated with even one therapist seeing both partners individually at times. Nonetheless there is a caveat to this parallel mode of treatment. The inevitable transferences to the therapists, whether acknowledged or not, may impose difficulties that can be enacted rivalrously either between the couple or split off elsewhere and for which therapists need to be alert.

Mr and Mrs F appeared to progress in single sessions in terms of their own particular difficulties in making emotionally resonant relationships. Their marriage had been intellectually based and they had used their formidable schizoid shells to protect them from emotional 'touching'. They could discuss at depth the latest play but not their own needs. Real difficulties began with the birth and upbringing of their son, whereby each felt that the care proffered by one was at the expense of themselves or that of their own parenting. Paradoxically, the emotional engagement with the individual work developed in inverse proportion to the increasingly intense competitiveness that was aroused over the upbringing of their child.

We would argue that couples who are concrete in the way described by Josephine Klein lack a 'third position'; their mental set, or psychic functioning seems to be one or two dimensional in a narcissistic sense. From that perspective it would be our view that we would not think it appropriate to separate them from their partner in couple therapy. Whilst they seem 'skinless', lacking a self-observing ego, and do need considerable supportive empathy, they also need slowly to become aware of the otherness of their partner, and their partner's relationship with the therapist. From that point of view, the concreteness of two therapists, as opposed to one, can create an optimal environment for ego development, as each partner can in phantasy believe that they have a therapist-parent to themselves. Indeed, this factor might well be a diagnostic indicator at assessment time as to whether or not to allocate one or two therapists to a case.

Britton (1989) well describes the necessity in psychic development for a third position which encompasses mature depressive position functioning. He sees the core issue as lying specifically within the primitive Oedipal constellation. For an individual to achieve a sense of internal space with his or her internal objects and therefore live out external relationships which would allow for space between subject and the external object, the person must be able to bear triangulation; to recognise, in all its love and hatred, the link between the parents from which the child is excluded; to not feel strangled by, or shut out by, or indeed damagingly excluding of the other person in a three person relationship; to be able to tolerate, without incapacitating guilt or shame or envy, the possibility of being both a participant and observed in a relationship as well as being an observer of a relationship between two others. Britton says that gaining this achievement 'provides a limiting boundary for the internal world'. It creates the capacity 'for seeing ourselves in interaction with others and for entertaining another point of view whilst retaining our own, for reflecting on ourselves whilst being ourselves'. Taking this perspective would provide a legitimate rationale for keeping couples together to work through the very issues of painful triangulation, as opposed to a phantasised and longed-for narcissistic oneness that troubled couples manifest.

Mr and Mrs G provide a good example of a couple who in spite of an unpromising start were ultimately able to find sufficient space in their relationship. They were a disabled couple who had lived most of their married life overseas. Both of them had suffered from early maternal loss in that both were unwanted and rejected babies and children. In the marriage, Mrs G had experienced a long history of sexual rejection by Mr G. By the time we met them her fury at what she saw as his callous insensitivity, domination and rejection of her knew no bounds. Mr G had withdrawn behind impregnable defences of silent passivity and hostile obstinacy, fearing to lose Mrs G but terrified to raise his head above the parapet. There was for a very long time a frightening paranoid atmosphere in the room. Mrs G could not tolerate for a second the slightest attention to her husband and likewise received every comment that invited space to think as a personal attack even to the extent of walking out of the session. Mr G was deeply embedded in a psychic retreat from which it was nearly impossible to draw him out. In this highly narcissistic environment where the fear of destruction was so acute that we would independently have phantasies of one or other of the partner's suicide or death, we never entertained a doubt that it was vital for this couple to reclaim their intense projections of vicious exclusion and attack together. Despite the potential danger, it seemed essential that they must eventually bear the piercing glare from each other's skinless sense of vulnerability and not leave the subsequently shared experience of painful exposure and dread of psychic annihilation to phantasy. When, however, the couple could experience each other's survival, experience the increased space between them, value each other's contributions to their shared endeavour then joy was in the room. Laughter, hope, and reparative trends emerged and the gratitude of Mr and Mrs G was touching.

In general, it is our view that only in exceptional circumstances would we choose to see couples intentionally in single sessions. Were we to do so we would think that optimally the couple needs both single and joint sessions to run in parallel so reflecting the psychic dilemma of needing to be both an autonomous and an attached individual. Phantasies and secrets arising because of single sessions are not necessarily that different from phantasies and secrets that can arise within conjoint work. But the lack of the known in the partners' minds exacerbates the phantasies and then creates its own problems. Above all the additional disadvantage of single sessions is that the couple will not be sharing all of the pain—and will be missing some of the joy—of a joint experience!

Breaks in the framework

In this section we explore the impact of one-off or expedient absences that arise in the course of the therapy either by one of the partners or one of the therapists and that come with notice, a last minute warning or no warning at all. It is self-evident that any absence from the therapeutic endeavour always comes with a meaning, no matter how well rationalised—and this can be true for any party to the work. It is always the meaning, conscious and unconscious, behind any absence and the responses to it that need understanding and in particular close attention to the therapist(s)' counter-transference.

Absence of one of the partners

Again, on the face of it, there may be as many conscious and unconscious motives for the absence of one partner, or indeed both, from a session as there are couples. However, it is the transference and counter-transference that needs exploration in these delicate situations where nothing can be taken at face value.

In cases where only one partner attends the session, that partner could sometimes be expected to use the session as an opportunity to attack their absent partner. It may be a cause for wonder if an anticipated attack does not occur. Although there may be many reasons, sometimes it is as if the attending partner desires to have the session to (and perhaps for) themselves, but when faced with the opportunity for making out their own case, or getting the therapists on their side, seems to feel acutely the loss of or risk of phantasised damage to their partner. This effect seems to mirror the acute ambivalence in which coupledom has to survive—the profound desire for autonomy and selfhood on the one hand, together with the dread of loss and damage to the deeply needed object on the other. It also mirrors the great danger the child may feel, in phantasy, if Oedipally allied with either parent, of damaging the other. Conversely a triumphant attack on the absent partner can also demonstrate the internal Oedipal drama being played out. The absence of one partner or one therapist is fertile ground for working in this area.

Ms H often attended sessions on her own whilst damning her husband Mr I for copping out of them with business excuses. She was unstoppable in her apparent hatred of her husband and used the time to execrate him mercilessly. The suspicion was unavoidable that she also did not want him to attend and managed to keep him away with her incessant attacks on him or by pleading child care problems. In the transference the therapist was both the preferred mother with whom she could belabour her neglectful father/husband, and also the longed-for idealised father, with whom she desired a relationship to herself, without her mother/husband to spoil it.

The single session may also be used passively against the absent partner. The therapist(s) needs to be alert to the possibility of being drawn into just such an overt or covert 'attack' on the absent partner with its potential for splitting the therapy, should the single session either not be alluded to subsequently in the presence of both partners or the material from it kept out of the conjoint sessions.

Mr J attended one session on his own following several months in conjoint work. He spoke more freely and frankly than ever before about his own distress and the reasons for it over the couple's lack of sexual relations and the problem, as they both saw it, that lay with his inorgasmic and uninterested wife. The therapists subsequently colluded with the unspoken assumption that this information was private and privileged and it was never brought into the conjoint sessions. This was a massive transference and counter-transference enactment in the case that perpetuated the unconscious phantasy that the husband/fathers had no needs that required to be overtly expressed and acknowledged. Only the wife/mothers were meant to be needy and deprived.

This case example raises clearly at least three other issues that arise out of expedient absences. One such issue is that in the absence of their partner the attending one may well speak more freely. Whilst this may be taken as a sign that the couple should be seen in single sessions, this is obviously not indicated. It is rather a manifestation of the degree of splitting in which the partners engage. There are evidently no-go areas in the marriage, and the problem may be connected with an Oedipal configuration.

A second important issue that arises is the whole question of confidentiality. This matter refers also of course to couples who are divided into single sessions for a particular period of time. The question is what may be known by each pair? Technically, the two therapists hold the marriage and therefore exchange information. How is this information to be used in subsequent conjoint sessions? A particularly stark example is the implicit or explicit knowledge of affaires.

A third important question is whether or not partners should attend on their own when they are in conjoint therapy. Couple therapists differ in their thinking about the wisdom of seeing only one partner. To do so may collude with all kinds of splits being enacted in the couple relationship. Not to do so creates difficulties as it enables a potentially reluctant irregularly attending partner to hold the power and apparently work against the therapy. However, seeing the attending partner does allow the problem to be worked with in the room. This was the dilemma ultimately faced by Ms H and Mr I. A relatively irregular attender can in concrete enactment expose the reality of the marriage. Without facing this reality and allowing the partner to come who wishes to do so, a collusion could be unconsciously entered into by the therapists with the partners that there is something called a marriage, or a viable coupledom, that may be able to be treated. The avoided issue might be that there are two very split and fused partners who prefer to use each other as vehicles for their projections in an unsatisfactory relationship which both on an unconscious level seek to perpetuate, rather than attend together to find a more satisfying relationship. Of course any risk of change implicit in attending therapy should not be underestimated.

Absence of a co-therapist

Absence by one of the therapists, whether planned or inadvertent, arouses similar conflicts to those exposed by the absence of the partner. This is not surprising, given that the unconscious is formed on the bedrock of primitive Oedipal stresses which are reflected in the transference. The present therapist will be on the alert for loss being turned into attack—or idealisation—of herself or the absent therapist.

In the course of a long therapy, the Ks had never missed a session, and were never late. One week one of the therapists had been unexpectedly absent. The following session, the Ks rang up beforehand to say that their son, due home that morning, had not arrived and they were unable to come to that week's session. There was not the slightest suggestion that this story was untrue. But there was evidently meaning to be drawn from it. This was a couple whom we knew well defended themselves against the pain of loss with powerful retaliatory defences.

Couples can be fearful quite overtly of damaging the remaining therapist who is perceived as vulnerable and weak without their partner. A common comment is: 'will we be too much for you?' Conversely the anger with the absent therapist and the present therapist who is left for better or for worse, can be expressed very subtly in a passive negativity by which little, or even no fresh work can be done. Invariably, the material from the lost session will be reworked quite unconsciously on the return of the absent therapist. This response, at the least, reflects a protest at the loss of the parental couple in the transference. For those couples who have failed to internalise a good creative couple, such a loss can lead to a valuing of that which is suddenly not available to them.

In their different ways neither the Ds nor the Gs previously mentioned had internalised a creative couple and for each of them the absence of a co-therapist and loss of the therapy 'marriage', did lead to positive change in their relationship.

Mr and Mrs G worked with us for at least two years without us acquiring any sense that we meant anything to them at all. We felt ourselves to be undifferentiated in their experience of us, just two professional heads, and barely noticed except for our words that either hurt or soothed. They never called us by name and we were convinced that the absence of one of us would scarcely register. This was reflected in our co-therapy relationship at a particular stage in the therapy. Unusually, we paid no attention to it and we rarely referred to them between ourselves once their sessions were over. After a long time, one therapist was unexpectedly taken ill and could not attend. To the therapists' surprise, the couple expressed concern about her to the remaining therapist, referred to her by name and sent her good wishes. This proved to be a turning point in the therapy. Valuing the therapist translated into valuing each other for the first time in the work.

Mr and Mrs D disagreed revengefully. They did nothing together and nothing apart and were inordinately envious and attacking of each other's activities. Occasionally, one therapist was absent. It was a shattering experience to both partners to be faced with the realisation that nevertheless the two therapists spoke to each other about their session. The couple could not take it in, and indeed the two therapists were themselves shocked at the time, having assumed that the couple would naturally think that as they worked together the therapists would obviously communicate with each other. It transpired thereafter that in the inner world of this pair, not surprisingly, there was no internalised working couple. In their inner worlds both mothers had succeeded in emasculating both fathers and Mr and Mrs D as only children. Their shared unconscious phantasy emerged as that articulated by Mr D, whereby the autonomy of one partner is death to the other. In this case the revelation of this phantasy elucidated much and the couple were enabled to make some progress.

As these examples of expedient changes suggest, an alteration in the framework can and does paradoxically produce change, provided always that the overall container is secure. The alteration creates an emotional crisis around difference, which forces itself upon the couple as a catastrophic change (Bion 1984) which can at best be mobilised and at worst is never forgotten. This catastrophe takes its meaning from being experienced in the face of an ever-present internalised object, externalised in the shape of a partner. In this Oedipal configuration a move towards or away from either of the transference partners in phantasy presages unconscious danger. Put reductively, the danger is of being possessed or rejected—terrors that must be avoided at all costs. Absence of any one of the participants can expose more clearly or distort more heavily the Oedipal issues which coalesce to keep couples stuck.

Conclusion

In all the preceding examples the therapists participated in the couple's interaction in numerous different ways which were crucial to any process of change. Of course in couple therapy not all interventions are directed at the couple. Sometimes a therapist will engage directly with one spouse, but at all times the couple therapist holds in mind the couple dynamic, thinks about and shares with the couple what idea of an internal marriage is being made manifest, what either partner is doing in his mind to or with the image of the other partner, or to or with the image of the therapist and the therapy pair. Some couples with a destructive image of an internal marriage will unconsciously try to split the therapist couple, idealising one, denigrating the other. Such was our experience with the Ks. On the one hand they made it clear that they liked the idea of us as a pair of therapists, appreciating our differences and needing the containment of us both. On the other hand they were very quick to attack us both, or divide us by sidelining one therapist and idealising the other. In the early days of their therapy we found ourselves disagreeing and quarrelling most of the time about interpretation of them, and holding strong feelings that the other therapist was insensitive or cold. At other times, we were more aware of our envy of the other's ability. Alternatively, a very narcissistic couple will obliterate altogether the idea of a couple, so that the co-therapists find themselves fused in their thinking, finding themselves feeling and speaking with one voice. With such couples the ability of both partners to retain their own voice and be in touch with the other therapist's voice is a barometer of the movement the couple are able to make towards a healthier and more creative idea of an internal marriage. We remember one couple where we found that time after time we divided the session neatly between us, one dominating the early part of the session and the other the latter half, but never able to speak together.

When co-therapists and couples take a decision to move into singles over a length of time the co-therapists have their work cut out to hold onto the couple's marriage, their own 'marriage' and the idea of marriage. One of the therapists working on his or her own with one member of a marriage has to bear his or her feelings about her partner's work with the other spouse. It is easy to imagine that one's co-therapist is doing much better work with the other spouse, or that the other spouse would be easier to work with if only they had chosen you! Conversely, one therapist may be very happy working with one spouse and contemptuously forget about or denigrate the other therapy pair. Working with the Bs in one to one work certainly exposed the therapist working with Mr B to rivalrous feelings in the conjoint foursome session that were held every few weeks. She was anxious for Mr B to show that he had learnt and changed from his sessions with her, lest in phantasy she and he were the 'bad' ones in this relationship. This phantasy was further fuelled by the fact that Mr B seemed to his therapist to turn not to her for support in the joint meetings, but to his wife's therapist. However, Mr B's therapist was also able to notice, with a touch of triumph, that Mrs B turned to her rather than to her own individual therapist.

But to think about every nuance of feeling in terms of an internal marriage is the task of couple psychotherapists. And excruciating as it sometimes is to come across one's phantasies of an internal marriage made flesh in the shape of a co-therapist, we think it is easier to work with couples when the phantasies can be tested against the external other in the shape of a known co-therapist. Co-therapists, especially if they have the good fortune to work together regularly, have the benefit of being able to think about alterations in their style, perceptions which seem distorted, behaviour which is unusual, and can then think about these issues in terms of counter-transference experience. Ways in which they find themselves clinging together, disregarding the other, enjoying the other's contribution, are vital clues to the internal world of their couple. Meeting regularly to discuss such counter-transference clues is even more important when the foursome conjoint framework is broken into single sessions with each partner.

Indeed it could be argued that in theory it matters not whether couples are seen at all times together or whether at different stages in the therapy they are seen individually, or whether there are unplanned absences of therapist or partner, as long as at all times the therapists have their transference and counter-transference antennae attuned to the idea of an 'internal marriage'. In practice, however, as we have argued, we believe that the capacity to develop an 'internal marriage' is optimally managed in conjoint co-therapy work. This may involve the co-therapists in examining the minutiae of their own relationship, but that is the tool of their trade.

This is a tool not available in the same way to unconnected therapists who are working in parallel, i.e. in a situation in which couple therapists are seeing a couple in couple therapy at the same time as one or both of the partners may have their own individual therapist. If these parallel therapists, who are not 'married', are unaware of, or ignore, or blur the boundary of their own therapeutic relationships with their client(s), then they are in difficulties because they are not working partners in the same way that marital co-therapists are. They may come together to discuss a couple with no background of knowing each other's work, and with no joint session to test out their patient's or couples' phantasies. In such circumstances projections may ricochet between the professionals. From the perspective of couple workers dealing with the myriad projections that make up the cat's cradle of couple work, we feel that the invisible matrix that would be created if the boundaries around concurrent therapies were breached would need an extremely firm outer container to ensure that phantasies could be lessened rather than multiplied.

CHAPTER SEVEN

COMBINED THERAPY—A GROUP ANALYTIC PERSPECTIVE

Jason Maratos

Jason Maratos is a consultant psychiatrist working in a South Buckinghamshire NHS Trust with children, adolescents and families, and is a training group analyst working at the group analytic practice. He is particularly interested in, and has published and lectured in various countries on attachment theory, self psychology, philosophy and culture. As a group analyst he is interested in the relationship of 'self and other', 'the other' being a parent, a partner, a group member, or a different culture.

Jason Maratos gives us a closely argued account of combined therapies from the point of view of a group analyst who also works within the National Health Service. He provides a comprehensive review of the indications and counter-indications for membership of a therapeutic group, and also for combining membership with another form of therapy. In this authoritative and very interesting chapter, he writes of his wide experience as a group analyst, and lets us know his thoughts on working with group members individually when this seems appropriate. He describes the experience of working with group members who are also in another therapy, and offers a comprehensive review of the literature on this topic. Approaching the concept of the invisible matrix from the perspective of group analysis, Jason Maratos offers a pragmatic acceptance of combined therapies, and writes about them with a refreshing clarity.

* * *

The group of therapies

Psychological development progresses through interactions of the *self* with the *other* from the beginning of life. Some of these interactions will be growth promoting, some will be damaging and others will be corrective or in other words, therapeutic. In this sense, any therapy can only be combined.

Combined therapy existed, probably, long before it was written about. Hobdell (1991) cites Foulkes (Foulkes & Lewis 1944) as the earliest author on the subject. In the early days of group analysis, there was uncertainty about the effect, ambivalence about its advisability and concern about its effect on each of the two combined therapeutic modalities. One concern was that the combination may detract and dilute the patient's efforts and that one therapy may 'contaminate' the other. The same concern was expressed, as late as 1980, (Scheidlinger and Porter, cited by Praper 1997) by focusing on what they saw as the potentially damaging effect on transference within the group. Such reservations are understandable when group therapy, as a new therapeutic modality, was not yet secure in its own identity. Perhaps even today, some of the reluctance of therapists to recommend combined work may be related to their own uncertainty about their identity as therapists and to seeing the 'other' intervention as a threat.

A boost to combined work, however, came from the therapeutic community movement. Hobdell reminds us that in the first therapeutic communities, there were many therapeutic influences taking place at the same time, such as community groups, small groups and individual work; combined therapy, therefore, seemed to be the norm.

Is there a rank order of therapies?

In considering combined therapy, one needs to address the issue of rank ordering of therapies. As rivalry and splitting are endemic dangers in combined therapy, rank ordering has to be taken into account and, certainly, is not to be dismissed with a facile statement such as 'all therapies are of equal importance'. Some highly experienced therapists operate under a conscious (or even unconscious) rank ordering of therapies. The primary therapy is occasionally thought to be individual psychoanalysis followed by other psychotherapies and by counselling.

Though rank ordering is important in the choice of one therapy, in the case of combined such considerations become paramount. Interestingly, a training analyst with the Society of Analytical Psychology (Hobdell 1991) writes that:

> ...in conducting combined groups I have always worked from the major premise that the group is primary... the integrity of the group has to be maintained at all times. (Hobdell 1991: 141)

In the same spirit, Hobdell named the individual sessions 'the satellite group'. In the case of combined therapy, this clear position is not without its risks. If we use the metaphor of a surgical operation, one therapy may be considered like the work of the surgeon while the other is reduced to that of a theatre nurse who hands him the instruments.

Some professionals feel demeaned or despoiled if they are expected not to address the internal world of their client directly; they may see themselves as 'hand maidens' of the primary therapist. The basis of competition for primacy would lead to actual re-enactment of a real external split and its transfer into the internal self of the patient as an internal conflict.

Is there a more important and a less important therapy? Ideally one would wish to see all therapeutic interventions as mutually enabling and potentiating, but in reality, it is difficult for therapies to operate at this finely balanced point. Therapies acquire different significance at different times. For example, there can be occasions where the interactions within a group are too intense for a borderline patient to manage. In this case, individual therapy may be the setting in which more direct therapeutic work is carried out; work which brings about change by itself and not only through enabling the group therapy to continue. Readers are aware of examples where the opposite is the case.

This temporal rank ordering is different from that which exists in the minds of some patients and therapists. Rivalry internal and external, between therapists and between those offering therapy proper with those offering interventions with a therapeutic effect is a dynamic which if left unaddressed may lead to anti-therapeutic consequences. This rivalry may be expressed (or experienced) as idealisation or denigration of therapists or of therapies.

Implicit in the notion of combined therapy is the understanding that two forces act on the same subject. These two forces will need to be considered and managed if they are to work together, for the same purpose without undermining or duplicating each other. Porter (1993) (cited by Benjamin et al 1995) takes the optimistic view that 'combined therapy offers the twin advantages of complementarity and potentiality' (the latter taken to mean *enhancement* of the effect of one by the presence of the other).

Difference from concurrent, parallel, sequential and incidental therapies.

In the literature on combined therapy one encounters terms which are used with different meanings. Some reserve the term 'combined' only for the case where both therapeutic modalities are delivered by the same therapist (Praper 1997) while others consider therapies which are concurrent or even sequential as combined. Praper uses the definition of two therapies by different therapists as conjoint; a term which has been used for description of therapy of one unit (say a family) by two therapists present at the same time in the same sessions. It is only with time that terminology will crystallise; the present author will not attempt here to impose his own understanding; this would be a futile exercise. Instead, we will only highlight the issue in order to prevent misunderstandings from arising. The dynamics of therapies by the same or different therapists obviously vary, as do the dynamics of therapies with essentially similar philosophy from those based on widely different principles as, for example, the combination of a psychoanalytical variant of therapy with systematic desensitisation for a specific phobia.

Dynamics of combined therapy

The parental metaphor, though hackneyed, retains its usefulness. The child may benefit from the differentness of her parents; may feel and become enriched by their different qualities if the parents themselves value and enjoy their diversity. If, on the other hand, the parents relate in a conflictual, antagonistic manner then the child will be placed in a position of having to choose one instead of the other. The result will be internal poverty and conflict. The same principle applies to combined therapy irrespective of whether it is carried out by the same therapist (in which case the potential for destructive conflict is between the therapies) or by different therapists (where the potential for gain or loss is even greater). The potential for splitting is so well recognised that it is unnecessary for me to add further to the existing literature.

The special case of group therapy

It is worth considering how two concepts developed by 'individual' analysts apply to group therapy; these are the related concepts of self-object and transference.

A key concept in the psychology of the self is that of the *selfobject* (Kohut 1971; Maratos 1996). Aspects of the therapist's self may be internalised by the patient; these will form the patient's new selfobjects. One can see that in the case of group therapy the sources of selfobjects are more than one, and in the case of combined therapy even more. If the patient is to avoid some internal chaos, disorganisation, fragility and enfeeblement, some effort needs to be directed at enabling the patient to select and organise his new selfobjects. Without such effort, the self will not be able to function effectively and will be vulnerable to fragmentation and breakdown.

Freud introduced the concept of transference (Freud 1912) as an unconscious perception of the therapist and the unconscious experience within the therapy situation of feelings which originated in early childhood and are misapplied towards the therapist. In an analytical group, there are more therapists in addition to the conductor and such misapplications occur in many forms. Porter (1993, cited by Benjamin et al 1995) refers to 'multiple transferences' which can be explored simultaneously. Patients often 'see' other group members as persons of their early life and relate to them as such. Resolution of these transferences is a cornerstone of therapy.

In the case of combined therapies, especially in the case of two therapists, transference acquires a further dimension (Dagg and Evans 1997 and Horwitz 1994). Some hold reservations that transference may be diluted while others see that in combined therapy there is the unique opportunity for the development of transference towards the therapeutic *couple*. Porter (1993) (cited by Benjamin et al 1995) warns about the danger of what he termed as 'transference splitting' a process through which different therapists/therapies are idealised or denigrated. Transference towards two therapists may be problematic, if the original parental couple had an antagonistic or conflictual relationship. The patient may experience a transferential wish to get therapists together. Such transference could be considered as a possible source of resistance towards combined therapy and as a possible destructive force within it. Resolution of such transference will add a further dimension to therapy. There is always the danger, though, that the prevailing transferences may be more than the single patient can process at one and the same time.

Acting out in combined therapy

Acting out refers to the enactment of unconscious feelings either within or without the therapy setting. Combined therapy is a rather more open system than unimodal therapy and therefore lends itself more easily to the enactment of affectionate, sexual or aggressive feelings.

Attempts of patients to create an 'unholy' alliance with one against the other therapist or to get the therapists together may represent transferential acting out. We have referred earlier to the phenomenon where pre-existing splitting of the internal world is acted out in the external world of therapists who may become unwitting participants in this anti-therapeutic process.

What is appropriate material for individual sessions and what for group?

The received wisdom is that individual material is dealt with in individual sessions while relational material is dealt with in groups. Such a notion may serve as a useful rule of thumb, but can be anti-therapeutic if applied too rigidly. Relationships with other group members may need to be discussed in individual sessions if the group member is too anxious to explore or negotiate them within the group setting. If the process were to stop there, then there would be no indication of a real resolution; there would be no experiment which would validate the theory. If the exploration in the individual session is followed by exploration and negotiation with the other group members then the therapeutic objective will have been accomplished. Indeed, the issue of feelings towards the other group members is a very good example of how combined therapy can help a patient over an otherwise insurmountable block to therapeutic resolution of internal difficulties and an example of how individual can complement the group work. Boundaries are there to be negotiated not to block treatment.

The mirror image of the above eventuality is the case in which early personal or dream material arises within the group setting. Normally this would be considered material for individual sessions. Nothing would be further from the truth. Many group therapists have encountered sessions in which group members share early material which (to their surprise) has striking similarities. Such material had been brought into consciousness by the intensity of the shared group experience. This is one therapeutic objective achieved in groups (making the unconscious conscious). Group members can develop a deep and full understanding of each other's intensely personal material thus achieving a second therapeutic objective: acquiring a new understanding of previously unconscious material.

What group members often find striking is that in a group session they present a dream, which they think of as an exclusively private experience, only to discover that other group members had similar dreams. This is a powerful therapeutic experience on many dimensions but the one I would like to stress here is the experience of the communality of human nature. This 'I am not alone – even in my private moments' feeling is not only restorative of the sense of self but also is formative of new bonds; both powerful therapeutic forces.

Dr Hobdell (1991) introduces another dimension of combined therapy: that it reinforces the idea that therapy happens 'in a couple'. Freud himself (1910) alluded to this in his uniquely fresh style: 'To-day things have a more friendly air. The treatment is *made up of two parts,* out of what the physician infers and tells the patient, and out of the patient's work of assimilation, of 'working through', what he hears'. (my italics). This notion of the co-operation of 'the couple' needs to be explored (and can be explored constructively) openly in therapy (both in the group and in the individual sessions). The couple, in this case, is the couple of therapies as well as the couples of subjects and carers. The dyadic nature of therapy is similar to the dyadic nature of development. The basis of development is the dyadic relationship of infant and maternal care. It is this relationship which led Winnicott to utter, at a scientific meeting of the British Psycho-Analytical Society (circa 1940), the extraordinary phrase, 'There is no such thing as an infant' (cited in Winnicott 1985).

The internal world of the therapist

Counter-transference is being understood by different authors to mean not only the unconscious feelings which the therapist experiences specifically in response to the patient's transference (as Freud originally intended 1910) but 'the whole of the analyst's unconscious reactions to the individual analysand' (Laplanche & Pontalis 1983). A whole host of feelings, irrespective of whether they arise out of the therapist's own experiences or in response to the patient's transference can be included under the same term, reducing, in this way, its specificity and usefulness.

We use the term 'internal world' at the heading of this section in order to highlight that feelings and beliefs, conscious, pre-conscious and unconscious play a determining part in relation to combined therapy. For example, some therapists feel more comfortable with unimodal therapies; some have difficulties in sharing while others prefer combining approaches and efforts. These elements in the internal world of a therapist will influence whether they engage in combined therapy themselves, whether they recommend this kind of treatment and whether they accept to see patients in this context. The Benjamins (1995) claimed that their relationships with the group members who they did not treat individually as well, were not as intense, and express the view that it may have been preferable if instead of combined, they offered conjoint therapy. It seems to me that such a contribution, which contains feelings and thoughts of the authors, is valid and should be distinguished from counter-transference.

The feelings of a therapist towards a patient in combined therapy in response to the patient's transference may be initially unconscious (and, therefore true counter-transference) and, in due course, be brought to consciousness by the experienced therapist or in supervision. Hobdell advocates that therapists need to beware of the possibility of recommending combined therapy out of counter-transferential hate. One can see how a therapist, troubled by such difficult feelings may seek the comfort of sharing these feelings in a wider therapeutic circle (with other therapists or other patients); such a move may not be counter-therapeutic in itself; it may indeed be a way of making feelings which are intolerable for the therapist more manageable and therefore no longer a hindrance to analysis. The danger is that a referral for combined therapy made on this basis may be defensive and may lead to avoidance of such feelings and may, therefore, compound in the therapy situation the client's original trauma.

Therapists who are about to recommend additional therapy could do well to consider that it is possible that their recommendation arises out of a whole spectrum of feelings arising from the patient such as feelings of not being a good enough therapist, of not being 'contained' enough, feelings of intense depression as well as the above mentioned feelings of hate. A recommendation arising out of such feelings is nothing short of acting out on the part of the therapist. Therapist acting out is not often cited in the literature, but therapists who work unsupported, isolated, stressed or who are newly qualified and may be poorly supervised, are all liable to such behaviour.

Issues around combined therapy

It is unusual for clients to be referred for combined therapy immediately after assessment. The most common pattern is to recommend one treatment modality and during its course, recommend the addition of a further therapeutic modality because of difficulties or lack of progress. Perhaps it is more difficult for a therapist to recommend that a patient devotes every week 50 minutes in individual therapy and 90 minutes in a group than to recommend that he/she devotes 150 minutes (the equivalent time total) in three times per week individual therapy or analysis. Although the explanation may be more complicated, when there is a clear understanding of what the combined therapy has to offer that is specific to the needs of the particular client, the recommendation may flow more naturally. Starting therapy in the combined mode may prevent early therapeutic 'drop out' and may save the client (and the therapist) from unnecessary angst.

Modulation of level of arousal

A neurophysiological finding, often ignored by some therapists, is that an organism is in an optimal position to learn and to negotiate the environment when at a reasonable arousal level. Too low arousal, as in relaxation or sleep at one end, or too high arousal, as in the case of panic, are not conducive to learning. Too high arousal is painful, and the subject will direct his efforts to reduce it or avoid the arousing environment. Therapy cannot be sustained if the patient (or the therapist) is persistently excessively anxious within the sessions; it is equally unproductive if the client is too relaxed and 'cosy'.

A therapist aims to make a judgement about this factor during assessment. If a client is likely to experience arousal at either extreme of the above continuum, then combined therapy may enable him to shift to a workable level. Such a consideration remains valid both before the beginning of treatment as well as during therapy of any modality. Combined therapy can serve both to increase anxiety by confronting the patient with neglected aspects of his self as well as reduce anxiety to workable levels in patients who feel too threatened or exposed in a unimodal setting. Hobdell (1991) advocates that combined therapy is initiated when anxiety in the group therapy sessions is so high that it inhibits the therapeutic process. He suggests that it should be available to all who can afford it.

The notion of expenditure in therapy is well worth separate consideration. Therapy does not represent only something that is provided to the patient. In order to access it, the client needs to expend time, effort and, often, money. Therapists often ignore this factor and interpret a client's reluctance to undertake therapy (or more extensive therapy) as resistance or defensiveness. Some therapists are puzzled about why those who need therapy most, are less likely to avail themselves of it. One of the reasons may be that they are near the point of exhausting their resources. I hope I will be forgiven if I use a simplistic metaphor, which in spite of its simplicity illustrates this point quite clearly: we, as therapists, are on a ship; we see a person overboard struggling to stay afloat. The person is moving about in the water in a way that causes him to expend a lot of energy without making much progress towards safety. We know that the only way they can stay afloat is if they learn to swim. We shout instructions on what to do, but he is too tired and too anxious (maybe in a panic) to follow them. In real life, we are not always in the position to throw a life-saving rope and then instruct in swimming, even though this course of action is highly desirable! Therapy can only provide the equivalent of swimming instruction and the therapist who attempts to be a life saver and an instructor at the same time often drowns with the patient.

Combined therapy is often thought as a mode of treatment that is more 'expensive' than unimodal therapy. It is easy for one to forget that it may also represent a 'saving' of expenditure in cases where the patient would have otherwise needed more intensive treatment as, for example, in-patient treatment. Combined therapy does not always represent more therapy. Combined therapy represents a specific mode of intervention with its own dynamics (strengths and difficulties and risks); it should be engaged in for the right reasons – neither as a cheap alternative to treatments which though more costly would be more appropriate for a particular patient at a particular time, nor as an unnecessarily costly over treatment when briefer interventions would have met the patient's treatment needs.

Diagnostic categories are often useful if they are used not as absolute rules but flexibly. Borderline personality organisation is such a category which has been thought to be more likely to respond better to combined therapy (Wong 1988). Review articles, such as the excellent paper by Praper (1997), refer to the work of numerous authors who have considered the advisability of combined therapy for patients suffering from obsessive compulsive disorders, from excessively schizoid personalities, those in a manic phase of a manic depressive illness, those who are severely masochistic and those in an acute crisis. But, while some authors refer to these conditions as indications for combined therapy, others refer to the same conditions as contra-indications. The reason for this apparent inconsistency in the literature is, I believe, that each diagnostic category includes a wide spectrum of disturbance, both in terms of severity but also in terms of variation. Even the most psychotic patients may have relatively healthy parts to their personality, which sustain them in therapy (and in life).

Rather than indications and contra-indications, the present author would advocate the use of the following guidelines: combined therapy can be engaged in by clients who are able to use or are likely to respond to psychotherapy, and have (or are likely to have) difficulties in unimodal therapy which will lead them either to drop out, to stagnate or to leave areas of their personality unaffected (untreated). Awareness of the above factors may take place before or during one form of therapy and introduction of combined therapy may proceed respectively, from the beginning or during the process of one therapy. The decision will depend on numerous, and not only dynamic factors.

Consideration of factors extraneous to the patient

Various authors often advocate that the decision for a particular treatment should only depend on the needs of the patient. This objective is as idealistic and desirable, as it is often unobtainable. Therapists live in the real world of funding, contracts, policies of insurance companies and priorities of health services. It would be unrealistic to ignore all these factors, especially when a major objective of therapy is to enable the recipient to make the most of their real life (rather than feel unhappy because their situation is far worse than that of others or of their hoped-for or imagined world).

Extraneous factors are not only practical/material but also those related to the therapist or the institution or agency responsible for the care of the patient. Management of therapist or institutional anxiety is one of the factors which is often thought of as an inappropriate consideration. Obviously, one should not simply overtreat a patient for the sake of reducing therapist or institutional anxiety, but alternatively, high-handed advocacation that the therapist should manage their own anxiety independently of their patient is equally unrealistic. One cannot forget that therapist anxiety is rarely independent of the state of the patient, and may be a healthy signal of patient needs. Therapist and institutional anxiety should neither dominate clinical decisions nor be ignored but needs to be seriously considered as a signal of the dynamic between client and therapist, and to be taken account of in the complicated process of deciding to engage in combined therapy. Therapist anxiety is a powerful factor influencing the level of arousal within therapy, a parameter which has already been considered briefly in this chapter.

How to set up combined therapy

Equally important to the selection of patients is their preparation for combined therapy. Boswood (1976) highlighted the need for the establishment of a good 'bond' between therapist and patient if therapy is to be sustained. The concept of a bond is very complex but it contains at least two elements: the first is some degree of liking or affection and the other is some degree of trust. The therapist needs to earn a reasonable level of trust from the patient. Just as the therapist assesses the patient during the early interviews so does the patient assess the therapist.

The present author believes that trust is best when it is only *reasonable* and not when it is absolute. When patients tell me that they trust me I become anxious. Absolute trust (especially when genuine) implies that the patient has handed a large part of their thinking or critical power over to the therapist and this is not a helpful step. I make a point of telling my patients that I approach them having 'done my homework' and having acquired a reasonable level of competence (and when appropriate, that I have no intentions of taking advantage of them), that I am reasonably 'good' (meaning competent and well intentioned). But I also point out to them that I am human, that, often, my interpretations will amount to hypotheses for them to consider and that they should accept them only if they think that they really apply to them. Therapy is inconceivable without the active and critical participation of the patient. Absolute trust is equally unhelpful as its opposite, paranoia. This paragraph should not be read to mean that I advocate that one should generate unnecessary anxieties in one's patients.

Trust is, at least, bi-dimensional. Trust does not imply only that 'the other' is perceived as benevolent but that 'the self' also is perceived as competent. Persons with a seriously damaged self find it virtually impossible to experience trust because they perceive themselves as incapable of coping with any conflict of interest. These persons find it very difficult to establish the reasonable trust required for therapy to begin and if they do engage in it, they run the risk of ending it prematurely. A large part of the art of psychotherapy is taken by the therapist's efforts to develop in the client a sense that he/she is competent enough to cope with the vicissitudes of therapy and that the therapist and/or the group (that is, the therapeutic setting) are reasonably 'good'.

Blanket statements about the safety of the group or of therapy often fail to reassure clients – quite justifiably. The therapy situation (individual, group or combined) can be as safe as the landing of an aircraft in a storm; it is exciting and usually safe but only if the pilots are 'good'. In group therapy, there are more than one pilot and it has always been recognised that the process can be constructive as well as destructive. Statements about the therapy situation being secure or safe serve only to reduce the credibility of the therapist.

Reassurance can only be reached after a thorough investigation of the client's anxieties about therapy. Will therapy unleash pain, which the patient will not feel able to cope with? Will the group members detect the clients' unacceptable internal world? Will the other group members place demands which the client will not be able to meet? Will the client have to fight to get any attention? Will there be repetition of earlier traumatic experiences, like scapegoating or manipulations? One cannot give a false reassurance that such dynamics will not take place – they do. A more realistic approach is that such dynamics can occur in groups as in real life and that the setting of client-group members-therapist operates with an interest, common to all, that of therapy. It is the common objective, the shared interest, which gives to the therapeutic situation greater security than life, which is at least perceived as full of actual conflict.

In recommending combined therapy, one gives the impression that one therapy is not enough! Such a recommendation may, thus, become an anti-therapeutic move. Especially when additional therapy is recommended, this may be a statement of inadequacy of the first and that something 'better' needs to be brought in for the rescue of treatment. Care needs to be taken because this perception is partly true; one therapy or unimodal therapy has indeed been considered inadequate for the needs of this particular patient. It is very difficult for patients to differentiate between the notion that a combined modality is more appropriate for them and the perception that one form of therapy is a poor therapeutic tool. The risk is that the therapy that is introduced second is seen as the more 'real' or 'powerful' method, that the client will disinvest or de-cathect from the original therapy and will end up receiving only the second therapy, thus defeating the whole objective of receiving combined therapy.

Timing

Hobdell (1991) recommends that clients already in group therapy could be offered combined therapy if their early material cannot be adequately explored in the group or if the analysis of their dreams may take time at the expense of the group. Other authors recommend that group therapy be added when there is a need for the client to develop their way of relating to others.

A number of authors advocate that individual therapy should be added if there is a need for exploration of early material and personal material, like dreams, while group therapy is added when there is a need for the client to develop their way of relating to others. Such an approach implies that the internal world is separate from the way in which a person relates to others. How could this be so? How could the relationships not be based on the internal world and how could the internal world not be shaped by relationships? One is a function of the other; perhaps not an equation but certainly a function.

Therefore, neither can we accept the notion that a group patient is offered additional individual therapy in order to address early material nor that an individual patient be referred to a group so that they can develop their relatedness. The deciding factor in considering the timing of the introduction of an additional therapy is not the therapeutic target but the method. Relatedness can be helped in individual settings and dreams are analysed in group settings. Additional therapy is considered when the client finds it very difficult to make progress in the existing therapy.

The same, or different therapists

The aim of this section is not to conclude with a recommendation about the preferable method but to touch upon the different issues highlighted by the two approaches. We will refer to confidentiality between the settings later on but here we can point out that information in the mind of the therapist is obviously optimal in the case of same therapist combined therapy and there is no problem of communication towards the therapist. Attention needs to be paid to the type of information, which the therapist can disclose to the group. The patient may well be anxious that the therapist may inadvertently disclose to the group information before the patient is ready to disclose himself. Such anxiety may act as an anti-therapeutic force in the individual session. A therapist who sees a number of her group patients individually will be taxed to remember what material to which she is privileged she may use in the group setting and what not. As the group members are the therapists, they will need to know material which may be relevant to them so it is the timing of the disclosure which is important more than the fact that information is disclosed or not.

As the relationship between patient and therapist will be different in the two settings, the same therapist will be experienced differently in the two therapeutic situations. The exclusively attentive therapist of the individual sessions may be unresponsive and may be perceived as withholding or depriving when in the group sessions. Such difference may be puzzling for the patient who will need some help to think this through before it gives rise to pathological dynamics. One most obvious misinterpretation may be that the therapist is not genuine, or two-faced. It is difficult for some patients to understand how the same person can behave differently towards them in different settings and maintain the same relationship.

The experience of the differentness of the same can be quite a useful introject for some patients, who feel that they can only be true to themselves and others if they behave in the same monolithic way in all situations. Such persons tend—for example—to treat their children or their seniors at work as their friends, with counterproductive consequences. Such persons also have difficulties in differentiating what is private and what public and when it is so. Introjecting this experience will enable them to adopt appropriate roles in diverse settings and feel honest with themselves at the same time.

Relationship between the therapists

The concept of splitting was introduced by Freud (1940) and further developed by Melanie Klein in 1932 (1975a) and referred to an unconscious process internal to the psyche of the patient. This attempt at coping with internal ambivalence by perceiving one person as good and the other as bad (my apologies for this simplifying expression of this complex mechanism) can be projected with such force that it can be adopted as reality by the perceived subjects. In a combined therapy situation, there is a risk that one therapist will see herself as the good object and will think of the other therapist as the bad one. A therapist runs the risk of falling victim of this process, and the present author is no exception to this, especially if he is the recipient of benevolent projections. One is less likely to wish to re-examine perceptions of oneself as a bad therapist than as a good one.

In the combined therapy situation, one is faced with a multi-dimensional counter-transference: the feelings of each therapist about themselves, about each other and about their patient. If this counter-transference remains unconscious it can be experienced by the therapists as conflict between them. If therapists do not know each other well or if they do but do not hold each other's skills or theoretical orientation in high regard, then the risk of actual conflict is even greater. The patient's splitting can then be mirrored and enhanced by the therapists' rivalry. The destructiveness of this process is obvious.

Not all conflict between therapists is counter-transferential in origin. Attributing all differences to the shared patient is nothing short of a 'therapeutic cop-out'. The two therapists are bound in the same venture of treating one patient. Their professional identity and reputation depends on the good outcome of the treatment. If one feels that their work is undermined by the work of the other he will not be satisfied with interpretations of splitting and counter-transference. There will be times when the client is deteriorating or simply not making progress. It is possible that one or other therapist intervenes in an unhelpful way. This is precisely the time for therapists to communicate with each other.

Communication between therapists and therapeutic situations.

Confidentiality is of equal value to good communication when more than one therapeutic situation is involved, even though one is opposite to the other; the one withholds while the other imparts information. Withholding information opens the road to manipulation, splitting and other unhelpful defences, which ultimately delay or work against treatment. Without confidentiality, the patient feels inhibited and cannot use the session properly. Openness of communication compromises the privileged position of the therapy session.

The patient in combined therapy is, therefore, faced with a dilemma: openness inhibits, secrecy delays resolution. This is true in the case of different, as well as same, therapist combined therapy. Cohn (1986) seems to favour confidentiality of the individual session, but accepts that group material can be dealt with individually.

It seems to me that in this situation, principles and guidelines are more useful than rules. The first principle is that the patient needs to feel that she is in control of who she imparts information to, and when. This is the essence of confidentiality and a cornerstone of therapy. The second principle is that withholding information from either therapeutic setting deprives the therapists of an opportunity of becoming helpful and is therefore to be avoided. The 'working formula' could be that the patient will maintain control of information but will aim to share material which is thought to be relevant.

One needs to define what is relevant. This task is impossible in absolute terms; a few attempts towards definition ended in unhelpful tautologies. My rule of thumb is that material is relevant if any of the involved parties experience ambivalence or unease about the 'confidential' information. It is precisely for such unease that individual sessions can be an invaluable complement to group therapy. Such ambivalence cannot be resolved within the group, as such a move would break confidentiality. Such ambivalence may not arise in individual sessions. In situations like this combined therapy genuinely offers something that neither single modality can provide.

It is precisely in such situations that the therapists need to be able to hold a frank and honest exchange of views. The unease may arise out of defensiveness or manipulation by the patient but may also spring from an erroneous approach by one or other therapist. Mature therapists can benefit from the combined therapy situation because by having an opportunity to discuss their shared patient they can acquire an understanding which may be deeper and more thorough than they could have reached thinking through the patient's psyche on their own. Even in supervision, the supervisor would not have the same wealth of information as the other therapist and therefore may not be able to reach such a deep understanding.

Communication, which may involve criticism, but may also involve the sharing of the feelings of the therapists, can be a source of genuine support for the therapists as well as an experience that promotes professional growth.

Some risks of combined therapy: contamination and dilution

Some practitioners are concerned that the therapy they provide may be contaminated by another. Such fears have been expressed that the purity of therapy will be lost and that the patient will be confused by ideas and interpretations which may be incompatible. In such situations, the 'other' insights are seen as 'foreign bodies' to the 'real' therapy. Of course, neither therapists nor therapies are clones to each other and differences will arise. Such differences may be conflictual; it would be defensive of combined therapy (probably a manic defence) if we did not recognise that this is a real risk. Differentness does not always automatically lead to complementarity; it may do so but it will require some active thinking through.

A more benign concern is that the combination of two therapies may make it difficult for a patient to engage wholeheartedly in one and that the experience will be diluted. The patient runs the risk of thinking that the real therapy will take place in the 'other' session and thus spend considerable time being 'in between' therapies. Any patient who has intensive therapy runs the risk of 'stretching' the therapy and as a result may have long but not intensive therapy.

The above mentioned are only risks and should not be seen as disadvantages of combined therapy. They are stated here to caution against a false sense that more is necessarily safer and better; combined therapy can be so but only if the risks are negotiated appropriately.

The effect on the whole group of added individual therapy for one patient

A very disturbed patient absorbs considerable time and energy from the group; the group members are relieved when additional therapy addresses some of the personal difficulties of one patient. The group is pleased when it is able to work better. Hobdell (1991) found that in his groups, patients occasionally recommend that a member has some individual sessions as well.

Naturally, one does not expect group members to consider matters always in such a mature manner. Feelings of envy and rivalry will almost inevitably arise as well as feelings of superiority in those who are not thought to be so disturbed as to need 'extra' therapy. In a setting of private practice, the feelings of envy for those who can afford additional therapy will bring to the surface earlier feelings of fairness or otherwise in early years. For patients who still confuse equality (having equal amounts of everything with everyone else, at least, within the sibship) with fairness (meeting the different needs with different amounts and different kinds of care) can learn a lot from the experience.

Unfortunately, 'things' are neither equal nor always fair in real life and re-enactment of this simple truth in therapy provides an added opportunity for the patient to learn how to progress without being overwhelmed by feelings of envy, sadness, loss and anger. If negotiated successfully, the combined therapy of one member can be therapeutic for the whole membership of the group.

Who is 'the case'?

With the influence of family therapy and systemic thinking, the notion of 'who is the case' has taken a wider dimension. For a family therapist, the case is the family, just as the couple is for the marital or sexual therapist. Although the case can be the family, treatment need not always be of the family as a whole through sessions in which all the members are present. In some families the dysfunction may be addressed by separate sessions in which one therapist sees the child on her own while another sees the parents, at least for a phase of the treatment. If the 'case' is the family, then this approach is combined therapy. If the family re-unites in conjoint therapy, then the dynamics mentioned above may prevail and inhibit progress, if they are not negotiated constructively. This is particularly so in the case where one section of the family received therapy of a different approach and philosophy than the other.

Pace of therapies

The pace at which therapy progresses is a concept which is often talked about, but not written on. This is probably due to the difficulty in defining this concept. Patients refer to feeling under pressure when the therapist or the group expect them to change before 'they are ready' to do so—whatever the term 'ready' may mean. Pace has to do with change, and living organisms are affected both by no or too little as well as too much of it. No change can only mean death and 'too much' leads to stress and breakdown. Change is an inevitable part of development, but the change which is part of therapy requires greater adjustment and energy as it aims not only to promote growth but also to 'demolish and reconstruct' patterns which have proven to be unhelpful in the past. Parting with even painful patterns can in itself be painful, and there is only so much pain that a person can process at any one time.

Ideally, the pace of change in therapy is negotiated jointly between the various parties. The therapist and the group read the signals of distress from the patient and 'ease off' the pressure. The emergence of primitive and pathological defence mechanisms are often such signals of distress. Unfortunately, the need to 'ease off' is not always recognised nor is it always respected by group members (or even over-ambitious therapists). In combined therapy the opportunities for this fine tuning to go wrong increase, the patient may feel that she is 'persecuted' from both group and individual therapy situations and may suffer a counterproductive response. This is the risk of making combined therapy 'too much therapy'. The ambitious therapist(s), the over-anxious group or the uncontained disturbed patient in the group can become for an individual patient a re-enactment of early trauma from parents of similar psychopathology.

The case of training

It is highly likely that most existing courses prepare trainees in the use of combined therapy rather inadequately. Some courses devote one seminar to the subject and I doubt that any offer supervision to trainees engaged in combined therapy. To my knowledge, experience in conducting combined therapy is not a requirement for qualification in any course and a requirement that trainees should experience combined therapy as subjects is almost unheard of. A number of training courses expect their trainees to gain experience in more than one mode of treatment irrespective of the focus of the course. Trainees in group analysis in London are expected to gain supervised experience in individual psychotherapy and other authors (Dagg and Evans, 1997) recommend that trainee psychotherapists be exposed to group psychotherapy. The same authors advocate that trainees should do so in co-therapy. In the group setting, the authors claim, unconscious processes are more visible through the interaction of participants with each other. Furthermore, the trainee can observe in group therapy the different aspects of the patient's self, gain a more whole/total understanding of the patient and carry over this learning in their work with individuals by expecting that their individual patients have aspects of their self which may not be apparent in the individual analytic situation.

The co-therapy setting is an approximation of combined therapy, in the sense that it gives rise to some of the dynamics prevalent in combined therapy but in a setting which is safe as it takes place in the presence of an experienced therapist.

Conclusion

Combined therapy adds an extra dimension to unimodal therapy; it may enable, enrich and sustain therapy; it carries its own risks and places special demands on therapists and patients alike. In the case where one of the interventions is group therapy the demands and the rewards are to the other group members as well.

CHAPTER EIGHT

SQUARE DANCE: INVISIBLE MATRICES IN CO-THERAPY COUPLE THERAPY

Mary Ann Dubner & Joyce Lowenstein

Joyce Lowenstein is Co-Chair of the Psychoanalytic Object Relations Couple and Family Therapy Training Program at the Washington School of Psychiatry, and a member of the Faculty of George Washington University Medical School. She is a member of the Steering Committee on New Directions in Psychoanalytic Thinking at Washington Psychoanalytic Institute, and is a founding member of the Couple and Family Section of Division 39 of the American Psychological Association. She is in private practice in Washington D. C.

Mary Ann Dubner is a faculty member of the Washington School of Psychiatry and founding faculty member of the Institute of Contemporary Psychotherapy. She is in private practice in Washington DC. Her recent publications include 'Envy in the Group Therapy Process' (International Journal of Group Therapy *1998), and 'The Incubator: the Therapist's Attachment to her Internal Bad Objects'* (Voices *1998). She has presented papers about hate in the group therapy process to the American Group Psychotherapy Association, and to the Eastern Group Psychotherapy Association.*

We invited Dr Joyce Lowenstein and Dr Mary Ann Dubner to contribute to the book from the perspective of the American object relations school of couple psychotherapy. These two psychotherapists work conjointly and separately with couples and with the individuals in the couples. They describe this framework, delightfully, as a 'square dance', a formalised pattern within which the practitioners can take up different positions in relation to one another. They consider their institutional setting in Washington DC, its principles and methods of couple therapy, and some of the historical background of its approach. They describe their model in use in casework with a couple, and think especially about how the shared unconscious phantasy of the couple appears in the transferences to the two therapists, and affects the relationship of the co-therapists in the counter-transference.

* * *

This chapter will be written from the perspective of two therapists who work as a co-therapy team with a couple. We are psychologists in private practice which means that we work on a fee-for-service basis. To give you a picture of our work setting, we, together with four other psychologists, rent office space in an apartment building about three miles north of the centre of Washington, D.C., near a metro stop. We all are independent practitioners having different specialties, interests and theoretical orientations. The authors of this paper share an object relations point of view. When one of us gets a referral that we cannot take, we may refer to someone in our suite if appropriate. We all refer to other therapists as well and they refer to us. When doing couples therapy, we often collaborate with therapists who are seeing one of the partners individually. Sometimes this collaboration is minimal, with little contact, sometimes we work more closely, always with the patient's permission. We have found that this model of couples therapy works well if the individual therapists have an understanding of couples therapy, otherwise it is more likely to be problematic.

We present a different model in this chapter. It consists of each of the individuals having their own therapist with whom they meet once a week. In addition the two individual therapists acting now in a co-therapy model meet with the couple on a weekly basis. Each therapist has a dual role/relationship with her patient; she is both the individual therapist and her patient's couple therapist, but has only one role/relationship with the other partner. In addition the two children are in individual therapy with therapists who were recommended by the couple's therapists. One of the therapists acts as a coordinator with these other therapists as well.

Our model of each partner meeting with two individual therapists and then meeting together as a patient couple and therapist couple is not new and actually comes out of a model developed at the Tavistock Clinic. In the 1950s couples therapy was usually done by two therapists seeing the couple separately. Under the leadership of Henry Dicks, what he called conjoint couples therapy (one or two therapists meeting with the couple) became more popular. The model that we describe in this chapter combines the two.

Since the couple we describe here resorts to considerable projective identification, blame and denial, seeing them together enhances the possibility that the splits can be contained within the couple rather than remain as split-off aspects of the individual. Having two therapists work with the couple presents the opportunity for us not only to witness and experience the splitting and to process the projective identifications but also to 'offer ourselves up' so to speak as containers to receive and work with the transference, the projections and the defenses in an effort to understand the shared internal world of the couple (*qua* couple). The goal of our work is not only to understand the purposes and meanings of these defense mechanisms for each couple but to enable them to transform their internal representation of a couple to one that is more workable.

This model reinforces the notion that it is the relationship which is being attended to, but that each individual has internal object relations and dynamics which cause problems not only in the couple relationship but also in their worlds outside the relationship.

In this chapter we will not delve into the complexities of Mr and Mrs R but will use the couple to show what this model of couples therapy contributes to thinking about invisible matrices. We will attempt to elaborate the multiple invisible matrices, the multiplicity of internal worlds as they interact, intersect and come to play in the analytic space. We will approach this with special attention to the holding environment and boundaries, the therapeutic container and the countertransference.

The holding environment

The holding environment is the setting and the format that we consciously provide for our patients. It is the scaffolding which supports the therapeutic process within which the space can then be used creatively to assist our patients' understanding of their internal worlds. The holding environment denotes not only the actual holding. but also the 'total environmental provision' (Winnicott 1985, p. 43).

Two aspects of the holding environment are space and time.

Space

We believe that the combination of individual and couple therapy with the same therapist provides a special kind of space for thinking. Couples often come into therapy dancing a very reactive tango, which ever way one moves the other responds, with no space to think. Our model is more like a square dance where several partners dance the same dance. The presence of a third (one therapist) offers space but the presence of another couple (the co-therapist team) offers even more and different space. This idea of a square dance can be very threatening to individuals. It means that you and your partner will be dancing with others, but that you trust at the end you will return to your original partner. The couples work brings up issues that can be explored in the individual session and then be brought back to the couples session and vice versa; issues brought up in an individual session can be further explored, even practised, in the couples session and then be brought back to the individual session to think about. In the individual sessions each partner explores his internal conflicts in the presence of the individual therapist. This provides them space to be curious about themselves separately and in relation to their partner (therapist or spouse). Each goes into the couples therapy feeling known by their individual therapist which enables them to use what they have gotten in the individual therapy as they switch partners back to their spouse. It is this model of the square dance, this particular holding environment, that allows for the reduction of anxiety, helping them to risk the frustration of confronting their partner in an attempt to be known. The following illustrates how Mr and Mrs R use the back and forth of the individual and couples work to explore what they are finding out about themselves. In her individual work, Mrs R is beginning to understand how controlling she is of her own feelings. She does not let herself know how hurt she is for fear of expressing it through anger. Mr R carries all the angry feelings in this relationship. He is aware of his anger which he says is always just below the surface and has been working on understanding the roots of it in his work with Dr D. In an individual session, Mrs R realises how resentful she is of Mr R. She reflects on the times she treats him with disdain like a child. These are feelings she has not allowed herself to know about. She has always been aware of being afraid of his anger but now she sees it is her own anger she also fears. She decides that she is going to try to tell him in a couples session about her anger. Fortified by knowing that their therapists are present they spend the next couples session talking about their fears, anger and hurts with very little interaction from either therapist. The patient/therapist couples have changed to the patient/patient couple.

Another spatial dimension of the holding environment is that usually we form a foursome; the patient couple and the therapist couple. For each of the partners in the couple seeing his/her individual therapist as part of a couple carries complex meanings which are related to each partner's unconscious internal representation of a parental couple. In the beginning of our work together, Mr and Mrs R brought up that whenever the four members of their family were together it was disaster. They worked much better in twosomes or threesomes (one parent and two children or two parents and one child) but when the four were together they did not do well. When we wondered aloud about the foursome in the room (Mr and Mrs R and the two therapists) Mrs R said that she felt much more anxious when we met as a foursome than when the couple met with one or the other of the therapists, as would sometimes happen in the couples therapy when one of us was going to be away, or in individual therapy. This model helped the couple to explore the meaning of two parents working together. For Mrs R this created a great deal of tension. Her parents separated when she was four and remained constantly contentious. She couldn't even mention her father's name in her mother's presence and vice versa. She talked about how terrible she felt when after her father died, her mother drove her out to his farm to get some things. The idea of their occupying the same space even after his death made her feel unsafe. For her being able to express these feelings about the therapist couple helped her to differentiate the external couple (us) from the internal couple (her parents) and to work towards being able to contain the idea of a couple as an imperfect but not totally destructive unit.

Using a co-therapy team/couple enables the couple to encounter a relationship that is different from their own. We work together as an individuated couple and we work separately as individuals, reinforcing the idea of separate individuality and individuality within the couple. Mrs R began therapy with the image of a couple being a single mass, a oneness which would eliminate conflict. Mr R started therapy with the image of a couple being two completely separate individuals, a separateness that would avoid conflict. For example, Mrs R's idea of being close was to use her husband as a receptacle for her emotions. Mr R often felt flooded by her attempts to use him in this way and was amorphously angry but unaware of why. In his individual therapy he has begun to reflect and to be more curious about himself. As he explores what *he* feels with Dr D in his individual sessions, he prepares to share with his wife his curiosity about himself. The mirroring and containment Dr D provides reduces his anxiety enough so that he can create space to hear himself and to think about himself in the presence of Mrs R. The more he does this, the more she feels his presence thereby reducing her anxiety. The less anxious she is the less she needs to project her emotions into her husband as a way of remaining connected to him. She is becoming better able to individuate and to separate her feelings and needs from his. Not only does this reflect her work in her individual therapy but also her experience with and of us, the co-therapy couple. We have become the external couple that each of them has begun to internalise.

Mrs R feels anxious that Mr R doesn't keep her in his mind. We find that by referring back to each other we model holding each other and the other sessions in our mind. In a recent couples session, Mr R was talking about a lunch he attended when he saw a street musician playing the clarinet. He said that he became so sad because he remembered the story Mrs R told him of always wanting to play the clarinet and never being allowed to. Mrs R was moved by the idea that her husband had remembered that story and had thought about her in that way. This parallels the therapists holding of their individual patient's worlds and bringing them into the couple's session.

Time

While we, the therapist couple, endeavour to meet the patient couple once a week at a set time our schedules make it difficult to keep this model consistently. Our arrangement is that when one therapist is unable to be present we meet as a threesome. However, if one of the patient couple cannot make the appointed time, we do not meet. While this presents certain problems, it allows us to meet with the couple more regularly than if we cancelled when one of us was gone. It also gives us the opportunity to hold the other in our mind even when absent. We always leave the absent therapist's chair empty. At times we feel that the couple sees us as interchangeable, that is one can be substituted for the other as if one is the same as the other. When this appears in the material of the session we try to address it and understand it as a defense against mourning a loss.

Boundaries

We find this model works well for us, because our exposure to multiple internal worlds in the same room, with each partner and each therapist present, offers rich opportunities for further elaboration and understanding. We draw a boundary around the interactive matrices of the couple and individual work. Just as we perceive the individuals as individuals and as part of a couple, also we perceive the couple as a unit comprised of individuals. We want to emphasise that boundaries do exist. They are permeable and become more so as trust builds. In the beginning of the work we would not consciously initiate bringing in material from the individual sessions to the couple sessions. We believe, however, once information is shared with us in the individual work it is always present in the couple work because it has become part of what we know and therefore part of all that is known in the invisible matrix. Even so the therapist's holding of information raises issues of crossing boundaries and violating the frame.

There are many times in the couple work when information is revealed about one of the partners without it first having come up in the individual work. While this happens often when one partner tells about something the other partner did, it becomes more complicated when one therapist brings in information that she knows from another session. Motives for bringing issues into the couple sessions can get confusing. For instance, one partner may bring something up in a couple session in the hope that it will get addressed by their partner's individual therapist in the individual session.

Dr D had been away for a couple session in which Mr and Mrs R talked about their holiday visit to their parents who lived in another state. Mr R said that he had been very depressed upon leaving his family home. In the subsequent couple session (in which both therapists were present), the couple discussed their differences in planning ahead. This led to understanding how Mr R doesn't prepare for having feelings about a given situation or upcoming event and finds his feelings erupt in him. Dr L wondered aloud whether this is like his becoming depressed after the visit with his parents which he talked about in the previous couple session. This is the first time Dr D learns Mr R was depressed after the visit. It didn't come up in their individual session. Did Mr R want her to know this? Did he want to tell her in his own good time? Will she bring it into the individual work with Mr R? A boundary has been crossed. Nevertheless, because now Dr D knows something about Mr R's experience, it will influence how she holds him in mind and how she works with him. Now Dr D also knows more fully something of Mrs R's experience with Mr R, where she often feels uninformed.

Boundaries are further complicated by the presence of two individual therapists for the children. One of the couple therapists serves as a co-ordinator for the children's therapist. What happens when one of the children's therapists reports to one of the couple's therapists about an incident that the couple had never discussed? While there has not been a lot of contact back and forth there is some. It was made clear from the onset of making referrals for the children (requested by the parents) that we would be in contact but not in any pre-defined way. In fact it was often very unstructured (talking after a meeting that the two therapists might be at, or during a telephone conversation that was made for other reasons). The information of the contact but not necessarily the details of it was always brought back to the couple session. This was met at the conscious level by the couple feeling relieved that we were working jointly in their behalf; however when one of the children's therapists told them something they did not like, the couple would get upset with us for not making the other therapists more knowledgeable about 'the truth'. There were also times when the couple requested that we talk with the children's therapists so that we could help them (the parents) understand what was going on. In this way the couple tried to use us as parents to intercede on their behalf (like a child asking his/her parent to go to school and talk with their teacher). Since one of the therapists acted as the contact person this also resulted in feelings of competition between the therapists which needed to be openly discussed and occasionally became enacted in the couple's session.

A complicated situation arose when Dr Y, the nine-year-old child's therapist told Dr L that Paul (the child) was very frightened of his father because of his violent outbursts and his hitting. While the couple had discussed Mr R's anger and rage which they said was expressed in hitting a wall, slamming a door etc., they had never admitted in either their individual sessions or in the couple sessions that the rage resulted in striking any family member. Dr Y had a meeting with the parents to talk about this and called Dr L as well. In the following couple session in which Dr D was absent, Mrs R talked about their meeting with Paul's therapist. Mr R reluctantly responded that he and his wife disagreed about how to punish the children. He felt physical punishment was fine as a way of teaching the children to stop fighting. When asked if he hit the children because he was thinking at the time it was good for them or as a release for himself, he admitted it was for himself. He then said he was going to stop hitting them, and in fact went home that night and told the children that hitting them was wrong and he was not going to hit them any more. Prior to the next couple session, Dr L told Dr D about the session. Mr R had never discussed this with her. In the following session with both therapists present, the couple does not bring the issue up. How do the therapists deal with it? Does Dr L bring it up in the couple's session? Does Dr D bring it up in the individual session? Several boundaries have been crossed with complications which are not easily understood. Once the information is in the therapists' minds it becomes part of all that is in the room. It influences the work and needs to be spoken about in the room.

The therapeutic container

Related to the holding environment but not synonymous with it is the therapeutic container. We distinguish the therapeutic container from the holding environment because it involves active internal emotional and cognitive processing whereas the holding environment is more about the provision of an external environment within which to do this. In this active process aspects of the other's internal world co-mingle with aspects of the internal world of the person doing the containing. This involves a struggle to make meaning of the contained contents and in so doing modifies those contents.

We offer some clinical material to illustrate. The background to this session is that the couple have decided they are going to get rid of their cat because it threatens the future health of one of their children. The couple have had this cat for sixteen years. Paul, the older of their two sons, has asthma and the pediatrician said they need to get rid of the cat or Paul will have severe health problems in the future. Damon the five-year-old son is very attached to the cat and Mr and Mrs R are quite concerned about how he will handle the loss. The couple has agonised over what to do about the cat and what to tell the children.

Mr R begins by looking directly at the therapists and saying rather forcefully, 'We need advice about what to tell the kids about the cat'. In lieu of containing his anxiety he tries to evacuate his feelings, put them into the therapists and not experience or think about them. Dr D comments on what she perceives as Mr R's process which gives her some space and time in which to think rather than to react. She identifies at first with Mr R's anxiety and feels the cat must be gotten rid of right away. However, she experiences the presence of Dr L who seems non-anxious. This helps her to contain the anxiety she is feeling, thereby permitting her to be more of a container for the couple. She attends more to the process going on in the room at that moment, can think about Mr R's anxiety and what he is doing with it (projecting it into her) and how that process so often shuts down communication between the couple. Instead of giving advice, she asks them to say more about what they are feeling, which they do.

It is easy to get caught up in our individual patient's feelings, but in our model as we come together as a foursome we are better able to contain the anxieties and think together as good enough parents do for each other and for their children. Initially we each swallowed their projections whole. (Dr L, identifying with Mrs R, her individual patient, felt dubious about getting rid of the cat.) By asking them to talk about what they feel the projections and the projective identifications were brought to light; the whole was broken down into smaller parts which we all can now chew on and think about without the pressure to act right away. The process in the room resulted in the couple's being able to return to their family and to process with the children the pain for all of them of dealing with loss.

Another example includes the intersection of the children's therapist and the couple's therapists within the invisible matrix. The other child's therapist, Dr X, notified the couple that she is no longer able to work with the child because she is ill. Here emerges the complexity of the internal worlds of all parties as they come to play in the analytic space. Each of us has heard her individual patient's version of Dr X stopping her work. Each of us also has her own fantasy and emotions about what is going on with Dr X. Dr D knows from her individual session with Mr R that he was very upset about the phone call. He was concerned about what was going to happen to Dr X and about the loss for his child and for his family. Mr R has a positive transference towards Dr X whom he says sounds and acts like his own mother. All this emerged in the individual session, but not when he talked at home with Mrs R or when he initially brings this up in the couple's session.

Mrs R, in her individual session, expressed annoyance toward the child therapist. She reported to Dr L that she had taken Damon to his therapy appointment only to find that Dr X was not there. When she telephoned her, Dr X's husband sounded surprised that no one had called Damon's parents to tell them that Dr X was ill and was not going to be working for some time if at all. Mrs R had mixed feelings. On the one hand she was concerned about Dr X, on the other she felt forgotten and unimportant. Why hadn't anyone called her? Why, she wondered, was she so forgettable? None of this emerged in the couple's session.

Mr R begins the couple's session by talking about the telephone call he received from his child's therapist. His voice tone is flat as he tells us Dr X sounded weak. He imagined she felt badly. He could relate to that.

Mrs R: 'You didn't tell me that.'

Mr R: 'Yes, I did.'

Dr D: 'What seems to be missing from this conversation is the emotions that were expressed in your individual session.'

Mrs R: (sounding upset and annoyed). 'This is typical. I get so little of you. If you expressed more of your feelings I wouldn't feel so lonely. We could discuss and share our feelings and be more a couple.'

Mr R looks confused. We ask for his reaction to what Mrs R is saying. He doesn't seem to understand. This is a dynamic in the couple. She pursues him and he begins to withdraw. We have called this (between us) 'Pacman'.

As we, the therapists, sit in the couple session we are containing our own external and internal relationship with the child therapist, as well as containing Mr and Mrs R's emotions from their previous individual sessions. A parallel process is going on between the therapist couple and the patient couple. We are identifying with the couple in experiencing anxieties about sharing feelings with each other. This couple is terrified of expressing affect toward and with each other and therefore omit it from their conversations. We, the therapist couple, have not shared with each other our own feelings about Dr X even prior to her ending therapy with the child. This has created a strain in and between us which in this session we are just beginning to realise. Once we can process our own reluctance to share our feelings with each other we can begin to understand what is going on in Mr and Mrs R. The above illustrates the complexity of the invisible matrices created by this multiple relational field, and the stress it produces on the containing function. In this instance, there was a parallel process between the patient couple and the co-therapist couple regarding non-communication of feelings. Silently, in the session, each of us was being curious about our lack of communicating to the other our feelings about Dr X. After the session had ended, we acknowledged our own anxieties about expressing our feelings to each other over this issue. In acknowledging our anxieties about disappointing and hurting the other we could better understand something about the couple's reluctance to share feelings with each other.

When Dr D brought into the couple's session the difference in Mr R's presentation about the phone call, an opening was created for Mrs R to think that Mr R is capable of expressing feelings but doesn't with her. She felt annoyed but eventually could become curious about that. She also felt that Dr D and Mr R have something together as a couple that she wants to have with him.

In a subsequent session, Mrs R talks about being able to 'be' more with Mr R. She is better able to contain her emotions and therefore Mr R is not as afraid of her. She is using Dr L as a container and is internalising Dr L's containing function. She also experiences that Dr D is not anxious when Mr R doesn't know what he feels, or when Mr R withdraws. She is internalising some of Dr D's containing function, too.

The clinical example we gave concerning the child therapist Dr X illustrates how parallel processes occur in the couple and in the co-therapy couple. We try to attend to these processes as they are enacted within the therapist couple and also as they are enacted with the other couples in the room (the individual therapist of one partner and the 'other' partner). In their working relationship, the co-therapists may experience dynamics which the patient couple experience. This requires that the co-therapists monitor the dynamics in their own relationship, contain and process them. Doing this can bring to light a more full picture of the patient couple's shared internal world. However it is often the case that such parallel processes go unrecognised until there is an enactment of them in the room.

Another example of parallel process between couple and therapist occurs when Mrs R brings into the couple session her interest in living in a foreign city. Her therapist, Dr L, gets excited about it too. Dr D holds some reservations about their moving now. In the room Dr L picks up on our difference (our different affects). This helps her to be curious about her excitement, work with it internally (in the moment) and come to recognise that this family is not ready to relocate anytime soon. Both therapists have lived in foreign cities and have enjoyed it. Dr D is able to contain the affect and not be overwhelmed by the excitement. This helps Dr L to de-centre from being the individual therapist and to re-focus on being the couple's therapist.

It helps the couple to experience that the therapist couple can have different ideas, affects, etc. and still go on being a couple. For example as Mrs R accepts her own identity and can contain more of her affect she does not need Mr R to be merged with her or for him to be a depository for her uncomfortable emotions. This helps Mr R to feel less suffocated by Mrs R and therefore he does not withdraw as readily.

Transference and counter-transference issues

We believe, as do all therapists who work from a psychoanalytic object relations model, that the crux of couple work is in helping the couple understand the unconscious overlay that is placed on their views of each other as well as onto us. These 'perceptions of the other' are the results of trying to re-create earlier familiar, even painful relationships from their childhood in an attempt to work them out in the here and now. This is done through the process of projective identification and is experienced in the transference and counter-transference.

In our model, having the same person as the individual therapist and as part of a couple co-therapy team means that the therapist offers herself up for both mother/father and parental couple transferences. The invisible matrices are composed of these multiple transference-counter-transference configurations.

Being a couple presents tension between one's individuality and one's couplehood. For many the fear of losing one's identity in being part of a couple keeps them very separate. For others the fear of being an outsider, always alone, makes them want to merge. Some couples are both on the same side, that is each wanting merger or each wanting total separateness. This may not present a problem for the couple until some change occurs in their external or internal life which pulls one of them in a different direction. It is these couples or those who from the start are attracted to each other because of their differences who often find their way into our consulting rooms. The couple that we are presenting are split in this respect in that Mrs R wants merger while Mr R wants separateness.

Our model addresses these issues of individuality and couplehood in the transference and counter-transference thereby making them more accessible. The model allows each member of the couple to be experienced by their therapist as both an individual and as part of a couple, and for them to experience their therapists as both an individual and as part of a couple.

When working as an individual therapist only, the patient's significant other becomes known to us through the patient's eyes as that knowledge mixes with our own internal objects. In traditional couple therapy, we know each partner only in the presence of the other.

Counter-transferences are based and explored in the here and the now. In our model we experience each partner in a variety of ways; as part of a couple, as part of a foursome and as an individual. At times, as their individual therapist, we have been caught up in situations in which we are identified with our individual patient, that is we feel as they do *vis-à-vis* their partner. At other times, we are identified with their object; that is we feel as their partner or other feels *vis-à-vis* them. This affects our feelings and perceptions of the partner who is not in the room. When we enter into the couple work our own counter-transferences become multi-dimensional. Instead of viewing this as total chaos, we experience it as an expansion of the holding environment and containing function, allowing us to gain a better understanding of the complexity of the couple as a unit and as two individuals with separate histories. We can then process their projections and think about them as individuals and as part of a couple. Our model also gives us the opportunity to experience ourselves as individuals and as part of a couple in the *presence* of our co-therapist. We know *in vivo* that being an individual and being part of a couple are two different experiences thereby expanding the transference-countertransference matrices, potentiating their availability for work.

The following are examples of some of the unconscious invisible matrices which appear in the transference and counter-transference. The first is an example of how the therapists' counter-transference to the individuals helps in their understanding of the couple.

The session begins with Dr D telling Mr and Mrs R that she will not be here for the next three weeks. We then go over our schedules. Rather than take a long Christmas break, we discuss who will be here during the next few weeks. Because of Thanksgiving and Christmas holidays during which Mr and Mrs R will be away; and the absences of Drs D and L we will not meet as a foursome again for six weeks, a highly unusual occurrence in our work. Except for the two sessions when the couple will be away, they will continue to meet with one of us but both therapists will not be together for our sessions until after the Christmas holidays. Mrs R will continue to see Dr L during this time but Mr R will not meet with Dr D for four weeks. The session proceeds with no comments by either Mr R or Mrs R about this scheduling. Mrs R then turns to Mr R and says: 'I'd like to bring up something that I'm scared about. I've been discussing it with Dr L in my individual session. I'm feeling upset that I'm not able to be as supportive of you as I'd like.' Turning to us, she continues 'Mr R is having problems at work and I want to be there for him. I get upset with myself that I'm not feeling more supportive although I try. Actually, it's even worse that that. I get angry at him when I think he is not fighting for himself.' (Dr L is feeling good that Mrs R is bringing up something which is very difficult for her to do). In her last individual session, Mrs R said she was afraid to tell Mr R how she really felt because he would get very angry and depressed which scares her. She then associated her fear of Mr R to her feelings as a child of always tip-toeing around, afraid to stir up any feelings. She prides herself on being able to go into a room, assess the situation and act in a way so as to keep things calm, but in so doing she has become aware of how she hides her own feelings. As Mrs R continues, Mr R in fact does get angry saying her timing is really lousy. He doesn't understand why she has to bring this up now, if his passivity bothers her she should bring it up at another time. He then becomes quiet and withdraws. Meanwhile, Dr D is growing annoyed with Mrs R. As her negative counter-transference mounts she places herself more as Jack's individual therapist, losing touch with the couple. Dr D, however, is not quiet and does not withdraw. Giving words to her counter-transference feelings she says, 'Mrs R, you say you want to talk about your fear of your anger but right here and now as you're talking to Mr R you're making an attribution about his passivity rather than showing curiosity on your part about your fear of expressing yourself'. As Dr L hears Dr D put into words her experience of Mrs R, she feels that Mrs R is being misunderstood and encourages her to elaborate on her feelings. Dr L, realising that Mrs R is making not only Mr R but Dr D angry, aligns with Mrs R in her wish to assess the situation and make it calm. The pairings that exist now are Mr R and Dr D (feeling angry with Mrs R) and Mrs R and Dr L (assessing the situation and wanting to create calm). As Mrs R talks more about her fears and relates them to her early experiences of being fearful of disturbing her father for fear he would get depressed and drink, as well as her anger at having a passive mother who would not stand up for herself, Dr D is able to expand her empathy to include Mrs R while still remaining empathic to Mr R. Dr D's identification with Mr R's anger allows him to feel understood. Dr D's sense that her co-therapist understands her, helps her to shift back to being the couple's therapist. Dr D feeling more a part of a co-therapy couple allows Mr R to become more of a couple with Mrs R. As Mr R is able to be more understanding of Mrs R, he also feels less suffocated by her and can elaborate his feelings. Each therapist's understanding the internal world of her individual patient helps each of the couple to elaborate, thus creating space for a contemporary couple rather than a historic couple acting out their pasts.

The next example shows how the transference from the patient to the therapist informs the therapist about her counter-transference toward her co-therapist. Towards the end of this same session, Dr L says, 'I wonder if earlier today you were feeling deserted by Mrs R in your time of crisis as you might have felt deserted by your parents, when as a teenager you got in trouble at school and they abandoned you?' Mr R moves to the end of his seat and in a very cold and deliberate voice says 'No! Couldn't it just be possible that I'm angry at Mrs R because the people at work are turning against me and I need the one person I trust to be there for me?' When Mr R expressed his anger toward Dr L she realised that just as the couple had not been talking about their feelings towards the co-therapy team for the disrupted scheduling, neither had Dr L realised how upset she was feeling toward Dr D for taking time off. She felt Dr D was abandoning her. It was through her experiencing of Mr R's anger towards her that she was able to get in touch with her anger at Dr D rather than just to attribute the feelings of abandonment to the couple. Dr L said 'I think you are not only angry with Mrs R about abandoning you but you are also angry at us.' Mrs R sat quietly back in her chair. Dr D said: 'Mrs R, what are you feeling?' Mrs R: 'I'm feeling mortified. I feel that Mr R's anger is scary and that he shouldn't have gotten so angry in here.' Dr D: 'I wonder if you wish Mr R had stayed more passive in here. When he expresses his feelings, it frightens you. You started by saying that you wanted to be more honest with your feelings, but it is hard to be honest when you are worried about being abandoned.'

In the processing after the session, Dr L talked about how abandoned she was feeling by Dr D. This processing can help the couple not to have to carry the therapist's anger as well as their own. The following week Mr and Mrs R reported that they got along much better after the session. This vignette is an example of how transference of the couple to the therapists helped the therapist get in touch with their own feelings toward each other.

The co-therapy team

The co-therapy team itself provides a holding presence for us and for the couple, but is very labour intensive. Careful maintenance is required which takes time, space and hard work. Between us all kinds of feelings like love and hate, competition and envy have to be sorted out. Our differences have to be recognised and worked through. Consultations with other therapists involved with the family take time and affect us.

We are members of an ongoing peer supervision group that has been meeting for many years. This group provides a container and a holding environment for us. It was here that we came to intimately know each other and our work. In addition to the group, we meet regularly together to talk about our work and about ourselves. We share with each other our internal worlds. We set aside time before each session to 'touch base' and afterwards to process the session. When there are differences or issues between us we try to sort them out although not always successfully.

The model of the co-therapy team is very difficult to maintain and is not consistently held. We meet with the couple even when one of us is absent. At one level, this provides an opportunity for the couple to experience us as being able to go on being without the other while remaining mindful of the other. However, at another level, it adds to the invisible matrices and makes the holding environment, boundaries, containing function and transference-countertransference issues even more difficult to track.

The fact that we are two women must also affect the unconscious invisible matrices. It influences our patients' phantasies about us as a couple. We have wondered whether certain topics like sex or aggression would emerge differently if we were two men or a man and a woman. We consider the transferences to be fairly malleable with regard to mother or father, feminine or masculine; each of us appears to get a fair share of both, but our patient couples do not get the actual live experience of a male and a female or of two males working together as a couple.

CHAPTER NINE

WORKING TOGETHER: ASPECTS OF A THERAPEUTIC CONTAINER AT WORK

Stella Pierides

Stella Pierides is a psychoanalytic psychotherapist in private practice, a team leader at the Arbours Crisis Centre, London, a teacher and supervisor. She is a co-founder and member of the Arbours Psychotherapists Borderline Workshop, and Art and Psychoanalytic Thought workshop. Her main area of work involves borderline psychotic conditions, crisis intervention and assessments, and her areas of interest include artistic creativity in the visual arts and in literature. She recently co-edited Even Paranoids Have Enemies: New Perspectives on Paranoia and Persecution *(Routledge 1998).*

This chapter gives us an insight into the working of a therapeutic community which aims to help people in deeply disturbed states of mind by means of therapeutic team-work and milieu therapy. Stella Pierides describes how, working and thinking together, the therapists of the Arbours Crisis Centre are able to know about their guests' very powerful projections, which are received into their professional matrix. She writes about how the therapists adhere to rigorous analytic thinking about the group process, whilst allowing themselves to be immersed in the life of the community. She is describing an almost unique situation in which the workers depend upon the healthy functioning of their matrix to enable them to work alongside a community of people who from time to time act out their deep distress. Within this professional matrix the staff group help each other to think about and process acute psychic pain and minimise enactment of the disturbance, which sometimes appears reflected within their group. Stella Pierides describes how the strength of a therapeutic community lies in its capacity to hold a member's unthinkable anxiety, which can then be processed by all its members together.

* * *

Severely borderline or psychotic patients requiring institutional, therapeutic community or hospital treatment have several professionals working with them: psychiatrists, psychotherapists, nurses, general practitioners, art therapists, among others. Whenever these professionals work together in the same environment, say a hospital, the therapeutic matrix is multi-levelled, often structured and hierarchical and it involves communication between those professionals such as note-keeping and exchange, staff meetings, telephone conversations, attendance of case conferences, referral procedures. Although clear structures exist in these situations, difficulties often arise through powerful counter-transference reactions in the treatment staff due to the intense splitting and projective mechanisms these patients employ.

Complications also arise at the times when different professionals work with the same patient concurrently, albeit from different therapeutic programmes. A psychotherapist might be seeing a patient who might also be under the care of a psychiatrist, a social worker and a community psychiatric nurse. What is being communicated, and how, becomes vitally important not only for good practice purposes but also for the actual health, and at times, survival of the patient. Collapse of professional co-operation under the influence of the projective mechanisms of the patient is not unheard of, and indeed often becomes the catalysing agent which is rarely thought about in a constructive way among the suffering professionals. Put simply, psychotherapists and psychiatrists stop communicating essential information to each other, or more conveniently, stop referring patients to each other; nurses become denigrated, and also denigrating or idealising of psychiatrists and so on. Of course, the same process takes place within the same profession; psychotherapists behave in similar ways towards other psychotherapists, psychiatrists to other psychiatrists and the unprocessed insanity circulates in the wider shores of the helping professions with the result of their becoming less helping. Furthermore, our increasingly litigious culture makes it harder for essential information to be communicated under a climate of paranoia and fear of blame. In addition, the context of treatment of these patients, so far removed from the consulting room treatment of individual psychoanalytic psychotherapy, gives rise to interesting as well as pressing conundrums. For psychotherapists thinking about these issues, communication of thinking becomes imperative as these patients challenge and stretch the concepts that we hold most important in our work; those of confidentiality, boundaries, transference and counter-transference, containment and identity.

In this chapter, I will be approaching this area with some thoughts on the concept of containment of the severely disturbed, and disturbing, patient. In particular, I will be discussing the nature of some aspects of the container/contained relationship in the light of Bion's work, using as my basis some of the dynamics of the Wednesday staff meeting of the Arbours Crisis Centre. The Centre is a small psychoanalytically informed facility, utilising its own unique blend of psychoanalytic thinking with group and community therapy. This is underpinned by the principle of co-therapy or working together of several professionals to provide a containing environment for these particular patients. The Centre therefore provides a microcosm of those diverse professional relationships encountered in the mental health world. Before I discuss the Centre further I will briefly summarise Bion's view of the infant's development and its vicissitudes.

Bion charted the development of two apparatuses in the mind: one for thinking and one for projective identification. In 'A Theory of Thinking' (1962) he elaborates on the way an infant develops a mental apparatus for thinking; and also, how, in pathological development, an apparatus for excessive projective identification is developed. A baby, for Bion, comes into the world with what he calls pre-conceptions: innate expectations, like the expectation of the mouth to be filled with the nipple; innate awareness, like the awareness that the mouth has found the breast and feeding is taking place. These pre-conceptions, when matched with realisations, the nipple in the mouth, through awareness of the satisfactory experience, become conceptions. Further, these conceptions become available to the baby as further pre-conceptions to be realised; they become in a way a store of satisfactory experiences that can be drawn from. In one sense, they become expectations to be fed, based on previous experiences of feeding. If they are always realised, a state of bliss—but no thought—is achieved.

When the pre-conceptions are not immediately realised—no breast—and if there is capacity for toleration of frustration, a thought—of no breast, and eventually, of absent breast—arises and an apparatus for thinking develops to cope with the thoughts. The thought of no breast, in itself, makes the frustration more tolerable or more containable. However, if there is little or no toleration of frustration, instead of a thought, a bad object is created, which requires an apparatus of projective identification to evacuate it. A pathological (excessive) hypertrophy of this apparatus results in the need for evacuation and its satisfaction, which becomes the equivalent of obtaining sustenance from a good object.

When thoughts are thus equated with a bad object, the need for satisfying evacuatory contact, not thinking, becomes vital to the person in this state of mind. Furthermore, the dominance of excessive projective identification disables the ability to distinguish between self and external object; space and time are equated with bad objects to be annihilated and awareness of them is attacked. Two-ness and separateness are not tolerated (Bion 1962).

Now the cycle of pre-conception—realisation—conception involves sense and emotional experiences. These primary impressions on the physical and psychic space (hunger, an unknown sensation, for the baby a yet to be processed sensation) through meeting with a live object (mother's nipple) which contains them (through feeding), give rise to a new experience (satisfaction); this is an alpha-element. This is stored as such in the unconscious; we do not remember all the meals we have had. The mother's intervention, her alpha-function, has processed her baby's (physical) need and raw sensation of unidentified hunger and transformed it to a mental experience. Mother's alpha-function extends to include the baby's sensations of the self; for the baby, awareness of herself is the result of mother having accepted and processed baby's sensations of baby's self. Too long a wait for the baby through mother failing to respond, or other factors, would have meant mother failed in her alpha-function and the baby experienced hunger—for instance—as what Bion calls, a beta-element, an unprocessed and undigested sensation resulting from failure of alpha-function, sitting uncomfortably in the psyche.

However, mother's function is more than providing alpha-function. Her input as a person consists in providing personal, receptive presence, what Bion calls reverie, a receptive state of mind that empathises with baby and baby's needs, feels and understands them; mother's reverie is then sensed by the baby who, using projective identification as an exploratory psychic tentacle, finds herself in the presence of someone moved by, but not shaken by her need. Her undigested and uncontained sensation has been contained by mother's reverie and transformed through mother's alpha-function into a liveable experience. The baby has now the experience of containment and contentment. The impact of this experience on the baby is the first knowing which is introjected, 'installed' as Bion calls it, and used subsequently as a model. Accumulation of contained experiences allows the baby to learn from experience. Put differently, containment results from baby having being offered by mother a safe space to project into and a presence willing to make sense of baby's sensations: sanctuary and meaning (Britton 1998). Furthermore, the experience that the mother undergoes with her baby is beneficial to her as well, she, too, grows mentally through it. This is what Bion calls the commensal relationship between the container and the contained; it is beneficial to both parties and affords them no harm.

Disasters in the provision of containment, which include, besides failures on behalf of the mother to be receptive and processing of baby's need, excessive envy originating in the baby, or other factors, result in the mental configurations of our psychotic and severely borderline patients. Mental evacuation becomes a way of life, or rather psychic death, while ways of producing emotional involvement with the therapist are felt as safer, and therefore much preferable, to those of involving her thinking capacities.

From this short summary of some of Bion's views, it follows that the nature of the container, the nature of the contained or un-contained and the relationship between the two, is vital in the understanding of what goes on whenever there is need for understanding a patient's development, or arrested growth, and her needs. For instance, Bion's baby which has developed a mental apparatus primarily for deriving satisfaction from evacuation will be looking for a suitable container and will be running away from thinking which, more often than not, she will experience as persecutory. We could say this is a fact of this particular baby's life. Any attempt at containing this baby will have to acknowledge, expect and be willing to work with this fact; there will be splitting, projection, excessive projective identification and confusional states at play. However, this container will not only have to be flexible enough, but also should have made the necessary arrangements for this to take place. It could be said that the very development of therapeutic communities owes its inception to some intuitive understanding of the needs of this category of patients.

Looking at it from another angle, all patients who need the support of therapeutic community living, carry failures in the nature of the relationship between the container and the contained. For that relationship to be beneficial to both, it has to involve flexibility. When there is none, either the contents explode the container or they themselves suffer further damage. In the former case, the treatment and treaters suffer, and inevitably the patient, while in the latter, the patient is left feeling that she has further proof of the uncontainability of her thoughts and feelings. Hopelessness and despair lead to a conviction, in some of the treaters, of poor prognosis for some of the more ill of these patients.

In what follows I shall describe briefly a therapeutic container which has evolved taking into account the nature of the psychological development of the patient. The Arbours Crisis Centre consists of a group of therapists working together as a matter of course to provide an intensive therapeutic intervention to people with a variety of diagnoses, from depression to psychosis. The space where this working together takes place, the Arbours Crisis Centre, was founded in 1973 to provide intensive support to those in crisis. The name of the Centre originates from the idea of the temporary dwelling places where the Israelites found rest during their wanderings in the desert; it implies a place where exhaustion, whether mental, emotional or psychological, or that experienced physically is taken seriously, thought about and translated in a way that aims to make it tolerable.

Three therapists live-in at the Centre making it their home for three years. They are supported by ten psychotherapists who work as team leaders, a nurse manager, a psychiatrist, a clinical assistant, a financial administrator, and a number of other staff including psychotherapists-in-training. With the exception of the resident therapists who change every three years, and the trainees who attend for a minimum of six months, the staff turnover is extremely low. Five of the ten team leaders have been at the Centre for over ten years. The Centre has space for six patients at any one time who are invited to stay as the 'guests' of the resident therapists. Guests at the Arbours Crisis Centre are treated as guests to a sanctuary, as well as with the respect with which *xenoi* were treated in ancient Greece. The resident therapists invite them by offering them more than a room and a bed: a space in the existing group of the Centre. The guests stay at the Centre for varying periods of time, from approximately one month to one year.

Each guest, after being assessed for suitability of placement and a grant secured for them, is then offered a moving-in date. Upon their arrival, apart from the practical details of the Centre, guests are given information about the formal structure of spaces and timetable of meetings. Thus they are told about the team meetings. These are meetings attended by the guest, their allocated resident therapist and team leader. Team meetings take place from three to five times a week. Guests are also told about the house meetings. These take place four times a week, are attended by all those living in the house and facilitated by the resident therapists. They are also told about the once weekly art and movement therapy meetings. Berke (1990) has described the structure of the work of the Centre as a multi-systemic approach of working with those with intra-psychic, interpersonal and situational problems. The three systems are the milieu, the team and the group. The milieu is the total interpersonal and inter-systemic environment of the Centre. The team is the individual guest's therapeutic space where he or she takes his or her emotional and psychic baggage to be unpacked and thought about. The group is the total of the people living in the house, therapists and their guests; its focus is the space of the house meetings, where the problems as well as the joys of living together are discussed, negotiated, understood and digested. The weekly Wednesday clinical meeting, is the space where the group of therapists involved in different capacities with the Centre meet formally to monitor, review, discuss and generally think about the ongoing work. In a sense it is the space which contains, supports, reflects and informs the direction of the work with individual guests. The director and associate director, the team leaders, resident therapists, trainees and other therapists feed into it their own experiences, interactions, feelings, perceptions and thinking to help form a picture of what is going on in each individual guest as well as in the group and milieu.

The model of the Centre based on co-working, brings together various aspects of technique, professionals and settings. Individual, patient-centred work takes place together with group work, psychoanalytically informed psychotherapeutic work together with movement therapy and art therapy; aspects of psychoanalytic technique rub shoulders with principles of therapeutic communities. All these ideas, techniques and professionals work together to inform and enrich one another so as to offer a suitable container for the needs of severely ill patients.

This diversity of meetings, therapists and approaches forms a major part of the identity of the Centre. The Wednesday clinical group, much like an effective and functioning ego, relies on this diversity of perspectives and input; with the awareness, at the same time, that under the pressure of immense projections from the work with the guests, the same group will be split, at times, along the lines of marriage of perspectives. For instance, between those who emphasise therapeutic community aspects and those who emphasise working with individual psychoanalytic perspectives; those favouring group and those who favour individual work; those who work with non-verbal and those who work with verbal therapies; those who live-in and those who only visit for meetings. I say at times and not often, because the history of the group has allowed for 'personalities to emerge' (Hinshelwood 1994) who, taking on various projections from the guests, relate in various and complex ways in the Wednesday meeting. However, this very important aspect of the life of the clinical group is not relevant to the purposes of this chapter. Nevertheless, how it is that this group—which is a microcosm of the wider mental health field—only temporarily splits and fragments and then reconstitutes itself rather than disintegrates, is an interesting and productive line of enquiry. In other words, how does the Crisis Centre staff group manage to be containing?

For the purposes of this chapter I am identifying the following factors: it is a stable group with a common history, where a 'reflective space' (Hinshelwood 1994) has been established which allows it to withstand and weather the storms of the patient's psychotic worlds; it is a group with common interests and aims, a clear delineation of roles and responsibilities and a commitment to working psychodynamically with, rather than for the patient.

The therapists of the Centre share a history together and having gone through several ups and downs, have learned to know and accept the different aspects of one another. This shared history of the Centre involves a collective working alliance of its members, who have known one another over time, especially calm time, and who, when regressed in working with borderline psychotic guests, although feeling confused, blaming of or cut-off from one another according to their patient's state of mind, do not act out too destructively, but are more able to treat the counter-transference feelings in themselves through the use of the Wednesday meeting. This history of contained experiences, this acknowledgement of the past too, in the group's collective mind, is what makes it possible for it to work well in the present, and to feel hopeful about the future. This also involves a commitment to working with each other, not in general terms, but together with the specific individuals that make up the Centre. In this sense, the Wednesday group has developed over time the emotional linking between its members which forms a fertile space for reflection, what Hinshelwood (1994) calls, in the context of group therapy, 'reflective space'. Although too much fear, intrusiveness or destructiveness attack this space and temporarily may fragment it as a mental container for its members with the potential of a temporarily psychotic intervention on the part of the therapists (Berke 1995), the clinical group through its shared common experience over time reconstitutes itself.

Furthermore, the Centre therapists share common interests and aims. Through their involvement with the Centre they have made the commitment to working with borderline and psychotic patients in need of specialist residential care on minimal or, whenever possible, no medication. This means that they have learned to accept and work with not only one another, but also their patient's specific difficulties as they are stirred up and emerge in and through themselves. McCready (1987) coined the term 'milieu counter-transference' to describe the collective phenomenon in which the treatment staff as a group experiences regressions in functioning that, because of the operation of the patient's ego defences, essentially mirror the level of the functioning in the patient. This counter-transference is a useful tool, when properly identified and treated, that benefits treatment both in terms of understanding the patient's experience as well as intervening in the patient's pathological view of the world. Such a view could be said to be taken for granted by the staff at the Centre who go further to examine and consider, in addition, their own individual transferences and counter-transferences to the guests. Underlying this is acceptance of the fact that, working with such severely ill patients, one does not remain untouched. Berke (1990), in delineating the Centre's therapeutic goals, writes: 'What we can do is help guests to tolerate their underlying despair, to identify their underlying difficulties and conflicts, and to expand in some small ways their relational capacities—the possibility of intimacy, empathy and trust. In order to achieve this we do not remain passive onlookers. Rather, we are active participants in the experiences they are trying to disgorge. Sometimes it seems that the main difference between them and ourselves is that we are more able to ask for help in struggling with intolerable feelings and states of mind.'

In addition, or perhaps because of the preceding factors, the therapists work within a clear delineation of roles and responsibilities, including the built-in ambiguities in their roles, and respect each other's space. The structure of each team is set up before the guest comes in and it remains unchanged, with the exception of the occasional recruitment of an additional team leader for extended staff supervision meetings. Thus an identity develops which is specific to the team. With this identity in place, and within the wider context of the whole therapeutic environment of the Centre, they are ready to be tossed about in the storms of the guest's—and their own—transferences and counter-transferences. During this time, there will be uncertainties, splits, projections, that will inevitably result in the therapists taking on their guest's disturbance to varying degrees (Berke 1995), with security in the knowledge that they will be held by the wider clinical Wednesday meeting.

Furthermore, there is a shared commitment to working with the patient. As part of the origins of the Centre draw from the therapeutic community background, the ethos in the group is directed to seeing the patient as involved in the treatment, whatever their level of disturbance might be. There is an understanding that, however much the patient may be in the throes of psychosis, there is always a non-psychotic personality present to which verbal and other comments and interpretations may be directed (Bion 1957).

All these factors together lead the clinical group members to communicate with one another in a thoroughly open way. Boundaries are the boundaries of the Wednesday clinical group and confidentiality is held by it.

Holding this background description of the clinical group—of which I am a member in my capacity as team leader—in mind, I shall now describe a clinical vignette where some of these factors and the emotional linking of the clinical group were under attack.

Robert, a thirty-two year old man who spent many years in hospital with the severest of diagnoses, came to the Centre for an initial six-month stay. Soon after his arrival, Robert refused to attend team and house meetings, leave his room, or join in the life of the house in any way. The staff group in the Wednesday clinical meeting became divided between those who saw the option of allowing him to continue like this as providing a hotel room for a paying guest, as corrupt accomplices to his state of mind—with the suggestion for the stay to be discontinued—and those who felt that we as a group should make an effort to accommodate his different needs to those of the other guests. How could Robert benefit from the Centre as a therapeutic community if he did not attend the house meetings and what message would we be giving to the other guests if we allowed Robert to miss meetings, was the argument of the former sub-group; whereas the latter sub-group argued for acknowledging his individuality in terms of his history, severity of disturbance and needs through finding a suitable, to him, form of therapeutic intervention. Though split, the group had the space for doubt and tolerance of the different positions and allowed Robert to continue his stay utilising the milieu, focusing on his resident therapist in the treatment programme.

This decision, based on a tolerant attitude of the group that has a long history, bore fruit and Robert started to come out of his room. In one of our clinical meetings, just after Robert had attended one of his team meetings and had spent some time in the house, we noticed how excited we all had got arguing about him from various emotional and intellectual standpoints. There was hope in some of us, disbelief in others, while perhaps not surprisingly, keeping an open mind seemed to be the most difficult state to be in. Suggestions on how to approach this new situation started pouring in: we should reduce his medication or take him off it altogether, involve him more with the other guests, encourage him to clean his room and so on. In addition, a letter had been received by our director from the guest's mother (a very intrusive woman who in the first weeks of his stay had insisted on visiting daily to clean his room, dress him and prompt him to do things) asking various questions, including about the state of Robert's gums, thus bypassing the therapists on his team. His own team leader had been quiet thus far in the meeting and moreover overlooked by everyone who had his or her own suggestion to make. Once this was noticed, we understood how we had been led to 'act' rather than think. The group realised we had to make room in our thinking as a group for his team leader and resident therapist and the work they had been doing with him, which had just born fruit, rather than intrude, at this very point, with our projections and anxieties. On that occasion, the group seemed in danger of becoming the impersonation of a very uncontaining and intrusive mother who would take over and mould Robert to what she thought was appropriate behaviour or treatment, and losing him/the patient on the way.

Still, Robert missed more meetings. In fact, his team meetings became one-to-one meetings between his resident therapist and his team leader. Finding ways of bearing the unbearable hopelessness, helplessness and contempt that were being passed on to them was the most important part of their work. The team leader had also to find a way of supporting the resident therapist on the team and the wider resident therapist group who, under the influence of enormous projections, often felt they were losing their way with Robert and their work with him. Once again, our Wednesday group experienced the split between those who wanted Robert to tidy up his smelly, by now mouldy room, who saw not keeping him tidy as our abandoning a baby in its own smelly mess; and those who wanted to allow flexibility by allowing him, and ourselves, space to become aware of the nature of his messiness while nurturing his attempts to grow. Helping him and his parents, who were offered family meetings, separate the gum problems from the psychological ones, as well as separate from each other, became the Centre's teething problems for a while.

When the time came for Robert to leave the Centre, the holding situation deteriorated. Partly due to holidays, it became near impossible to arrange a review meeting with his psychiatrist, social worker and ourselves to think together about his future. While the Crisis Centre clinical meeting had decided that Robert would benefit from another six-month stay here, this needed to be communicated and thought about with the other professionals working with him outside the Centre. Robert's leaving date approaching, he had his leaving meal—a standard procedure for all those who leave the Centre, even those who are offered a second stay—which proved to be a moving experience for everyone, and a week of saying goodbye. Without appropriate planning however it was not known when exactly Robert would leave the Centre, and whether he would be returning for another stay or going to another facility, short of us making a unilateral decision which we could not do. In the least, funding would have to be negotiated with the Health Authority for another stay. To make things worse, Robert's resident therapist, Marvin, who had carried the linking of the intervention, having reached the end of his contract with us, was in the process of leaving. Robert had become quite attached to him, as he had come to represent a major link between himself and his team leader, himself and the containing object of the team space. This meant that, even if Robert was to be allowed another stay by the review panel, he would still have to be allocated a new resident therapist.

Not surprisingly, Robert deteriorated at this point. He was now seen sitting for hours in the house conservatory mumbling to himself, impervious to people's approaches, or suddenly becoming aggressive and threatening. The contact he had made with people seemed to have evaporated and he vacillated between consuming rage and threat, and total apathy. At the clinical meeting, individual members of staff described their experiences of him. Marvin's wife, Cathy, also a resident therapist, who was finishing her contract much later than Marvin, described how she had asked Robert to turn the volume of the music he was playing down and he had stood in front of her, staring into her eyes in a very alarming way. Cathy had felt very frightened, but managed to acknowledge her fear to him. After a few minutes, Robert had said to her, 'You have beautiful eyes' and had sat down again. Another member of staff had taken a place mat on the table to put her coffee cup on, finding herself suddenly confronted by a threatening Robert who, grabbing it from her, said, 'This is my mat, that one is yours'. The group felt despondent and hopeless for him. His aggressively loud 'music' had entered our ears and filled our minds blocking our attempts to think. The decision made previously, that the Centre would recommend another stay for him got forgotten and indeed it became for a while unthinkable. Eventually, however, linking started. Cathy, as Marvin's wife, was indeed in Robert's way. Her 'beautiful eyes' that Robert connected to Marvin, in his identification with him, made a man of him again, not a frightened child. Indeed, it was Cathy who had been frightened of him. Her fear however, at that moment of confrontation, had been contained by her. This fact, having been observed by Robert, had allowed him to appreciate the beauty in the containing 'I'. He could sit down and relax for a bit. And so could we, sit together and think about him. The clinical group felt for him and his predicament. It was truly 'maddening' not to know what was going to happen to him, to the work he had done here, to the good experiences he had had. The threat was a threat to his whole world that was coming undone; no wonder he had pitched his whole existence on the mat that he could call his. At the same time, the mat and the other objects that he tenaciously saw as his, became parts of him that he protected with ferocious persistence from the him, and us, who were aware of the possibility of impending separation and loss.

This clinical meeting helped all those working with Robert to find once again the good contact they had made with him, to remember the decision to offer him a second stay and recognise in themselves Robert's crisis. The 'impossible'-to-arrange meeting was arranged, though Robert did not attend, saying 'you decide for me'. This was both a refusal to take responsibility for himself and his future as well as an indication of trust to those working with him. The principle of working with the patient in this instance had to be rethought in relation to him, with the therapists knowingly going the extra mile to carry for him not only his anger, despondency and destructiveness, but also his trust and hope. When they asked him for the purposes of the review meeting what his long-term aims were, he replied to 'get a flat and be able to drive a van'.

While the review group took on the responsibility to make a decision on his behalf, Robert felt freed to literally express through his behaviour how he felt about himself and the milieu he was in. Our clinical meeting gathered the information. Walter, the new resident therapist who was now replacing Marvin, had been invited by Robert to watch television with him, and on another occasion to have a cup of tea. Maria, a trainee, having offered to make Robert a cup of cocoa, reported how she had been asked by him 'How long will this take?'. She had replied with a question: 'Why, are you in a hurry?' and they had both laughed amicably. Robert had then proceeded to pace up and down the kitchen, keeping busy with his thoughts. Indeed, Cathy remembered times he had been asked to bring from his room the plates, cups and saucers he had accumulated there, when he had replied, 'Hmm, it's a matter of finding the time'. People's experiences of him were mulled over and thought about. We were all reminded of how Robert's time and space-frame was different from ours. Time and space, separating objects in the external and internal worlds, having been attacked by the him unable to face separateness, or frustration, were banned from existence in his mind. He was so busy in his mind with the traffic of thoughts he felt crowded by, thoughts he had very little sense of containing, that it was indeed an effort for him to find the time for activities that would involve him in the life, the time and space of the house. And yet, here he was, welcoming in essence the new resident therapist and trying to help him feel at home. Robert's behaviour towards Walter was the behaviour of someone who has a home and a place from where to invite and make welcome someone else. It was the behaviour of someone who has space for understanding what it is like to be a new group member. In the clinical meeting, even though we did not know whether Robert would eventually find the resources to 'have a flat and drive a van', we felt that it was likely that he would be able to find a space in his mind from where he would have the drive to acknowledge himself and others as existing in the same space-time context. The laughter he had shared with Maria, far from being a denigratory episode, had been a moment of realisation and of sharing the same moment in time with another human being.

This vignette illustrates a number of issues in the working together clinical group. Robert's distress was such that it stretched and tested the fabric of the Centre. Where the strands of community therapy and psychoanalytic work met, a rift threatened to open. In addition, the resident therapists felt their work de-valued when Robert refused to go to the house meetings facilitated by them. Group and individual therapists were in danger of being at each other's throats. However, under these enormous projective processes at work, though the clinical group was split, it did not fragment; it went from questioning and doubting its identity to understanding its mental state in relation to that of Robert, and so managed to contain the projective fragments of his mind.

In this case, it took the whole clinical group thinking together to understand and contain a complex situation, aggravated by a threatening relapse. In Robert's case, it was a 'leaving crisis' shared by our whole group and outside professionals who could not come together to arrange a meeting to think about him (Berke 1987), as well as a crisis precipitated by external to the patient factors: the actual departure of a member of staff. For containment to take place, the individual guest's needs had to be acknowledged and taken into account. The therapists too had to be able to question, pull apart and reformulate not only their sense of position and identity, but also the Centre's. The container had to be moulded specifically around the patient in such a way that the contents could be contained. Put differently, the whole therapist group had to avoid the temptation to bring up baby following the specialist's manual with the strictly prescribed ways of handling and times of feeding, and to develop a baby-oriented approach responding to the particular baby in question. Had Robert been able to make decisions on what was appropriate treatment for him, attend therapy meetings and be part of the social group, he would have been well on his way to recovery, perhaps not needing a residential facility but rather out-patient psychoanalytic psychotherapy. As he was, his needs were for an expanded therapeutic space that would allow for flexibility of thinking and in the treatment offered. For this to happen, the clinical group had to find a way of making the distinction between flexibility and an 'anything goes' attitude; while the latter colludes with the psychotic part of the personality of the patient, the former allows for thinking to develop rather than stagnate behind mechanically standardised rules of expected behaviour (Pierides 1998).

The bounded flexibility of the container allowed for this particular person, on that particular occasion, to have a good experience. It allowed the clinical group to have a good experience too, of doing good work as an expanded team, of thinking with and relating to a very disturbed and disturbing person for a period of time. For a while, the container and the contained, through mutual contact, grew together in what Bion (1957) refers to as a commensal relationship. Robert's needs had not been ignored by being labelled; nor had they been rejected for not fitting comfortable expectations of what the Centre offers and is about.

Unfortunately, but also predictably, the situation deteriorated once again around the next leavings, of both staff and guests. In the case of staff, it involved Cathy, Marvin's wife, who was now finishing her contract with us. The resulting upheaval in the staff group meant that for a while its containing capacities deteriorated. Like a preoccupied mother, the staff group became less sensitive and receptive to baby's needs. This happened at the time of Robert's father having left the country and his mother planning to follow by going abroad herself. The basis of Robert's life, the parental couple, literally, and in terms of the therapeutic team, was abandoning him. Similarly, our staff group was losing Cathy, and, through her marriage with Marvin, also losing both Marvin and the couple that for a long period had contributed a sense of stability to the Centre. At the same time, four of the six people of the guest group were in the process of leaving: a constant reminder of his own leaving coming-up. Under this pressure, Robert took leave of his senses in a way whose only organising principle was destructiveness. This time, it was not possible for the clinical group to contain him and he had to go to hospital for a period of time. The container that the Centre provided had been less stable in the latter period, with less to offer. The clinical group had to face once again the full impact of Robert's and our predicament, his and our limitations and relationship to reality, pain and loss; and the further injury to our omnipotence of our clinical group's holding potential deteriorating at a time of change and loss.

So what can we learn from the experience of the Arbours Crisis Centre model of working together? For working together to work, the separate professionals involved need to be clear about their specific roles or professional identities; they need to be clear about who is who in the therapeutic programme and who is doing what. This is particularly important when working with this kind of patients who have not had the opportunity to get to know who they are or indeed develop a sense of identity in themselves. It is also particularly important because the therapists working with them will, at different points in the therapy, forget, hopefully only temporarily, who they are. In the case of Robert, we had to work very hard to keep to our individual spaces when the pull was to get into each other's positions. One of the main reasons we managed to keep to our boundaries is the common history of our group. Even Robert's psychiatrist, external to the

Arbours, had happened to have been involved with the Centre previously, in an advisory capacity and, having had knowledge of our work, was helpful and supportive.

Obviously, this is rarely the case with other professionals referring patients to the Centre, or with other professionals in the mental health world working together with the same patient. In such cases, making oneself and one's work known as well as learning about other professionals' work through professional networks, publications, attendance at conferences are vital. Information, understanding and communication help bridge the gap between professionals who learn from experience as well as from each other's experience, so that when on the firing line of their patient's projections they have a reality to consult with. One might say, using Hinshelwood's (1994) term from group psychotherapy, that shared awareness of each other's work forms a public, to the professionals, 'reflective space' where reflectiveness and understanding circulates and from which they can replenish a receptive state of reverie suitable to the needs of the patient and the treatment. In such a mental space although splitting occurs it diminishes and the realisation of our common aims re-emerges. We are all in the same boat together.

To psychotherapists, the importance of thinking psychodynamically is clear. Where it needs to be emphasised is in situations in which different professionals, with different ways of working and agendas, come together to work with the same patient. For that 'team', in the helping professions, however diverse and perhaps unrelated it may appear to be, there is need for communication about the patient and sharing of experience. There is no doubt that there will be conflict, but the patient can only be held when that conflict can be expressed in a contained way, thought about and understood. If this coming together does not happen, the patient's need for evacuation gets satisfied, but she remains in the same, and often worse, predicament. Her projected distress, not modified at best, distorted at worst, returns to give rise to bizarre perceptions of her by the professionals in the mental health field who then feel they have further proof of her untreatability.

CHAPTER TEN

THE PRIVATE PUBLIC THERAPIST

Susie Orbach

Susie Orbach's interests as a psychotherapist and writer have centred around psychoanalysis, gender, counter-transference and the body, psychoanalysis and the public sphere, the construction of femininity and emotional literacy.

Her first book Fat is a Feminist Issue *is now twenty-two years old. It was followed by two books on eating problems, three on women's psychology with Luise Eichenbaum, and two collections of her Guardian columns called* What's Really Going on Here *and* Towards Emotional Literacy. *Her latest book is a series of imagined tales from therapy told from the psychotherapist's point of view, called* The Impossibility of Sex.

In 1976 she co-founded The Women's Therapy Centre, and, in 1981, The Women's Therapy Centre Institute, a training institute in New York.

She has a PhD from the psychoanalysis unit at UCL, an honorary Doctorate of Letters from Stony Brook University in New York, is currently a Visiting Professor at the London School of Economics, and is an affiliate member of the Society of Psychoanalytical Marital Psychotherapists.

Susie Orbach writes this chapter using her own experience of being a well-known figure, in order to explore the effect this has on her clients. She tells us how her own struggle with her 'little corner of fame' has helped her to be less fascinated by it in others, and shows us how her own thoughtfulness and understanding of it has made it available for use in the transference. She reflects upon the professional matrix which she holds within the consulting room and which is formed by the two aspects, private and public, of her therapeutic self. While the private therapist and her relation to her patient are contained and accessible to thought and interpretation, the public therapist can be experienced at any time through the mass media, and can impinge on patients who wish to keep her as their own. Her public self is also open to critical or envious attack in outer reality, and she writes about how this may affect the patient's negative transference within the consulting room. On the other hand, she describes how having a public persona can help people who are themselves in the public arena to make good use of her as a therapist. Susie Orbach's contribution to this book is welcomed for both her public and private therapeutic self, and of course for the combination of the two, which adds another dimension to our matrix.

* * *

Psychotherapists often enquire how my patients and I 'handle' my public profile. Embedded in the question is a sense that there is something not quite kosher about my public activities as a writer or an advocate for psychotherapy. Indeed, so strong is that feeling, that when it comes time for my publishers to promote a new book of mine, I, who like most writers suffer acute unease about the unpleasant work of promotion, try to resist the demand to be interviewed by melding my own discomfort to the (imagined?) judgmental voices who criticise those whose professional activities take them into the public sphere.

I have had a column in *The Guardian* for eight years, I broadcast regularly, have written about therapy for *New Woman* for five years and I have published several books for a general readership to do with psychotherapy, psychoanalysis, women's psychology, eating problems and the relationship between the public and private spheres of life. In addition, when Luise Eichenbaum and I started the Women's Therapy Centre in 1976, we contacted local and national newspapers, radio and television to disseminate information about the project and make it accessible to those who might be interested in using it. This public approach to the psychotherapeutic attracted and made possible the uptake of psychotherapy for many who would have been be put off by, or not even known how to find the discreet brass nameplate of the Institute of Psycho-Analysis's clinic.

Over the years I have made several different sorts of response to the question that psychotherapists have posed about my public profile. Sometimes I have answered that I've grown up as a psychotherapist with it. There hasn't been a before and an after. My professional life in Britain started with the Women's Therapy Centre which attracted considerable attention because it highlighted an area of experience that had previously gone unrecognised. When my first book was published and became a best-seller, I did go through a fundamental change in the level of personal recognition I received (and a great deal of personal difficulty around this which required considerable psychological work on my part), but as far as the people I was seeing in therapy were concerned, a good third of them had no idea that I had published a book, a few felt they should develop eating problems to be more interesting to me (the book was on women's relationship to food, fat and femininity) and several others had responses that required exploring in the therapy relationship.

If I reflect on my present practice, my patients divide into these same three categories. Several have or had no idea that I have a public profile. Although for a few years between 1994 and 1997, my persona outside the consulting room could not escape the attention of my patients, because from time to time my house was under siege by photographers and journalists, this has now passed. Obviously in this period there were some references to who I was in the world by all my patients. But in the last eighteen months, my sense continues that among new patients, a third are absolutely unaware of my public persona. A few discover during the course of therapy that I do write and broadcast and are interested in that, and a few come to me having sought me out because of my work outside the consulting room, which then becomes a feature of the analytic relationship, a matrix which becomes more visible as we try to understand its meaning in the room.

Sometimes, of course, sensing more than curiosity when a colleague asks me about 'how my patients handle the problem of having a well-known therapist', I become defensive. I feel deeply relieved to be able to remind them of Winnicott's and Guntrip's BBC broadcasts. What surprises me in my gravitation to this historical fact is that both myself and my interlocutor require this. I have taken on some guilt about my desire to communicate the beauty of what our profession has learnt, to give back to people what we have been given in the consulting room. The resort to respected figures in the analytic world is a way to assuage this guilt, as though I have committed some misdemeanour. Meanwhile, I believe that my questioner feels reassured that there is a precedent, a way for him or her to think about the phenomenon apart from their feelings towards me.

In truth, the issue is complex and extremely interesting to me at a clinical and technical level. There are a variety of experiences that can occur for a patient during the course of a therapy in relation to my 'well-knowness'. My experience, does not, I believe thread through into a theoretical position or understanding; what I have to say is simply a set of reflections. In general, I view my public profile and its significance in the therapy as another sort of lens for looking at aspects of the clinical encounter and the issues that are both embedded within it and can impinge upon it. However because several of my patients or former patients are well known themselves, my own position does offer some useful insights into the experience and mental representations of 'the famous'.

A patient, herself a beginning therapist, would tell me about the negative (mainly nasty) things her friends (also therapists) said about me (friends who knew she was seeing me). It was always shocking and not something I could immediately respond to within the transference-counter-transference. I would feel socked in the stomach, privately furious at the behaviour of her friends, surprised that she would allow them to talk this way in her presence, as though I were simply a piece of public property and not someone with whom she had an important intimate relationship. When I could recover from what felt like an assault, I would wonder, sometimes to myself, sometimes with her, about her involvement in these attacks on her therapy and herself and also wonder what she couldn't manage directly between us.

This use of me was, I came to understand in time, a way in which the problematic aspects of her attachment could be expressed. A seductive father had barely mitigated the effects of a narcissistically treacherous and wounding mother, and in her attempt to make a relationship with me, an older, more senior psychotherapist, she was trying to manage the moments of hope she experienced in the therapy without them terrifying her and making her feel quite mad. Her adhesion to her bad object relations was such that anything at odds with it had nowhere to go. As long as she could hate me, or have others hate me, she could feel safe enough to eke out some small moments of positive connection inside the consulting room. These rare moments were so overpowered by her terror around her developing attachment to me that she sought security through the emotionally known route of hate.

This patient's use of my outside-the-therapy persona as public property which was being kicked, savaged and insulted, was extremely painful. I was also susceptible in the counter-transference to some guilt that I had somehow injured her by being who I was. I had to keep reminding myself – and once in a while reflect on this fact to her—that she was in the profession and had chosen me; that her choice might have a significance for her. (For example, she might have hoped that I would especially understand her; she might have felt that someone who had a large presence could contain her; she might have been attempting to confirm that no-one, however experienced or well regarded, could be of any use to her.) Although in common with any patient, a training patient knows not where or how her transferences will unfold in any given therapeutic situation, nevertheless I found it curious that my public persona was quite such an issue. If she discovered that I was speaking at a conference, she would be alarmed or highly critical, as though the professional territory which we inhabited should somehow be forbidden for me. There was an attempt to control me or at least censure me and in the counter-transference I felt accused, as though I had done something wrong by having a contribution to make to our field. It was as though she needed to see whether I would withstand her attempts to denigrate me and limit my capacities and activities outside of the consulting room.

She was not yet a sufficiently experienced therapist to know that post-qualification encounters between training therapists, trainees and former trainees are common, and even if she could conceive of such an idea, it was of no help to her, for I had become a figure who could magnetise her hate. The possibility that my presence outside the consulting room could ever be consoling was beyond consideration.

I felt on my guard to be vigilant and meticulous about my own hurt responses to the meanings she was creating in splitting me in this way. If she had been a patient who had divided up her positive and negative feelings between the private and public aspects of our relationship, I would have found the situation more manageable. It was the fact that hate was her idiom and that it permeated both parts of the divide, that made it so terribly difficult. It wasn't possible to hope that she could simply integrate her hate with her more positive feelings and have those co-exist inside of her both in relation to me as therapist and me as outside-the-therapy persona. That would have negated what had salience for her around attachment. My struggle was to recognise the hate as what she would have brought to any therapy, whether or not the therapist had a public presence.

With this patient, I faced the temptation to describe her defence structure as one marked by envious attack. And although descriptively, this was without a doubt the case, it wasn't a sufficient answer to her intrapsychic or interpsychic struggles. Such an explanation would simply have alleviated the transference situation for me, rather than constituting a therapeutic understanding for her. We had to work harder to see the ways in which her desire for something good for herself was itself entwined with powerful anti-libidinal impulses (Fairbairn 1955). Our work was to enable her to experience her continuing allegiance to an inner set of relationships which had so failed her. With this in view she then had the possibility to let go and mourn. Her use of my public persona then had the potential to conform less to the menace in which she habitually lived, and become more simply a fact about who I was, rather than an attack on her.

By contrast, there is the patient who wished to protect me. Or perhaps I should say wished to be protected from me, or the me outside of the consulting room. Although this patient was one who did know of my reputation before she saw me, during the course of therapy she has found my public appearances surprisingly disturbing and disagreeable.

Andrea grew up in a family in which her father was a clergyman who played a prominent and very visible role in the community. He was greatly respected in the small town in which they lived but he wasn't often home and Andrea and her sisters fed off the attention they received from others as his daughters. It wasn't that he was a caring man in the community and another way at home, but he was infrequently at home so that much of her relationship with him was by proxy. She admired him for being so wise and well respected but there was something missing. She wanted more of him. She was left at home, as she saw it, with mum and the endless boring visitors to the vicarage to whom she had to show kindness and be nice. Andrea was brought up to be selfless and caring for others and she was, but there was a part of her that hankered for a more direct relationship with her father rather than what she described as this 'truncated and reflected' view of him.

Andrea was initially very pleased that I was well-known. It gave her a sense of continuity with her experience of her parents and she found it protective. But she became very distraught when I turned up in her newspaper or unexpectedly on her television screen discussing this matter or that. She wanted me as she knew me, with all my attention riveted on her. Indeed, so distraught was she that I was commenting on matters other than her that she asked me to please inform her, where possible, of my appearances, so that she might have the opportunity to decide whether she wanted to see me or not.

I was not adverse to her request. I could well understand how disruptive it might be to be watching television with your husband or friends and have your therapist pop up, unannounced in front of you. Why should one's private relationship with one's therapist intrude in such a manner?

As we were in the midst of discussing this, a particularly unpleasant profile of me appeared. The profile writer was snide, discussed me as cold and included much about my personal history that she had researched and thrown at me in the interview. It was my first experience of being done over in an interview and I was rather shaken. It is one thing not to like the emphasis of an interview, but not to recognise oneself was disconcerting and unpleasant. I also felt that the information in the interview was presented in such a way that 'facts' about me were disclosed which were extremely personal and which I had not yet told my children. They were certainly not issues I would have chosen to have the public or my patients know, not because they were shameful but because they were not—told that way—anyone's business to tell. Nor were they the kind of information that in the ordinary course of things would be disclosed to a patient or 'discovered by a patient'.

Serendipitously then, Andrea's wish to know when I might appear in the press or on television and radio coincided with this unpleasant profile. She had not in fact read it. Her husband, mindful of how much distress the random popping up of her therapist caused her, informed her that there was a negative article about me in her newspaper, thus giving her the choice to read it or not. In the course of our discussions around this article and her general wish to be forewarned about my appearances outside the consulting room, she was able to disclose how much she felt a need to both be protected from me and to protect me. We explored together what it was in her that I needed protecting from. It transpired that she really needed me to be hers and having me with opinions outside of the consulting room or sharing me with a wider public was just too painful. It re-evoked aspects of her father that she wasn't ready to work on as yet. She wanted to have me as her therapist and nothing else. She did not feel sufficiently robust to have me exist both for her and for others in this visible way in the world. And she did not feel able to be angry at me.

In the event, I did agree to tell Andrea when I knew I was going to be on television. I was, and remain, unsure about whether this was the correct thing to do. My concern in acceding to her request was that I would be constantly intruding to tell her about my sometimes frequent appearances. At the same time it felt as though she could only get away from me by being informed. Another concern was that she would worry that she was asking me to think about her whenever I was broadcasting and that she might feel some guilt about this. Some of these issues we discussed and others we didn't because it either didn't seem possible or because she was in the middle of other issues that were more pertinent to her. Just because she had raised this agenda didn't mean that we would pursue it as thoroughly as I might have thought useful because that in itself seemed like I'd be imposing. In other words, I already felt somewhat culpable for causing this distress within the therapy and although we therapists are good at rationalising whatever occurs by saying that it is grist for the therapeutic mill, nevertheless I did feel that my agenda had been superimposed on her transference in a way that was unfortunate and I had some responsibility for not letting that take over her therapy. If Andrea had been in three times weekly therapy I imagine we would have explored these issues more fully but without that luxury we got as far with it as we could.

In Andrea's case, my presence in the world became a major feature of the transference but it could only be dealt with to a certain extent. My external presence highlighted and encapsulated certain key issues with her father but again I believe that we would have been able to work on this material in a different way if I hadn't had a public persona. What was interesting and perhaps not unsurprising was that she didn't read the negative profile whereas several other of my patients did, and this placed them in a dilemma for they now felt inclined to comment on it one way or another. In certain cases, it opened up the way for them to discuss issues in our relationship that had previously felt off limits, for others it was a chance to express their concern for me and their devastation that their therapist should be written about in this way. For some patients who could imagine or surmise that I might have been hurt by the profile, the significant therapeutic issues revolved around their perception of my vulnerability or its opposite, my imperviousness to maliciousness.

All patients who commented on the profile found it distasteful. In two patients, however, the sense that I had not been able to protect myself from such a vicious write-up produced a response of considerable contempt for me and for the fact that I could have 'allowed' myself to be so vulnerable. I found such a response intriguing. It was as though they had needed to see me as somehow invulnerable, and that recognition that I was neither invulnerable nor omnipotent forced forward into the therapy their personal issues around their own grandiosity and narcissism. Imagining themselves in my place, they were sure they never would have succumbed to such a negative profile. They believed that they would have had sufficient ability to either squash such a journalist or that such a profile could never—had they had the opportunity to have been written about—have evoked such negativity. They maintained a belief that they would be able to do it better and that I had failed them in having permitted this portrait of myself to appear.

Again, it would have been easy enough to take their attack on me as an expression of their envy, which indeed it was, but the issues involved demanded further understanding if we were not to stay in a position in which their narcissism operated as a successful defence against their vulnerability. Behind their contempt of me was the most terrible fear that I had been diminished and that I was now a nothing; someone who could not withstand either their hatred of me, or their or others' attacks on me. These two patients' difficulty in countenancing my vulnerability was of course indicative of their own difficulties and anxieties. They had not yet found a way to manage their own frailties other than by expelling them. They had extreme difficulty with the needy or pained parts of themselves which were almost invariably managed through anger. In their imagining of my response to the profile, they were disgusted that I should have put myself in a situation in which I was vulnerable and then they were further dismayed that they had put themselves in the hands of a therapist who could allow herself to be vulnerable. Their need for me to be inhuman—to be incapable of being hurt—gave us additional ballast for our understanding of how difficult any kind of need was for them personally. With these two patients, their own distress created a sadism within them. While they had contempt for my having been done down in this profile, they also rather enjoyed being able to tell me how dreadful I was for having let this occur. I hadn't actually seen their sadism in action, or much known about it, so having it appear within the therapy relationship was extremely useful. I believe it would have come into the transference-counter-transference at some point, but that the fact of the article propelled it forward. The article was used in the evolution of the transference, rather than my public presence having caused this particular transferential relationship to appear.

This leads me to discuss the patient who has found her or his way to me because they have read some of my work or heard me speak about psychotherapy. Although far less tyrannical, the range of positive responses to me-outside-the-therapy is something that also has to be negotiated, like the presence of a third party. For some people this can be quite straightforward. They have come to, or have been referred to me, as someone who is known, and therefore by implication trustworthy. The external acknowledgement of me as a therapist provides a structure of safety in which the work of the therapy can occur. In the course of their therapy they may encounter feelings about whether they are deserving of my time, since I must be so much in demand. They wonder about how long they can take up this place with me, how many others are waiting to replace them who are more deserving of help, more interesting, more troubled. They feel insecure and they discuss and conceptualise their insecurity vis-à-vis their right of access to me, as they perceive me as someone who has multiple important pulls on her time.

Although it would be easy enough to see this phenomenon concretely, as an expression of my actual position in the world, in fact the very same issues come up for patients of my supervisees, as well as for my patients who have no knowledge of my 'other life'. So this aspect of my existence in the public world is simply made use of in the development of the transference. It has to be addressed, and indeed as we do so it throws up many important issues around entitlement, recognition, and dependency, as one might anticipate. These are issues that I believe would come up in any therapy but which are framed slightly differently because of my public persona and as a result then provide an interesting solution for the individual struggling with them.

In other words, in the therapy the very fact of my having a public persona and, in the patients' minds, many other and often more important pulls on my attention, means that when they can recognise that they are also important to me, this recognition can have a particular intensity to it. At a technical level it is as though my presence in the external world highlights and augments the issues around recognition, polarising my recognition against their felt insignificance. Thus when patients can begin to believe that they are well regarded within the therapy relationship, when they can trust that they matter to me and are not insignificant or keeping their place illegitimately, this can have an intensified effect.

Akin to this issue is the way in which my public persona can come to represent an absent or elsewhere engaged parental object, while my presence and constancy within the therapy room offers the option of working on the internal object who has an external subjectivity (Benjamin 1995) and who can withstand the attacks that are foisted on that external subjectivity. One of the developmental tasks we and our patients face is the struggle to differentiate, to recognise the other, to see the other as separate from us rather than some kind of extension of us; an object of our own making, or under our fantasised control. As we work to enable our patients to achieve the capacity to have separated rather than merged attachments (Eichenbaum & Orbach 1988) we are constantly caught in the transference vacillations between the attempt to remake us in the way that their original objects have been experienced, and the attempt to experience us anew, as a new relationship which brings forth the potential for a different form of relating. My public persona does not change this issue, which is one that would come up in any therapy, it simply focuses its exploration in a different direction. It may precociously stimulate the issues of recognition, entitlement, abandonment, and availability, but I cannot be sure.

Another group of patients for whom there is a significance to my public persona are those individuals who are well regarded in their own field, may even be famous outside of it and who have complicated feelings about their own self-worth which involve feelings of doubt, feelings of fraudulence and a worry about how the various bits of them, the confident and the insecure, fit together. It has seemed to me, that such individuals can bring with them a sense of needing to see someone 'big' enough, that's to say, publicly regarded or known to be esteemed in their field, to match their own degree of recognition. I have several times encountered the experience of a well- esteemed or powerful individual in their field, who finds an initial and even an ongoing sense of comfort from the fact of my well-knowness. They don't—as one might imagine—project on to me a sense that I am as self doubting, fraudulent or divided, or that I feel as shaky as they do. Instead, they seem to see me as both senior in my field and sorted out. If they are competent and good at what they do in their own field of endeavour, they anticipate that I can perform for them as they do for others, and that I will be good at it. There are several points worth mentioning in regard to this group of patients.

The first and not inconsiderable issue is that being well-known is a peculiar thing in and of itself. Many people have a kind of prurient interest in fame, at whatever level the fame is (Rose 1998, Orbach 1997). The 'famed' person becomes someone other, a different category of person. They are of interest to others, their views or actions have a particular currency, they become public property. In many different ways they are scrutinised and looked at as well as looked up to and looked down on. They become the carriers for a vast range of projections, some of which they are aware of and some of which they are oblivious to. Nevertheless despite their own status, they regard others who have achieved a similar status as valuable. They project on to other well regarded people that they know or encounter, attributes similar to those of which they are themselves recipients. In other words they don't have a particularly developed understanding of fame. It works on them as it works on everyone, they are as caught up in it as are those who aren't famous. Just think of the comments of famous movie stars who encounter their peers on the set and who are reported as being so thrilled about it. This is partly a respect for craft but equally the workings of enthraldom to fame. Thus with a well known therapist they project a certain sense of safety: the feeling that they can trust me since I am seen as a kind of iconic good therapist. If this projection on to me can be explored, then their experience of trusting me, can be a precursor to a trusting of themselves. This, of course, is to run ahead to the latter part of a successful therapy when the impediments to trust have been deconstructed.

Of course, internally the well-known person may have or develop an extremely complex relation to self. They were once someone who was not particularly known and they have developed into someone who has now become known. For such patients, the transition to being well-known or famous creates a kind of personal disjuncture. Sometimes this is alienated and dystonic even though it may be wanted. In extreme cases they can regard their well-esteemed public persona as a valued self or they can relate to it as an idealised aspect of self almost akin to an idealised object. They require the regard they receive because they have little alternate access to good feelings about themselves. Their 'famous' self, operating as a good object for them, is both tantalising and reassuring. But at the same time, the split within them can make them feel ashamed of or unable to psychically negotiate with the parts of themselves which feel shaky, fraudulent or not so admirable. One of the things that is quite consoling in having a therapist who is well-known is the sense that the therapist need not be pruriently interested in them as a famous person. Their fame is of interest because of what it means to them, but that fame need not become a burden or be of a particular fascination to the therapist and hence to the patient.

I mention this point because I have encountered colleagues who have felt intimidated or just strangely caught up by having a well-known person such as a writer, an actor, a scientist, a model or a politician in treatment. The 'fame' of the patient can unsettle the therapist so that they are unable to explore it. They talk about the famous patient with a special reverence or protectiveness. They feel they derive a certain kudos because of the social standing of their patient. Perhaps the objective status of the individual in therapy intimidates the therapist. Perhaps the therapist finds their patient's fame extra-ordinary, which of course it is, but I have noticed a reluctance in the therapist to take on her or his counter-transference around this issue as a means to think about the peculiar experience of the patient. They are affected by the 'fame' but don't quite dare to think about it. This reluctance can unwittingly reproduce in the therapy the same difficulties that the individual can experience around their recognition outside of the therapy. The patient can be held in a kind of magical social position in which the disturbing and confusing aspects of their fame are occluded from the therapy, as though the fame had not become a salient feature of who they are. This kind of response on the part of the therapist can become an obstacle to the therapy, an unconscious part of the transference counter-transference relationship when the well-knowness resides in the patient but not the therapist.

A more substantial issue with well-known patients who feel that they compartmentalise themselves and don't quite hang together as a whole—despite their recognition in their own field—is that they often carry a deep distrust towards self and others. In so far as they feel they have got away with something or that their recognition is undeserved, or that they are waiting to be found out, they can feel a kind of contempt for those who take their elevation quite seriously. This would be problematic enough, but inevitably there is a simultaneous need to continue to be regarded in this way. They do not yet trust that they can be recognised for who they are, whatever the level of their accomplishment, as well as for the accomplishment that has created public regard. For a period of the therapy we have to work on various levels at once. We have to recognise those psychological imperatives that enabled them or indeed impelled them to pursue excellence or recognition (or whatever variant it is). To do so can be deeply relieving for it can open the way to work on the underbelly of that need and to an engagement with why recognition was required in that form. This will often almost inevitably turn (for patients that is, maybe not for other 'famous' people) to the feeling of disregard, of not being seen that may inform their thrust to be seen and heard by others outside of their personal milieu.

As we try to work on the delicate balance between their psychological imperatives and their sense of fraudulence or guilt for having acclaim, there is one possible advantage to them of my relative knowness. They don't, I believe, have to be looking after me to make sure that I am not envious or admiring, or peculiar about their recognition. They can experience me enjoying them and their accomplishments enough to trust that they, in all their personas, can be understood and looked at without this provoking shame. The job I have of trying to bring the disparate bits of them together is facilitated by my being well-known in that they can feel safe to explore their fame within the therapeutic space. Also, of course, they can discuss, again without much shame, the peculiar states of mind that recognition itself evokes in oneself and others. Although I believe this would be possible in any therapy, the fact of my public persona is somewhat helpful here because I believe they invest me with a knowledge about these phenomena which enables them to feel less reticent about raising what can be rather embarrassing issues. While these embarrassing issues might be raised in any therapy they might not be heard quite as accurately.

At the level of unconscious identification, I believe that I am sensitive to the peculiarities of fame. My 'fame', such as it is, has come from a combination of starting the Women's Therapy Centre, from publishing and from broadcasting. The ways in which this has separated me off from my colleagues and my prepublished sense of self has been disconcerting. For a long time I felt very uneasy about being 'known'. I was happy for my ideas to be disseminated, I was happy to have a platform for them, but I did experience a changed relationship to myself. I worked on this issue with my intimates and in my analysis so that I neither had to disavow the recognition I had gained nor absorb all the projections I received, especially from colleagues in the field. This worked well enough and I gradually came to terms with the peculiarities of my position.

At some point in the last few years however, my profile was raised. I felt in this instance that it was completely unwarranted and unwelcome. It wasn't something I felt I could easily work through as it had no place to settle. It had little to do with me per se and it had a very negative effect. The only consolation I had was that I could better understand the experience of patients, like actors or journalists who are newscasters, who are known not because their work is intrinsically better than that of other actors or journalists but because it is on television and therefore seen by a huge audience. The difficulties they experience with their relation to self is something of which I have a taste of understanding which I believe helps me in my work with them.

I do a great deal of referring. I don't know if this is a result of having a public profile as a psychotherapist or whether I would have found this niche anyway. Although when anyone rings or writes to ask me for therapy, I make it rather plain that I am unavailable for regular therapy but could do a consultation and make a referral, I think there are transference implications of referring which have an impact on the patient as well as on the therapist to whom I refer. These need to be explored if the therapist, especially, is to feel supported in the work that he or she will do with the patient.

Consultation is important because it sets the tone of what therapy is. It is an anchor for the patient. If the referral doesn't work out, they may return for further consultation. I have become perhaps overscrupulous in the consultation process in an attempt not to be too much of a presence myself. That of course is not straightforward because the very act of consultation involves facilitation and active engagement. One is not only endeavouring to make the prospective patient as comfortable as she or he can be to say what is on her mind and in her heart, one is also assessing suitability for psychoanalytic psychotherapy. Of necessity, the assessment interview is different from an on-going psychotherapy. The therapist must gently and skilfully probe into areas of life in a way that the patient may not have considered before. At the same time, the therapist is giving the patient a taste of what therapy is, thus taking him or her in new directions. This can be exciting for patients because, amidst the pain and anguish that has driven them to seek therapy, they are feeling understood or, more accurately, feeling the possibility of being understood. This initial interview can be thought of as a kind of courtship. The patient seducing with her or his story, the therapist showing what the two of them can do with what the patient has presented. The therapist is employing her or his talents, taking the trusting part of the patient and encouraging her or him to consider established beliefs in a different way. It can be an exhilarating hour for patients and a memory that stays with them for a long time. Because of this, the transference to the referring therapist can be acute, but if the receiving therapist, without feeling inadequate, can allow the patient to explore it, the referral can be extremely successful.

Some prospective patients express open disappointment about not being able to have therapy with me. I can sometimes hear tears on the telephone when I tell them the position as though it has taken whatever they have to make the telephone call and the effort is dashed by my reply. It is not the case however that when I have met the individual for the consultation she or he is unable to make a connection to a colleague to whom I make a referral. The referral may work well and the individual in question may articulate at the beginning of the therapy any feelings she or he may have about being passed on, being passed over or referred to just the right person. The ability to express such feelings to the therapist is a hopeful sign that the therapy can give voice to the salient issues in the patient's inner experience. What is intriguing and is really unexplored is not so much my presence in the mind of the patient and thus in her therapy, but my presence in the mind of the therapist to whom the patient has been referred.

When I follow up or speak to the therapists to whom I have referred I can sometimes catch a wan expression of discomfort that they themselves feel that they might be second best, not chosen by the patient and somehow less able than I would be to help this particular patient. If the therapist is in supervision with me, we are in a position to explore these concerns. From my perspective, I would not have referred the patient if I didn't highly value the therapist. That is a minimum condition for a referral. But in fact, so powerful is this issue of public recognition, that it can skew professional relationships or impact on the therapy of another within the invisible matrix. I know that the issues I am talking about now are not absent from any collegial referral. The receiving therapist may welcome the referral source but be wary lest the prospective patient is disappointed. The receiving therapist may feel a set of expectations transmitted to her from the referring therapist and from the patient. But I think there is an extra inflection in a referral from someone like me who is publicly identified with therapy.

So what am I saying? For the most part I think my knowness in the public sphere and its discussion within the therapy is an artefact, a medium for the transference rather than constitutive of the therapies I engage in. Despite this, it absolutely cannot be ignored, because it does in fact impinge on or shape aspects of the therapeutic encounter and through an exploration of the meanings the patient brings to it, much can be worked on for that particular patient. It is a matrix that does well in becoming visible for at least two-thirds of the patients that I see in therapy. For a particular class of patients who are themselves well-known or well-regarded in and or outside the field, my knowness would seem to constitute a benefit. I believe that my own understandings of the interpersonal and intrapsychic processes pertaining to 'fame', enables me to bring another dimension of understanding to this peculiar phenomenon of late twentieth century life where fame is desired by so many, and visited on (to a larger or smaller extent) quite a considerable number of the people whom I have seen in therapy. My own struggle with my little corner of 'fame' works to help me be less fascinated by it in others (although not less fascinated by how they feel about it and what they make of it). This offers the possibility that my approach to the patient can have a kind of neutrality – an invisible but perhaps benign matrix that allows me to think about this often vexing experience or moment of transition in an individual's life.

CHAPTER ELEVEN

THE SUPERVISOR AS THE HIDDEN CO-THERAPIST IN PSYCHOTHERAPY WITH COUPLES

Evelyn Cleavely

Evelyn began her professional life training and working as a State Registered Nurse, then entered the Probation Service, and served as a Senior Probation Officer in Inner London. Evelyn then obtained a staff post with the Institute of Marital Studies (now the Tavistock Marital Studies Institute [TMSI]) where she became a senior marital psychotherapist and the Institute's Training Co-ordinator. In 1989 Evelyn took a planned retirement and was invited by the TMSI to chair a Steering Group to set up and launch a professional body, the Society of Psychoanalytical Marital Psychotherapists, to support their graduates, maintain and develop standards of practice, and promote psychoanalytic marital psychotherapy. Since 1989 Evelyn has pursued the application of psychoanalysis to the understanding and management of organisational behaviour and has worked on and directed group relations programmes in this country and abroad.

In this chapter Evelyn Cleavely draws upon her long experience as a supervisor to define what she understands as the supervisor's most important work—knowing about the unconscious of the 'couple-patient' through the medium of her counter-transference. She describes a particular function of the supervisor as a sharer with the therapist of counter-transference experience, which gives access to the 'couple-patient's' unconscious phantasy. In this process, she proposes, the supervisor becomes a 'hidden co-therapist' to the couple, while also being available to understand and support her supervisee. She describes a 'dialogue in continuous interaction' between supervisee and supervisor, and suggests that within the containment of this dialogue a therapist can begin to 'think the unthinkable' on behalf of the couple with whom he or she is working. As we become aware of Evelyn Cleavely's 'critical and compassionate way' we can see how it enables the therapist to bring her clients for supervision in a way which builds on Freud's discovery, in 1919, how 'the Ucs of one human being can react upon that of another without passing through the Cs'. Through the process of supervision she makes conscious particular aspects of the client's relationship, and makes visible to us yet another facet of the invisible matrix.

* * *

In this chapter I consider the function of supervision in the varied journeyings of therapeutic relationships. I focus centrally upon psychotherapy with couples, although a great deal of what I explore is applicable to supervision in general. The thoughts and concepts which I offer in this chapter have involved a critical and compassionate examination of my own supervisory practice and are generally related to the clinical work of senior and experienced psychoanalytic marital psychotherapists.

I am indebted to my friend and colleague Peter Fullerton, for the title of this paper. Some years ago, at his request, I provided supervision, on a weekly basis, to his single-handed work with a couple, and during these sessions he began to refer to me as his 'hidden co-therapist'. I was captured by his phrase as I felt it accurately described the kind of supervision I valued for myself and always desire to offer to my supervisees.

Co-therapy, like any relationship between two people, may be a partnership. Partnership does not necessarily imply equality of status, or level of experience or even maturity but it does demand equality of commitment: commitment to the task and of working with the consequences of one's actions in relation to that task. Only this kind of commitment frees one from the captivity of having to get it right and the paralysing fear of being wrong.

I and my supervisee form a partnership which implies working at the therapeutic task from a standpoint of 'equality' even although there are differences of seniority, levels of experience and knowledge. It is not that I am more clever than my supervisee, although he/she and I might be collusively drawn into thinking that at times, just as a therapist and patient are sometimes given to believing that the therapist actually knows more of the patient's problem than the patient does himself. Neither of us could have got there easily, if at all, without the other.

To get there, wherever that is, demands suffering a process of interdependency which involves working 'in the dark' from a place where knowing and not knowing meet together in anxious but potentially creative uncertainty. It means thinking about supervision as a meeting point between two people who bring their differences to a shared commitment to the same desire, that is: to understand a couple's dilemma in pursuit of their shared struggle toward growth and development.

A play on the word supervision suggests a 'superior being'; one possessing the capacity for exercising 'vision', insight, wisdom and imagination. It contains the deep (but ambivalently held) yearning within all of us to continue learning. Some of my supervisees have had more extensive training than I and certainly possess more 'little grey cells'. And when, from my knowledge of their work, I note that their therapeutic skills go beyond my own, I know I experience both joy and envy. But in saying that, I do not dismiss or diminish what I provide in my supervision of their psychoanalytic therapy with couples. Although the supposed 'superiority' of the supervisor to the supervisee is often not borne out by reality when supervising senior therapists, the concept of a 'superior being' is developed as a myth, (often in the face of, and as a way of managing helplessness). Such a myth is often collusively held to and cherished by both supervisor and supervisee.

A myth may often become fixed and related to as an 'absolute truth', a rigidly held belief-system which robs the myth of its essential meaning and its power to direct the way toward integration. Related to as 'absolute truth' a myth serves its defensive purpose (that is, the management of the unpalatable), rather than its potential for embracing the unpalatable, and transforming the way we are and our relationships with others. The development of a myth, while defending us from the unthinkable, (for example, feelings of helplessness), at the same time, paradoxically, offers a way to think about and transform the unthinkable—so long as it is related to as a myth and not an 'absolute truth'.

Alongside the many 'collective' myths that human beings through time have generated, we each of us develop our own personal myths, which we cherish, which we live by, and which colour and influence the relationships we form and the way we view ourselves and the world around us. Couples in their relationship together develop shared myths in which repressed aspects of their individual inner worlds find a meeting point in the other; a place for, and of, continuous interaction. Access to a myth's transforming powers is gained through a process of dialogue. Joseph Campbell (1968), in his fascinating book *Myths To Live By* writes of Jung's definition of this: 'a dialogue by way of symbolic forms put forth from the unconscious mind and recognised by the conscious in continuous interaction'.

It is this concept of 'dialogue in continuous interaction' between conscious and unconscious that I find helpful in thinking about couple relationships and my supervisory practice. It is only as I take up my role as supervisor and my supervisee her role that we have any hope of engaging in a 'dialogue in continuous interaction' that will lead to 'super' 'vision' in relation to the work being presented.

To illustrate the meaning the 'dialogue in continuous interaction' has for both therapy and supervision I share my thoughts concerning the use of interpretations. Charles Rycroft (1968) begins his definition of interpretation as 'The process of elucidating and expounding the *meaning* of something abstruse, obscure, etc.' This implies that interpretation is an intellectual activity by the therapist which is received or rejected by the intellect of the patient. I have no argument with this definition, nor would I question the efficacy of the activity: it is the process I wish to draw attention to.

The kind of interpretative work that I believe can really make a connection to the unconscious regions of the couple patient's world, and which has a 'ripple effect on the whole' arises from exploration by the therapist of the emotional experience of her counter-transference. The intellectual work of exploring that emotional experience leads to an interpretation, which inevitably in my experience brings forth a further counter-transference experience in the therapist. It is *this* experience that leads to a further highlighting of the fragment of the couple's shared unconscious phantasy that it is necessary to confront.

This, of course, happens also in supervision. The supervisee's response to my comments often arouses an emotional response in me which when examined helps to refine the original interpretation and offer further meaning. In other words, it is not only the interpretation itself that is so important but the meaning hidden in the response to it, and further highlighted in the therapist's or supervisor's emotional experience in relation to that response, whatever it is—whether feeling ignored, dismissed as useless, as a persecutor, or as having got it right.

Necessary to allow this 'dialogue in continuous interaction' to take place is a willingness to engage with the dark forces within: within ourselves, within the couples who come seeking our therapeutic help, within the transference in the therapeutic relationship and in the supervisory alliance. A form of healing or transformation begins to take place when the struggles in those darkest places within find a sympathetic ear, an ear (which can be our own) that has the courage to hear the unthinkable and allow it to become a thought, to hear the unnameable and allow it to be named, to hear the unspeakable and allow it to be spoken; an ear that can hear what causes the heart to tremble and experience fear; an ear that is not overwhelmed by what it hears, and hears compassionately without judgement of another or oneself. Such is the nature and quality of this therapeutic hearing that firstly it is only possible in the containing environment of clinical supervision, and only then when supervisor and supervisee can engage in 'dialogue in continuous interaction'.

Part of my supervisory practice is conducted through correspondence—'a dialogue in continuous interaction' through the post with supervisees as far away as South Africa. When I was first asked to do this, I had grave doubts as to whether it was feasible to provide clinical supervision in this way—teaching, perhaps. Today, after several years' experience, I have fewer doubts and can value the advantages of written notes. What follows is a summary of therapy with a couple, generously provided by their therapist for this chapter, and excerpts from my supervision notes sent to her at the time the couple were in therapy with her. With her consent I refer to my supervisee as V to protect confidentiality. She writes:

'Sue first presented alone in crisis at the point of flying to another country to have an abortion. She and her husband Mark already had three children, and Mark was adamant that they could not have another child. The experience was of a 'life and death' struggle. Some grief therapy, in relation to the abortion, and which included Mark, was engaged in. The couple presented again in extreme crisis two years later. The issues presented were to do with their intensely felt differences in values and life choices. The couple would fight bitterly over these differences, pushing each other into extreme despair in which one or both would indicate that suicide was the better option. Mark would often say, 'Divorce is not an option; suicide is the ultimate solution'.

Mark's father had committed suicide five years earlier, for which Mark blamed his mother. Sue's father had committed suicide when she was ten after a prolonged depressive illness. Sue remembers his first suicide threat when she was three, when he threatened not only suicide, but also to take the family with him. Sue, herself, had attempted suicide by taking an overdose, shortly after the birth of their first child. Sue's sister had also attempted suicide. Both mothers were much maligned, especially by Mark, who blamed them openly for the suicides of their husbands.

The very first supervision of my work with this couple was a watershed for me. I was feeling on the edge of despair, extremely anxious, and feeling 'crazy' to have taken them into couple therapy. But the couple related warmly and respectfully to me and I liked them both.'

My supervision notes concentrated largely on helping V know what she already knew, but did not know that she knew, even though she had written it several times in her notes to me. In my first supervisory notes to V in relation to this couple I wrote:

> *How painful this couple's conflict and anxiety is and how sensitive your work with them. You mention or refer to suicide no less than eight times in your report and I think this is very significant. It is the substance of their shared anxiety and what lies behind the need to engage continually in conflict and crises. They each push the other to the* nth *degree, in order to be constantly reassured that the other will not commit suicide. The technical problem they present is how to work with the current crisis and at the same time focus courageously on the purpose it also serves, namely to draw attention to and defend against the shared anxiety concerning suicide.*
>
> *I am struck how monstrous mothers are perceived as being and I wonder about your counter-transference and the emotional experience they evoke in you. I would suspect that there is a huge difference between how they describe their mothers and their transferences to you. Exploration of your counter-transference to them may lead them nearer to restoring the realities of those maligned mothers: maligned, perhaps, only because of a need to make sense of the suicide of their fathers. If mothers were not such monsters, fathers would not commit suicide.*
>
> *Their despair at each other's differences, although a reality, is also, I think, a defence against and a way of managing the anxiety that they share in relation to suicide. Their relationship is based on a preoccupation with suicide and a defence against it—a constant and terrifying need to test out. It is as if they have to push the other to the edge in order to discover that edge, to experience it, to know it, name it and to survive it. I think you should grasp this suicide nettle firmly and bravely and make it the central focus—I am tempted to say the only focus. The less afraid you are of exploring it with them the less afraid they will become, and the less likely it is that suicide will be the consequence of their shared life together. If you can keep to this focus with them the work may be quite short. This is the kind of work where the heart trembles, but it is the very trembling of the heart that makes the work pos-*

> *sible and provides that something that will make a difference. My heart goes out to you.*

The initial attempts to 'grasp the suicide nettle' were resisted. There were, I thought, several reasons for this: the very high level of anxiety the couple were experiencing; the closeness of a pending break in therapy; and the need to know that their therapist was not so daunted by the problem as not to keep pursuing it with them. And that she did with great sensitivity and courage. At the third opportunity, the couple were enabled to make the link between the anxiety about suicide and the need for the 'constant crises' that pushed them continually to the edge. V writes in her summary of her work with this couple:

> *During the time I saw them over a period of nearly eighteen months, Mark lost his job, lost a great deal of money in a business deal, faced huge debts and two court cases. Sue discovered that she had been sexually abused by her father. These issues often took over the therapy and were important in their own right, but in holding to the central focus of the 'suicide nettle' I was able to help them reflect on the purpose and meaning of 'pushing each other to the edge' in the constant crises. Finally, on one occasion, near the ending of therapy, just after the second court case when Sue realised the full extent of their financial loss, she came alone terrified that she would indeed push Mark to commit suicide.*
>
> *In the final session, the couple came together, Mark with a long black scarf wound round his neck. Both were depressed. Sue could not see the future in the face of their financial disaster. Mark talked about how he felt he could never ever satisfy Sue, and would commit suicide. Again, we explored their shared need to push the other to the edge. They spoke of their respective fathers and this time noted how they were different to Mark. The couple did not come again, because of their financial pressures. I had to hold my belief in their capacity for survival and let them go. I have had reports over the years that they are still together and doing well.*

These excerpts illustrate how a couple's unconscious communication of a central issue: the fragment of their shared unconscious life that is most urgent to address, and the defence against confronting it, are *both* projected into the therapist, who, in receiving the projections as an emotional experience, cannot, until she has fully explored her experience, know what she knows. In her work with this couple, V demonstrated her capacity, (with the help of the supervisory notes 'read and reread' she would have me say) to hold the tension between the couple's defensive use of crises, and their unconscious developmental wish to 'grasp the suicide nettle'. To gain, or regain conscious access to their repressed anxiety means helping the couple to manage and tolerate the fear of revisiting that anxiety. Not to do so means having a large part of their lives controlled negatively, and for them to be only half alive to their potential.

To offer a therapeutic container which will enable a couple to revisit a repressed and shared anxiety may often require the containing space of supervision and the supervisory relationship for the therapist or therapist couple. Here, through the exploration of counter-transference, the therapist can understand the nature and quality of the couple's repressed anxiety; and is enabled to think the unthinkable on their behalf. David Whyte, (1997) a poet who brings poetry to his consultative work with organisations, writes: 'Our deeper struggles are in effect our greatest spiritual and creative assets, and the doors to whatever creativity we might possess.' Supervision is an extension of the therapeutic container, providing for the therapist a regular space and significant relationship.

The quality of work in supervision and the interactive processes that develop between the supervisor and supervisee will often, and most helpfully be 'reflective' of an important aspect of the couple's interactive behaviour (Searles 1965, Mattinson 1975). When this 'reflection process' is available for examination in the safety of supervision, it can sometimes reveal a hidden aspect of the couple's communication. At such times, the reflection process unfolding in the 'dialogue in continuous interaction' between the supervisor and supervisee uncovers a hidden emotional experience, often the very opposite of that consciously communicated by the couple in therapy. For example, an unconscious purpose of the persistent and lively fight between a couple, so resistant to interpretation and change, might be betrayed by a 'heavy deadness' exposed in the interactive process between supervisor and supervisee. The hard-to-relinquish fight can be then understood and responded to compassionately as a shared defence against an intolerable anxiety related to 'deadness'.

At other times, the reflection processes arising in supervision simply mirror what is observable in the room with the couple and consciously known between them. The function of the mirroring, however, is in the emotional experience it provides in supervision. Here, in the extended therapeutic container, the supervisee and supervisor can, in the presence of and in relation to each other, examine the nature and quality of the emotional experience aroused between them. By understanding it as an unconscious communication from the particular couple under discussion, they can gain access to some fragment of the shared repressed anxieties that lie so deeply hidden in the couple's defensive but meaningful interaction.

In working with couples it is always possible, I think, to find an astonishing connection between the inner, unconscious world of one and the outer, conscious world of the other. It is as if each selects a central fragment of their separate internal worlds to which the other is receptive, and is willing to express consciously. To put it another way, each unconsciously chooses a particular fragment from their inner world that can engage in a meaningful interactive dialogue with the external world of the other, and into which the other can project. Whatever the actual nature of that fragment, it is always a fragment that potentially contains an essential connection to the core wholeness of each, and to the hidden phantasy shared by both.

A couple described their very different childhood experiences. So opposite were they, in fact, that it had proved valuable to examine how each in choosing the other was unconsciously seeking something of the other's experience to balance what was lacking in their own. Each, however, was trying also to get away from a 'too much so' quality in the experience they had had. A 'push and pull' pattern of attachment developed between them as each tried to get from the other something of the very experience the other was trying to get away from. The demand each made on the other to gain something of the experience which made up the shortfall in their own, was felt at times to threaten their relationship. Each made the same complaint of the other; the demands and the withholding were felt by both to be 'too much so'.

My supervisee in bringing this couple to supervision would often open her comments with, 'Oh, this couple is just too much' and this I likewise, from time to time, echoed. In staying with our experience, however, and examining the nature and quality of it when it arose, we felt we discovered, in the experience itself and from the language we chose to describe it to the other, clues to the shared anxiety that lay behind the couple's interaction. As a direct consequence of this 'internal' work in supervision something immediately shifted inside each of us. We found ourselves thinking about and relating to this couple in quite a different way: our attitude toward them had changed. In understanding the emotional experience aroused in us by the couple as a communication from them, we were freed from the experience itself; it had served its purpose. Later in therapy, this internal shift in the therapist, alongside her understanding of her experience, seemed communicated to the couple without a word from her being spoken. 'It was as if', she reported later, 'the couple had themselves been at the supervision session: even the language they used was similar to our own'.

Unconscious communication, or communication at a level beyond that of language, is a two-way process and arises in therapy when a stage is reached—often supported, I believe, by an unconscious prompt from the patient couple themselves—when the therapists can allow themselves to discover what they know, and make an internal shift in relation to that knowledge. I have heard this described as a moment when the therapist catches up with her/his patient couple. In my supervisory practice and psychoanalytic therapy with couples, it is the unconscious phantasy, or as I prefer to say, 'the fragment of truth', of the couple's shared inner world, which emerges as a central characteristic of a couple's attachment and interaction, and which becomes the focus for psychoanalytic attention. I have commented earlier on how a central unconscious fragment of the inner world of each finds external expression within the pattern of attachment and interaction that develops between them. A fragment from the repressed unconscious of each discovers a meeting point in the conscious reality of the other: a meeting point which occurs where the inner and repressed of one finds conscious expression in the external responses of the other. A pattern of interaction is created in which each partner expresses consciously an unconscious fragment of the other's inner world. In a couple's relationship these individual fragments become reduced and refined into a 'shared fragment of truth'.

In therapy, this 'fragment of truth', helpfully goes through a process of further reduction and refining as it becomes manifested in the therapist's counter-transference and still further in the counter-transferential and reflection processes of supervisory sessions. This reducing and refining process serves to sharpen the focus on the couple's 'fragment of truth', and allows for a deeper comprehension of the couple's core inner darkness. And as something of that darkness breaks the surface of consciousness it spreads out to encompass more of the whole experience of the relationship, like the ripple effect of a pebble thrown into a pool.

In a group supervision, a therapist presented her work with a couple who shared an early childhood loss of the parent of the opposite sex. The wife described her 'heart being broken' when her father died unexpectedly when she was eight years old. Her husband's mother died of heart disease when he was twelve years of age. Both, also, were their parents first-born and both were quickly followed by the birth of a sibling. The presenting problem was the husband's frequent short-lived affairs. There was nothing untoward in the manner in which the therapist presented her work with this couple, other than her almost entire focus on the wife. The atmosphere in the room, however, became heavier and heavier and the only man in the room closed his eyes, heavy with sleep. It was difficult to 'stay alive' in the room. But what was killing us off? Or was being killed off?

I decided to prod the group into just sufficient life to reflect upon and share the emotional experience aroused in them by the presentation. I wanted each to stay with and 'alive' to their experience in order to be able to think about it. I quote their responses:

I am frightened to death by her fragility.

I want to shake her alive.

I feel deadened by the presentation.

They feel a dead weight.

I feel energised with anger (this from the man in the group who had been sent to sleep).

I feel angry with her.

Finally, I asked the therapist to describe her own counter-transference to working with this couple. She said 'I recognise my preoccupation with the wife. She makes me feel very sad for her. There is no one there for her. She fills my mind and I can't stop thinking about her. There is no space for anyone else'. By this time the atmosphere in the group room had changed dramatically. Members were leaning forward, alive to each other's counter-transference experiences and beginning to engage with some of the 'unthinkable' aspects of this couple's dilemma and shared 'fragment of truth'.

I focused the group's attention on their emotional experience of the presentation, as having meaning for, and being an unconscious communication from the couple. The couple's shared 'fragment of truth' as a focus for therapeutic attention began to emerge. She, whose heart was broken by the untimely death of her father, marries a man upon whom she can rely to keep her constantly alive to her broken heart. He, whose mother died of heart disease as he was entering adolescence, marries a woman whose heart he can continually break and who constantly re-assures him by staying alive. The pattern of their interaction, when explored, appeared to move between a quality of 'deadness' to a consuming preoccupation with a 'broken heart'. Fragile dependency and rage in relation to the early loss of a parent, and perhaps to an even earlier loss in the form of the birth of a sibling, were now re-experienced in a life together consumed by a preoccupation with 'deadness' and a 'broken heart', and which left no space for anything else.

My own role as supervisor to this group reflected, I think, the need for a 'container' which allowed members deeply to experience something of what lay hidden in this couple's unconscious communication to their therapist; and having enacted it in 'deadly sleep', as it were, to rediscover their capacity to think and speak to the unthinkable fragment of this couple's truth contained within their counter-transference. Much has been written concerning the understanding of transference and counter-transference phenomena, but in relation to this chapter, I describe the counter-transference as a significant unconscious communication from the couple by way of projections, which is made conscious through the therapist's awareness of the emotional experience aroused in him/her by the couple in the process of the therapeutic task. I am aware of the complexities and even dangers of the use of one's counter-transference, but I remain convinced of its efficacy and its quite magical potency in putting one's finger on the pulse of the unconscious. Its dangers lie in the difficulties inherent in judging and identifying just what belongs to the therapist's inner world, and what properly belongs to the couple.

In my supervisory practice, over many years, I have been struck by how often supervisees wish to claim the emotional experience aroused in them as belonging to themselves. And, of course, they are right to do so, for there must always be a receptive place for a projection, whatever it is, to make a meaningful connection. The tenacity with which the claim is held, however, most often serves the purpose, it seems to me, of diverting attention from or largely dismissing the unconscious communication from the couple. After all, the therapist is being put in touch with an emotional experience which has arisen, in this instance, from the processes of a therapeutic relationship.

The regularity with which I was coming across: 'this is my stuff, my baggage' or similar convictions in my supervisory practice, and which seemed to divert attention from the couple patient, alerted me to think that something else was being communicated by the couple themselves and reflected in the therapist's response to her/his counter-transference. For example, a couple may unconsciously communicate their wish to dismiss and divert attention from the very thing they are, at the same time, communicating the necessity to confront. The essence of what needs to be addressed is potentially available through the analysis of the therapist's counter-transference, but the defence against confronting that which has hitherto remained hidden in the dark recesses of the couple's inner worlds is also projected, and becomes part of the therapist's counter-transference. That which needs to be faced and the defence against doing so are both projected into and find expression in the emotional experience of the therapist, and the tension between the 'wanting and the not wanting' to confront the issue becomes at that moment the unconscious fragment that needs to be addressed.

The nature and quality of the tension can often be determined through the language the therapist finds him or herself using to describe the emotional experience of counter-transference. For example, 'this belongs to me' or 'the relationship is too fragile' or 'they are too vulnerable' may indicate both the therapist's unconscious anxiety, and the controlling defensiveness of a couple relationship.

Not infrequently in my supervisory practice, a process of splitting, clearly observable in the pattern of interaction between the couple, becomes manifested in the supervisory relationship. Splitting is often regarded negatively and as destructive: a defensive mechanism leading away from integration. But I find myself cherishing the experience when a process of splitting occurs between myself and my supervisee. For if I and my supervisee can tolerate staying with our different standpoints to explore them thoroughly and hold them in tension, it is, I believe, possible to reach a deeper level of understanding of the couple's dilemma and discover that shared unconscious fragment which requires attention. Splitting always involves a loss of integrity in that it implies not being entirely true to one's whole self. Paradoxically, when the polarities manifested in the split can be courageously explored, named, owned and held in tension, splitting can lead to integration, that is, to integrity restored with a conscious knowledge of its dual aspects.

It is hard, sometimes impossible, for a lone therapist to contain the tension of such polarities when receiving them as a projection from the couple patient, and difficult also for co-therapists always to contain and work with the projected split within the couple. Supervision provides a containing space for the polarities of a split to be held and explored. I think this is made possible just because the supervisor, although emotionally experiencing the projections, is not directly involved in working with the couple patient.

A supervisee in describing a couple with whom she was working moved me close to tears by the profound sadness of their story. Yet she, in working with them, felt quite unmoved and told me how she was made to feel constantly subjected to a 'performance' which kept her very much at an emotional distance from them. Together we pondered on whose experience was closer to this couple's truth. As I listened and stayed open to her experience of them and she did likewise to mine, we began to see that both our experiences held an important truth. This work led us to a different understanding of this couple's dilemma, and to seeing that their sad story which so held them together also served, because of the anxiety contained within it, to distance them from each other and to limit the comfort each could give and receive. I was able to experience their sadness and feel close to them just because I was distant and unknown to them.

Idealistic hopes and omnipotent desires of couples often, and helpfully, meet a connecting hope and desire in the therapist; just as each partner in a couple relationship had originally met a connecting hope in and for the other. Without such interconnecting hopes and desires, however unconscious they may at times be, therapy, like a couple relationship, probably will never begin. As supervisor I can view the therapist's omnipotent desires in relation to a couple, as belonging to his/her own internal world, but if such hopes, and feelings in relation to the couple persist in presenting themselves in supervision, I choose instead to work with and understand these desires as an emotional experience aroused in the therapist by a couple and as an essential communication from them.

At times, supervisees describe their work with a couple as 'stuck'; and as supervisor I am not immune from that experience, and sometimes find the exercise of my interpretative skills leads nowhere, except to an increasing experience of stuckness. Much of this experience of 'stuckness', I believe, has hidden within it an element of the omnipotent desire to make things right which, as for the couple, is difficult to relinquish. They and we are 'stuck'. These omnipotent hopes, that partially form and characterise a couple's relationship, are reflected in the emotional experience of the therapeutic and supervisory relationships. The work in supervision requires the supervisor and supervisee being able to explore their counter-transference experience and confront the meaning and significance of the stuckness rather than trying to search out means to try to change it. There is, of course, a paradox in all of this, which I hope will become apparent.

All my supervisees, from time to time, bring a couple for supervision and begin by describing the couple and their work with them as 'stuck' or 'I am getting nowhere, just going round in circles; nothing seems to change anything'. Coming to supervision is often an indication of a shift somewhere. It is as if the couple themselves have signified through an unconscious process that they are fearful, but ready to face the meaning for them, of the 'stuckness that will not go away'. In order to do that, however, they first require their therapist to do some internal work on the emotional experience of stuckness in the counter-transference. This is the work of supervision. The supervisory relationship provides a containing space in which, in the presence of another, the therapist can begin to face the meaning of this particular experience of stuckness and discover its many, and unthinkable, aspects.

I am not speaking here of the meaning in the therapist's own inner world, but the meaning in relation to the couple and the therapeutic relationship. The feeling of being stuck with something you cannot change is the very experience the couple have to face and grieve, and *know they cannot change it*. When this is worked with in supervision and internalised by the therapist, something important shifts in the therapist's relationship with the couple. The emotional and therapeutic energy, quite properly spent in seeking to change something for the couple, is now recognised and mourned as energy misspent in trying to change the unchangeable. The therapist's attitude and response to the couple changes; and this is communicated to the couple, through an unconscious process, often without a word being spoken and sometimes even before they are next seen.

The experience of trying to change the unchangeable is, itself, the very unconscious fragment in the couple's pattern of attachment and interaction, (now experienced emotionally in the therapeutic and supervisory relationship), that is struggling for conscious recognition from the dark recesses of the couple's inner worlds. The fundamental purpose of the experience in the present provides the opportunity to re-experience what could not be changed in the past; when instead of being grieved, it was denied and banished to find expression in a continuous and fruitless endeavour to change something; something that could always be relied upon to resist changing. The creative and developmental purpose of re-experiencing in the present something that cannot be changed, is that it allows one, at last, to grieve. As I heard on a television 'soap' recently: 'Grief is a friend, it lets you remember, mourn and cry'.

A couple's relationship holds within its containing boundary the potential integration of each. I am convinced that this is true, whatever the quality of that relationship. The wholeness of each, is potentially accessible in the 'dialogue in continuous interaction' of their shared life, at the centre of which is a significant meeting point. Discovering and facing what it is that is struggling for conscious recognition at that meeting point, takes conscious courage: in the context of this chapter, the courage of the invisible matrix of supervisor, therapist and the couple.

Conclusion

In this paper I have defined supervision as an extension of the therapeutic container, which provides a space in the presence of a significant other, for supervisees to discover what they know, but do not know that they know of their couples' struggles; where they can think the unthinkable, on behalf of their couples, and name their experience in relation to it. I have attempted to describe some aspects of my supervisory practice and in doing so provide an experience of it. What I have shared inevitably indicates something of where I am coming from; the influence of a Jungian analysis; the attraction of work with couples; the application of psychoanalytic thought to that work. Inevitably, also, it exposes something of my own internal struggles and journeyings to the dark recesses of my own inner world.

More hidden perhaps are the internalised influences of my own experiences of supervision. Four supervisors; Joan McCarthy, (to whom I am also indebted for her encouragement in the writing of this paper and for her patient reading of the drafts), Patricia Coussell, Mary Welch and Enid Balint have in various stages of my professional life and in different ways 'partnered' me in my work as my 'hidden co-therapist'. I know that I shall always appreciate their great influence upon the quality and direction of my work and I trust that I have internalised, at least something of their combined wisdom, warmth and encouragement and that this is apparent to my supervisees. Added to these substantial influences are those of my professional trainings, literature, friends, colleagues, my couple patients and my patient supervisees. All these influences and more, serve to make up the 'invisible matrix' that accompanies me in my supervisory practice. I do not consciously endeavour to bring any aspect of this matrix into a supervision session, neither do I consciously try to keep any out. I recognise my 'invisible matrix' as a presence; to make and find what connections it will. Wherever, and to whatever that may lead I welcome with gratitude, for it is at the point where two worlds meet that there is a possibility of a 'third something' being born; a thought perhaps, which will make a difference and transform each.

BIBLIOGRAPHY

Balint, M. (1968) *The Basic Fault*, London: Tavistock.

Bannister, K. & Pincus, L. (1965) *Shared Phantasy in Marital Problems*, London: Institute of Marital Studies.

Bayley, J. (1998) *Iris: a Memoir of Iris Murdoch*, London: Duckworth.

Benjamin, J. (1995) *Like Subjects, Love Objects*, New Haven, Connecticut: Yale University Press.

Benjamin, L.R., & Benjamin, R. (1995) 'A therapy group for mothers with dissociative disorders', *International Journal of Group Psychotherapy* 45, 3: 381-403.

Berke, J. H. (1987) 'Arriving, settling-in, settling-down, leaving and following-up: stages of stay at the Arbours centre', *British Journal of Medical Psychology* 60: 181-188.

Berke, J.H. (1990) 'Conjoint therapy within a therapeutic milieu: the crisis team', *International Journal of Therapeutic Communities* 11, 4: 247.

Berke, J. H. (1995) 'Psychotic Interventions', in *Sanctuary: The Arbours Experience of Alternative Community Care*, ed. J. H. Berke, C. Masoliver & T. Ryan, London: Process Press.

Bick, E. (1968) 'The experience of the skin in early object relations', *International Journal of Psycho-Analysis* 49: 484 - 486

Binnington, L. (1999) Personal communication.

Bion, W. (1957) 'Differentiation of the Psychotic from the Non-Psychotic Personalities', in Bion 1984.

Bion, W. (1959) 'Attacks on Linking', *International Journal of Psycho-Analysis*, 40: 308-315.

Bion, W. (1962) 'A Theory of Thinking', in Bion 1984.

Bion, W. (1984) *Second Thoughts*, London: Karnac Books.

Blum, H.P. (1983) 'The position and value of extratransference interpretations', *Journal of American Psychoanalytic Association* 31: 587-617.

Bollas, C., & Sundelson, D. (1995) *The New Informants: Betrayal of Confidentiality in Psychoanalysis and Psychotherapy*, London: Karnac.

Boswood, B. (1976) 'The letter to Dr. DeMare', *Group Analysis* 9, 2: 81-2.

Bowlby, J. (1979) *The Making and Breaking of Affectional Bonds*, London: Tavistock Publications

Britton, R. (1989) 'The Missing Link: Parental Sexuality in the Oedipus Complex', in *The Oedipus Complex Today: Clinical Implications*. ed. J. Steiner, London: Karnac Books.

Britton, R. (1995) 'Foreword', in Ruszczynski & Fisher 1995.

Britton, R. (1998) *Belief and Imagination*, London: Routledge.

Campbell, J. (1968) *Myths To Live By*, New York: Bantam.
Casement, P. (1985) *On Learning from the Patient*, London: Routledge.
Chiesa, M., & Brown, R. (1990) 'Introduction to repertory grid: theory and technique', *British Journal of Psychotherapy* 6, 4: 411-420.
Clulow, C. (1998) Personal communication.
Cohn H.W. (1986) 'The double context: on combining individual and group therapy', *Group Analysis* 19: 327-339.
Colman, W. (1993) 'Marriage as a psychological container' in Ruszczynski 1993a.
Coltart, N. (1983) 'Diagnosis and assessment of suitability for psychoanalytic psychotherapy', *British Association of Psychotherapists Bulletin* 14: 1-9.
Coltart, N. (1992) *Slouching Towards Bethlehem... and Other Psychoanalytic Explorations*, London: Free Association Books.
Cooper, J., & Alfille, H. (eds.) (1998) *Assessment in Psychotherapy*, London: Karnac.
Dagg, P.K., & Evans, J.B. (1997) 'The synergy of individual and group psychotherapy training', *American Journal of Psychotherapy*. 51, 2: 204-9.
Denford, J. (1995) 'How I Assess for In-Patient Psychotherapy', in Mace 1995.
Dicks, H. (1967) *Marital Tensions*, London: Routledge & Kegan Paul.
Fairbairn, W.R.D. (1952) *Psychoanalytic Studies of the Personality*, London: Routledge & Kegan Paul.
Fairbairn, W.R.D. (1955) 'Observations in defence of the psychoanalytic theory of the personality', *British Journal of Medical Psychology* 28: 144-156.
Fine, R. (1989) 'The Extra-Analytic Transference and the Analytic Triad', *British Journal of Psychotherapy* 5, 4: 485-504.
Fisher, J. (1999) *The Uninvited Guest*, London: Karnac Books.
Foulkes, S.H. (1971) Transcript of audio-tape: 'The Group Conductor', Institute of Group Analysis & the Group-Analytic Society, London.
Foulkes, S.H., & Lewis, E. (1944) 'Group analysis, studies in the treatment of groups on psychoanalytical lines', *British Journal of Medical Psychology* 20:175-84.
Freud, S. (1910) 'The Future Prospects of Psycho-Analytic Therapy', S.E. XI: 141-151.
Freud, S. (1911) 'Formulations Regarding the Two Principles in Mental Functioning', S.E. XII: 213-26.

Freud, S. (1912) 'A Note on the Unconscious in Psychoanalysis', S.E. XII: 255-66.
Freud, S. (1912) 'The Dynamics of Transference', S.E. XII: 99-108.
Freud, S. (1915) 'The Unconscious', S.E. XIV: 159-215.
Freud, S. (1940) 'Splitting of the Ego in the Process of Defence', S.E. XXIII: 65-69.
Garelick, A. (1994) 'Psychotherapy assessment: theory and practice', *Psychoanalytic Psychotherapy* 8, 2: 101 -116.
Gell, E. (1998) Personal communication.
Gittings, R., ed. (1990) *Letters of John Keats*, Oxford: Oxford University Press.
Haldane, D., & Vincent, C. (1998) 'The lone therapist, the couple and their problem: reflections on threesomes', *Society of Marital Psychotherapists Bulletin* 5.
Harris, J. (1998) Personal communication.
Harris, M., & Meltzer, D. (1986) 'Family Patterns and Educability', in *Studies in Extended Metapsychology*, Strath Tay, Perthshire: Clunie Press.
Hewitt, P. (1998) 'Boundaries and Difficulties in Assessment', in *Assessment in Psychotherapy*, in Cooper & Alfille 1998.
Hinshelwood, R. D. (1994) 'Attacks on the Reflective Space', in *Ring of Fire: Primitive Affects and Object Relations in Group Psychotherapy*, ed. V. Shermer & M. Pines, London: Routledge.
Hinshelwood, R. D. (1995) 'Psychodynamic Formulation in Assessment for Psychoanalytic Psychotherapy', in Mace 1995.
Hobdell R. (1991) 'Individual and Group Therapy Combined', in *The Practice of Group Analysis*, ed. J. Roberts & M. Pines, London & New York: Tavistock/Routledge.
Hodson, P. (1998) Personal communication.
Hodson, P., & Brookes, S. (1989) 'Learning through the looking glass', *Tavistock Gazette* 26: 7-11.
Holmes, J. (1995) 'How I Assess for Psychoanalytic Psychotherapy', in Mace 1995.
Holmes, J., & Lindley, R. (1998) *The Values of Psychotherapy*, London: Karnac.
Horwitz, L. (1994) 'Depth of transference in groups', *International Journal of Group Psychotherapy* 44: 271-90.
Judd, D. (1998) Personal communication.
Klein, J. (1990) 'Patients who are not ready for interpretations', *British Journal of Psychotherapy* 1: 38-49.

Klein, J. (1995) *Doubts and Certainties in the Practice of Psychotherapy,* London: Karnac.
Klein, M. (1946) 'Notes on Some Schizoid Mechanisms', in Klein 1975b.
Klein, M. (1952) 'Some Theoretical Conclusions Regarding the Emotional Life of the Infant', in Klein 1975b.
Klein, M. (1975a) *The Psycho-Analysis of Children,* London: Hogarth Press.
Klein, M. (1975b) *Envy and Gratitude,* London: Hogarth Press.
Knowles, J. (1995) 'How I Assess for Group Psychotherapy', in Mace 1995.
Kohut, H. (1971) *The Analysis of the Self,* New York: International Universities Press.
Konig, K. (1997) *Self-Analysis for Analysts,* London: Jessica Kingsley.
Krause, I. B. (1998) *Therapy Across Culture,* London: Sage.
Kuprat, Y. (1999) Personal communication.
Laplanche J., & Pontalis J.-B. (1983) *The Language of Psychoanalysis,* London: The Hogarth Press & the Institute of Psycho-Analysis.
Limentani, A. (1972) 'The assessment of analyzability', *International Journal of Psycho-Analysis* 53.
Lyons, A. (1993) *Psychotherapy with Couples,* in Ruszczynski 1993a.
Mace, C., ed. (1995) *The Art and Science of Assessment in Psychotherapy,* London: Karnac.
Malan, D. (1995) *Individual Psychotherapy and the Science of Psychodynamics,* second edition, London: Butterworth Heinemann.
Maratos, J. (1996) 'The emergence of self through the group', *Group Analysis* 29: 161-168.
Mattinson, J. (1975)*The Reflection Process in Casework Supervision,* London: Tavistock Institute of Marital Studies.
Menzies, I. (1970) *The Functioning of Social Systems as a Defence against Anxiety,* London: Tavistock Institute of Human Relations.
McCormack, C. (1989) 'The borderline-schizoid marriage', *Journal of Family and Marital Therapy* 15, 3: 299-309.
McCready, K.F. (1987) 'Milieu counter-transference in treatment of borderline patients', *Psychotherapy* 24, 4: 720.
McDougall, J. (1986) *Theatres of the Mind,* London: Free Association Books.
Mellett, J. (1998) Personal communication.
Meltzer, D. (1966) 'The relation of anal masturbation to projective identification', *International Journal of Psychoanalysis* 47: 335-342.

Meltzer, D. (1982) *Studies in Extended Metapsychology*, Perth: Clunie Press.
Milner, M. (1987) 'The Role of Illusion in Symbol Formation', in *The Suppressed Madness of Sane Men*, London: Tavistock & The Institute of Psychoanalysis.
Molnos, A. (1995) *A Question of Time: Essentials of Brief Dynamic Psychotherapy*, London: Karnac.
Mordecai, A., & Waydenfeld, D. (1998) 'The Assessment Consultation' in Cooper & Alfille 1998.
Morgan, M. (1995) 'The projective gridlock: a form of projective identification in couples', in Ruszczynski & Fisher 1995.
Morgan, M. (1998) Personal communication.
Morley, E. (1994) 'Using the Focus of Couple Psychotherapy in Work with the Individual Patient', unpublished MA thesis, University of Hertfordshire.
Nitsun, M. (1996) *The Anti-Group*, London: Routledge.
Orbach, S. (1997) 'The one and only you', *The Guardian*, October 11th.
Orbach, S., & Eichenbaum, L. (1988) *Between Women: Love, Envy and Competition in Women's Relationships*, London: Century.
Pierides, S. (1998) 'Machine Phenomena', in *Even Paranoids Have Enemies*, ed. J. H. Berke, S. Pierides, A. Sabbadini, & S. Schneider, London: Routledge.
Porter, K. (1993) 'Combined Individual and Group Psychotherapy', in *Group Therapy In Clinical Practice*, ed. A. Alonso & H.I. Swiller, Washington D.C.: American Psychiatric Press.
Praper, P. (1997) 'A case of combined therapy: some developmental and object-relations phenomena', *Group Analysis* 30: 331-348.
Rabe, M. L. (1998) 'How to Assess and Select a Patient for Group Psychotherapy: Group versus Individual Treatment', unpublished dissertation.
Rayner, E. & Hahn, H. (1964) 'Assessment for Psychotherapy', *British Journal of Medical Psychology*, 2, 4: 8-15.
Riviere, J. (1991) 'Symposium on Child Analysis', in *The Inner World and Joan Riviere: Collected Papers 1920-1958*, London: Karnac Books.
Rose, J. (1998) 'The cult of celebrity', *London Review of Books* 20, 16 (August).
Ruszczynski, S. (1992) 'Notes towards a psychoanalytic understanding of the couple relationship', *Psychoanalytic Psychotherapy* 6: 33-48
Ruszczynski, S., ed. (1993a) *Psychotherapy with Couples*, London: Karnac.

Ruszczynski, S. (1993b) 'The theory and practice of the Tavistock Institute of Marital Studies', in Ruszczynski 1993a.

Ruszczynski, S., & Fisher, J., eds. (1995) *Intrusiveness and Intimacy in the Couple*, London: Karnac Books.

Rycroft, C. (1968) *A Critical Dictionary of Psychoanalysis*. London: Nelson.

Scharff, D.E. & Scharff, J.S. (1991) *Object Relations Couple Therapy*, New Jersey: Aronson.

Scharff, J.S. & Scharff, D.E. (1998) *Object Relations Individual Therapy*, New Jersey: Aronson.

Scheidlinger, S., & Porter, K. (1980) 'Group Therapy Combined with Individual Psychotherapy', in *Specialised Techniques in Individual Psychotherapy*, ed. T.B.Karasu & L. Bellar, New York: Brunner / Mazel.

Searles, H. F. (1965) 'The Informational Value of the Supervisor's Emotional Experience', in *Collected Papers on Schizophrenia and Related Subjects*, London: Hogarth Press & The Institute of Psychoanalysis.

Segal, H. (1997) untitled, *Institute of Psycho-Analysis News* Spring 1997.

Sher, M. (1998) Personal communication.

Sinason, V. (1992) *Mental Handicap and the Human Condition*, London: Free Association Books.

Skynner, R. (1976) *One Flesh: Separate Persons*, London: Constable.

Stewart, H. (1992) *Psychic Experience and Problems of Technique*, London: Karnac.

Stokoe, P. (2000) 'Holding the Boundaries', this volume.

Stumpfl, M. (1998) 'Transference and Counter-transference in the Assessment Consultation', in Cooper & Alfille 1998.

Symington, N. (1986) *The Analytic Experience*. London: Free Association Books.

Tantam, D. (1995) 'Why Assess?', in Mace 1995.

Tatham, P. (1998) Personal communication.

Tonnesman, M. (1998) 'Foreword', in Cooper & Alfille 1998.

Turquet, P. (1985) 'Leadership: the Individual and the Group' in *Group Relations Reader 2*, ed. A.D. Colman & M.H. Geller, Washington: A.K. Rice Institute.

Vincent, C. (1995) 'Love in the Counter-transference', *SPMP Bulletin* 2: 4-10.

Vincent, C. (1998) Personal communication.

Wallerstein, R.S. (1999). 'A Half-Century Perspective on Psychoanalysis and Psychotherapy', in *Psychoanalysis on the Move,* ed. P. Fonagy et al., London: Routledge.

Whyte D. (1997) *The Heart Aroused: Poetry and the Preservation of the Soul at Work'*, New York: Doubleday Dell.

Winnicott, D. (1960a) 'The Theory of the Parent Infant Relationship', in Winnicott 1985.

Winnicott, D. (1960b) 'The True and False Self', in Winnicott 1985.

Winnicott, D.W. (1985) *The Maturational Process and the Facilitating Environment,* London: The Hogarth Press.

Wong, N. (1988) 'Combined Individual and Group Treatment with Borderline and Narcissistic Patients', in *Borderline and Narcissistic Patients in Therapy,* ed. N. Slavinska-Holy, Madison, WI: International Universities Press.

Wright, K. (1991) *Vision and Separation,* London: Free Association Books.

INDEX

For Product Safety Concerns and Information please contact our EU representative GPSR@taylorandfrancis.com
Taylor & Francis Verlag GmbH, Kaufingerstraße 24, 80331 München, Germany

www.ingramcontent.com/pod-product-compliance
Ingram Content Group UK Ltd.
Pitfield, Milton Keynes, MK11 3LW, UK
UKHW022026061126
477531UK00002B/54
9780367324834